LSWR CARRIAGES

VOLUME 3

Non-Passenger Carriage Stock

LSWR CARRIAGES

VOLUME 3

Non-Passenger Carriage Stock

G R Weddell

Kestrel Railway Books
PO Box 269
SOUTHAMPTON
SO30 4XR

www.kestrelrailwaybooks.co.uk

Printed by The Amadeus Press.

ISBN 0954485955

Front cover, top: 44ft Post Office sorting van No 4. (National Railway Museum)

Front cover, bottom: 44ft Post Office sorting van No 4, drawings 464 and 618.

Back cover: 48ft Army ambulance.

CONTENTS

PRICE FOURPENCE

LONDON & SOUTH WESTERN RAILWAY

U.S. 62

AMBULANCE
TRAIN

FOR USE OF THE

AMERICAN
ARMIES

IN FRANCE

Constructed at the Company's
Carriage and Wagon Works
at Eastleigh, Hants, · · 1918

H. A WALKER,   General Manager.

INTRODUCTION

Four excellent books entitled *LSWR Locomotives* by D L Bradley and others were published by Wild Swan Publications, followed by the present author's *LSWR Carriages, Volume 1*, which described the development of passenger carriages in the 19th Century. The second volume of that work was published by OPC under the title *LSWR Carriages in the 20th Century*. The goods vehicles that came into Southern Railway ownership were dealt with in detail in *An Illustrated History of Southern Wagons, Volume 1* by Messrs Bixley, Blackburn, Chorley, King and Newton, published by OPC. This book will be referred to quite frequently in the present work as simply *Southern Wagons, Volume 1*.

These seven books together covered the story of virtually all LSWR locomotives and rolling stock with the exception of what is sometimes referred to as non-passenger carriage stock and the goods stock of the 19th Century. It is the intention of this book, together with the next in the series, to close that gap, so far as is now possible, and thus complete the story. It was originally planned as one book but the content has expanded to the point that it now has to be divided into two volumes.

This book deals with non-passenger carriage stock (NPCS). It is not known whether that description was ever used in LSWR days but it describes vehicles designed to run in passenger trains or at passenger train speeds, such as milk vans, postal vans, horseboxes and so on. The next volume will include goods wagons from the 19th century, service vehicles and a variety of other associated subjects.

The numbering of drawings, photographs and appendix entries follows the style adopted in the LSWR Carriages books, that is, each subject is given a chapter and item number. Although this gives rise to some gaps, it automatically links the drawings to the photos and to the appendix entries without the need for a table of cross-references.

As with the carriages books, most of the information comes from builders' drawings, mainly LSWR and Metropolitan Carriage & Wagon Co, the latter by courtesy of Birmingham City Libraries (although it is understood that these are currently in the care of the Historical Model Railway Society), and from the LSWR company records in the National Archive (formerly the Public Record Office). Most of the earlier drawings, including those from Metropolitan, bear the LSWR drawing number (generally four figures). After the Carriage Works moved to Eastleigh, a new number series was started, commencing from 1.

The National Archive records include many, but unfortunately not all, of the LSWR Committee minutes books. There are also the Carriage Registers from 1904 and 1912, which include the luggage vans, horse boxes, and so on, but there is little or nothing on wagons other than a diagram book that only contains information on vehicles surviving at the 1923 Grouping.

Photographs, particularly of the goods vehicles, are regrettably scarce as so many photographers concentrated on the "glamorous" locomotives, and often took great pains to avoid including any of the revenue-earning vehicles. Several photos included here are of rather poor quality because they are enlargements taken from the background of such locomotive or station views, but they are all that I have been able to find for those subjects.

Several photos have either no credits or are shown as "Author's collection" because so many photos purchased many years ago had nothing written on the back as identification. If anyone recognises one of their photos, I trust they will accept my apologies and thanks for having made them available to the public.

I must express my gratitude to several people, particularly to Harold Tumilty and Ray Chorley, without whose help I would never have started on these books, and to various members of the South Western Circle who have helped to fill in some of the many gaps in my own studies. I am also extremely grateful to my wife Margaret, who has had a lot to put up with while I have been busily engrossed in this work!

Gordon R Weddell

Opposite: Cover of pamphlet produced by the LSWR in 1918 that described the Ambulance Train used by the United States Army in France. Ambulance carriages are discussed in Chapter 3.

S11 4-4-0 on the up "Day Mail" passing Worthy Temporary Signal Box. This was a "break section" box about a mile north of Winchester, half-way between Winchester and Winchester Junction, and only opened "as required", so the up and down signals were normally off. It was erected in the late 1890s, and –although described as temporary, it lasted (apart from closure between 1918 and 1920) until 1932. (South Western Circular Volume 13, page 192 et seq.)

(N Pomfret Collection)

CHAPTER 1

PASSENGER LUGGAGE VANS

Perhaps the title of this chapter needs a little clarification. In the earliest days, London & Southampton Railway trains seem to have been formed of passenger carriages and goods wagons all marshalled together. Quite early on, the passenger and goods trains were segregated, the passenger trains carrying only First and Second class passengers. Third class passengers, whose carriages were not much more than goods wagons with benches, were only carried by goods trains for a few years. Luggage, in the sense of being the belongings of the passengers on the trains, was at first carried on the rooftops of First class carriages, or squeezed in as best as could be managed by Second and Third class passengers. Quite soon, the amount of luggage forced the provision of extra accommodation for it.

The earliest specific reference that distinguishes between simple luggage vans and those containing a Guard's and brake section was a stock return in July 1848, which listed the total quantity of them as ten luggage carriages and three covered wagons for passengers' luggage in Third class trains, all of them being "old and in poor condition", which might suggest that they were downclassed original carriages. There was no suggestion of replacing them.

All other property and merchandise was carried by the goods trains, at first in open trucks, some of which later had tarpaulins to cover them, and later still in true covered wagons. As goods trains ran to quite slow timings, never faster than 20mph and with frequent stops at stations to either detach or attach wagons, or to allow passenger trains to pass, there arose the need for some commodities, particularly perishables, to be carried in some faster manner.

In *LSWR Carriages, Volume 1* it was recounted how, at first, brakes were only fitted on some First class carriages, then later on some of the Third class. However it was not long before there was recognition of the need to provide some special vehicles with brakes and accommodation for a Guard, so the covered wagons or vans built for this purpose became the logical place to put the extra luggage.

In 1848, it had been reported that the monthly average number of carriages per train varied between 5.4 and 10.0. From the stock return, the ratio of passenger Guard's vans to ordinary carriages was 1 to 12.5, which might seem odd until it is recalled that at that stage many of the early Firsts and Composites still had outside brakes and Guard's seats fitted to them. Further stock returns give the following Guard's van to carriages ratios: 1854: 1 to 13.9, 1859: 1 to 10.7, 1872: 1 to 5.4, 1874: 1 to 5.1 and in 1882: 1 to 4.8.

In LSWR records, the terms "luggage van" and "Guard's brake van" appear to have been

L11 class No 412 passing Esher with a down "churn" train, showing a variety of vans.

(HL Salmon/J Minnis Collection)

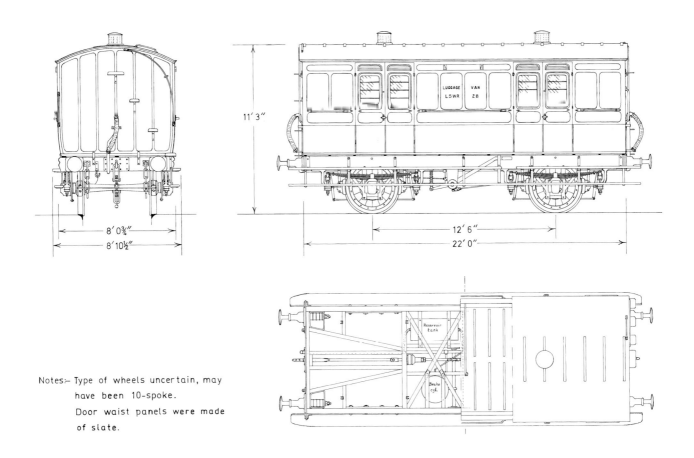

Notes:– Type of wheels uncertain, may
have been 10-spoke.
Door waist panels were made
of slate.

0   5   10   15 feet

Figure 1.1. 1883 22ft passenger luggage van, drawing DB97.

Plate 1.1a . 22ft luggage van No 45 of 1883 and 20ft brake van No 207 of 1864, behind which is a 14ft 2in horsebox of circa 1863 (see Figure 4.3).

synonymous until at least the early 1880s, and to have sometimes even been applied to Brake Thirds. As trains grew in length and weight, the provision of more brake power, by adding more brake vans, and presumably more Guards and "Breaksmen", as indicated by the above ratios, automatically brought extra luggage accommodation. Thus, there seems to have been no need for any vehicles to be built solely for carrying luggage in passenger trains.

The lack of any special vehicles for just luggage or perishables appears to be supported by several returns of rolling stock over the years and by some minutes in mid-1859, when it was first agreed to build twelve covered wagons for the conveyance of mails, fish, baggage, etc by passenger trains. In the end, it was decided that they should be built, but with "breaks", which must have included provision for a Guard to operate the brakes, so they were doubtless of the same general type as before. In 1869 it was ordered that communication cords should be fitted to "horse boxes, carriage trucks, specie and box wagons" to permit running in passenger trains.

The words specie and bullion were used to describe high value goods requiring good security. These included precious metals, gem stones and money. Britain imported huge quantities of the raw and refined materials from various parts of the Empire then manufactured and exported currency, both as coin and notes, to very many countries world wide. As a major trading nation there was also a considerable traffic of gold and silver between the banking institutions of the world. Much of this trade flowed through Southampton Docks.

The development of continuous brakes on the LSWR has already been mentioned in *LSWR Carriages, Volume 1*, and this caused a considerable change in the van stock. No longer was it necessary to have several Guard's brake vans on long trains, all that was needed was a Guard's compartment at each end of a train, luggage space could be as little or as great as the traffic required. Thus from 1882, a new class of "Passenger Luggage Van" (PLV) came into existence, all vehicles being fitted with the Automatic Vacuum Brake (AVB). Under this heading there were several subdivisions for milk, newspaper, flower, fruit, bullion and also for mailbags where there was no requirement for sorting. Post Office Sorting Vans are a separate subject and will be dealt with in the next chapter.

Thus arose a distinction between the types of non-passenger carrying vehicles that would normally travel in passenger trains, or run to passenger timings, and which became known much later as non-passenger carriage stock (NPCS), and those that would travel in the slow goods trains. The latter will be dealt with in the next volume.

Passenger brake or Guard's vans are sometimes considered as NPCS, but they were an essential part of any passenger train in cases where Brake Firsts,

Brake Seconds or Brake Thirds were not used. They have therefore been included in the previous volumes with the carriages at the appropriate places according to date and design –except for some fruit train brakes that appear later in this chapter.

The earliest record in the LSWR Carriage Register is for fifty 22ft luggage vans that were ordered from Metropolitan in 1882, delivered in 1883 and numbered from 1 to 50. They are recorded as being to drawing DB97, although this seems more like a drawing location (perhaps Drawing Box No 97) rather than a true drawing number. They are shown here at Figure 1.1. Plate 1.1a, which was previously shown in *LSWR Carriages, Volume 1* to illustrate the early Brake Third, shows one of them in original livery complete with communication cord. Behind the Brake Third is a 14ft 2in horse box of c.1863 (see Figure 4.3) with the upper part of the horse doors open.

The brake system fitted was naturally of the early LSWR pattern using a separate reservoir tank. Handbrakes were apparently not fitted at first since there is mention in the minutes of the Traffic Committee for 4th March 1885 of the necessity for having hand lever brakes fitted to the new PLVs, which were described as not having a brake. Since this was technically not the case, it is clearly another instance of confusion between the provision of actual brakes and the provision of a Guard's brake – at the meeting they doubtless knew what they were talking about, but the secretary merely recorded the facts using the minimum of words! The Engineering Committee was then asked to accelerate their fitting. Handbrakes were needed because, unlike most passenger vehicles, non-passenger carriage stock had to be handled and shunted in sidings where, once the vacuum brakes had been released, there was no way of restoring the vacuum to provide power to brake the vehicles for parking.

The underframes for these new vans were of composite construction like those of the first bogie carriages, that is, of mainly timber construction but with steel headstocks, and had similar buffers and other features. According to the Metropolitan drawing they were to have 3ft 7in wheels, which implies Mansell type, but one that survived on the Longmoor Military Railway until 1969 ended up with 3ft 8in ten-spoked ones; in-service photos seem to show both types. To facilitate washing out, the floor had a slight slope from the sides to the centre with a gutter and drain holes along the centre line. This was a feature of many of the luggage vans described in the rest of this chapter and was particularly important for those vans earmarked for fish traffic! This subject will come up again in Chapter 4. As was mentioned regarding the carriages of the period, the springs were connected to the J-hangers by chain links, but again, like the carriages, these links were later replaced with screw-ended rods.

Plate 1.1b. The nearest vehicle is 22ft luggage van of 1883, drawing DB97, and next to it is 24ft luggage van of 1896, drawing 636.

(Kenning Collection)

Plate 1.1c. 22ft luggage van of 1883, drawing DB97, at Longmoor in 1968.

(GR Weddell)

Plate 1.1d. 22ft luggage van of 1883, drawing DB97.   *(GR Weddell)*

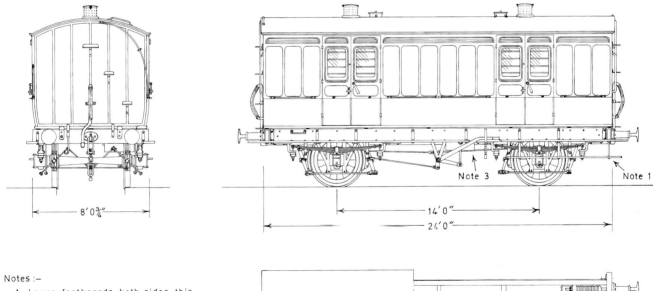

8′0¾″   14′0″   24′0″

Notes :—

1. Lower footboards both sides this
   end only.

2. Interior parts of underframe and brake
   rigging deduced from similar vehicles
   and photos.

3. Hand brake lever on this side only, not
   fixed on cross-shaft, connected to one
   wheel only.

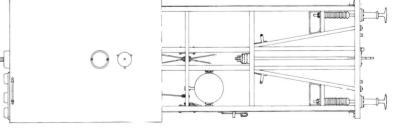

0   5   10   15 feet

Figure 1.2. 1887 24ft luggage van, drawing DB97A.

Plate 1.2a. 24ft luggage van to drawing DB97A of 1897, possibly No 63. There is some lettering below the LSWR and number that might read "Newspaper Van". *(Lens of Sutton)*

On 24th November 1886 the General Manager, Mr Scott, urged the Traffic Committee to agree to the provision of additional vans for the transport of parcels, perishable goods and luggage by passenger trains. It was decided that fifty should be ordered at once, and that they should be built at Nine Elms and have vacuum brake gear. They were numbered from 51 to 100 and are described in the register as being to drawing DB97A, but the design was substantially different from DB97. Was Adams following Beattie's practice of buying some and then improving on the design? The length was increased to 24ft and they had different panelling and different brake arrangements, as can be seen in Figure 1.2. It will be noticed that the hand lever appears to act against the vacuum cylinder. In fact the hand lever and the drop arm were loose on the cross-shaft, and the rod was connected to the top of the lever on the near left wheel only. At some later date, the brake arrangement was rebuilt on at least some of the vans. The cross-shaft was extended and the long lever fitted to the far side. On the near side, the drop arm

and link to the left wheel brake was removed and a lift link handbrake lever was fitted, connected to the cross-shaft.

It is very likely some of these vans that were referred to in a report in the April 1893 *South Western Gazette* of the record speed of landing mail from the liner New York. The mail gangway was fixed from the liner to the quay at 8.45am, and two checking boxes were prepared. The first bag was checked at 8.50am, and from that moment a continuous stream of men passed to and from the vessel. The whole of the mail, consisting of 898 bags was checked by 9.40am. The checking included directing to particular vans according to destination. The train consisted of the engine, a Guard's van and seven mail vans.

Another large batch of luggage vans was soon commenced at Nine Elms to drawing DB99, illustrated in Figure 1.3. Altogether 123 of these remained in the 1904 register, yet there is no mention at all in the minutes! It is possible that they were in fact commenced under the authority given in

Plate 1.2b. X2 class No 593, followed by a 24ft luggage van of 1887, drawing DB97A.   *(Lens of Sutton)*

Plate 1.2c. 24ft luggage van of 1897, drawing 97A, formerly No 79, in SR departmental service. Note the "skew brakes".
(Lens of Sutton)

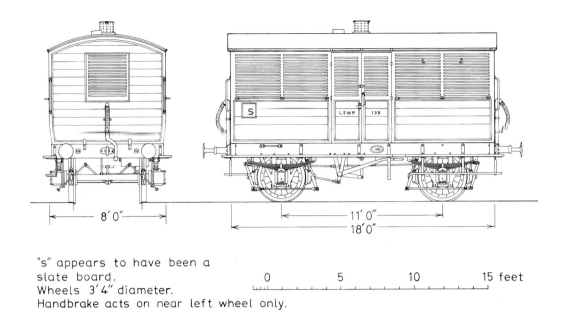

"s" appears to have been a
slate board.
Wheels 3'4" diameter.
Handbrake acts on near left wheel only.

Figure 1.3. 1887 18ft luggage van, drawing DB99.

Plate 1.3a. Pictured at Southampton, the nearest vehicle is 18ft luggage van of 1887, drawing DB99, and next to it is probably a 24ft composite and then a 28ft third. The photograph was taken before 1893.

("Hampshire and Isle of Wight", 1893)

Plate 1.3b. K10 class No 383 (built 1902). The vans on the right are 18ft luggage vans, drawing DB99, still in faded passenger livery. *(Lens of Sutton)*

Plate 1.3c. To the right of the PD&SWR brake van is an LSWR 18ft passenger luggage van. *(Lens of Sutton)*

Plate 1.3d. 700 class No 687 with troop train of LNWR carriages, 1899. The leading van, however, is an LSWR 18ft luggage van. *(Lens of Sutton)*

Plate 1.3e. New body built in 1904 on the underframe of 18ft luggage van No 136, drawing DB99, the only one so rebuilt.

November 1887 for 400 additional goods wagons and 200 cattle wagons on capital. If this is so, it might account for the odd fact that the first twenty were numbered after the rest. This could have happened if the first twenty were given goods numbers, but then a decision was taken that they were to be classed as passenger stock in view of their vacuum brakes and the intention to run them in passenger trains – in which case all those not completed or started upon would have received their passenger numbers from the outset with the first twenty then following them. Just a theory, but we shall never really know, and anyway it is not important enough to alter the cost of rail travel!

These vans were particularly noticeable for the fact that the upper half was almost totally louvred. They were similar to thirty 18ft meat vans, intended for running in passenger trains, that had been authorised at the end of March 1887 (illustrated as Figure 18 in *Southern Wagons, Volume 1*), the main external difference being that the luggage vans had a slight turn-under to the sides, like carriages, and were flush boarded on the lower half whereas the meat vans were flat sided and had outside framing. Although oil lights were provided there is no evidence of the provision of end steps, no doubt lamps were not often put in and when they were required somebody had to use a ladder to reach the roof, as in the earliest days.

They were originally painted in the carriage "salmon and brown" livery with the "LSWR" and number on the doors just below the waist. This can clearly be seen in a photograph of Southampton that was published in 1893, but in some other photos there is only a slight, and in some there is no, difference of shade. In most cases there is little evidence of varnish, since even the definitely brown parts appear as quite a light shade, on which the lettering hardly shows. One might deduce that they received passenger livery without the full quota of varnish coats both when new and subsequently, permitting early discolouration. It seems rather unlikely that they received any of the normal passenger lining out. In common with other passenger and goods vehicles the ends were the usual brown.

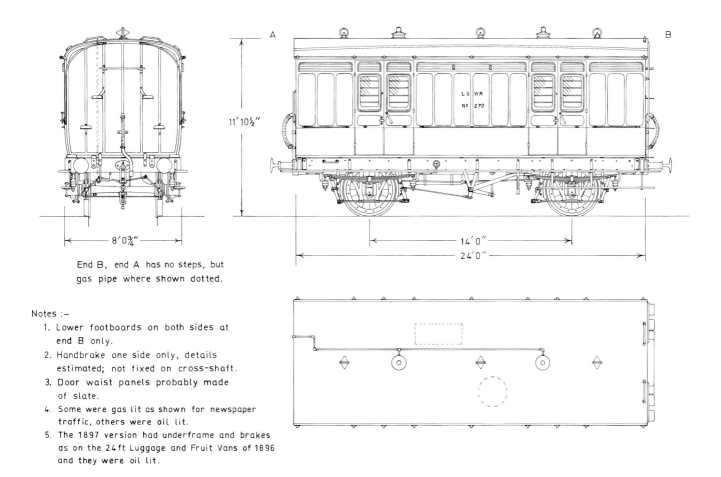

11'10½"

8'0¾"

End B, end A has no steps, but gas pipe where shown dotted.

Notes ;–
1. Lower footboards on both sides at end B only.
2. Handbrake one side only, details estimated; not fixed on cross-shaft.
3. Door waist panels probably made of slate.
4. Some were gas lit as shown for newspaper traffic, others were oil lit.
5. The 1897 version had underframe and brakes as on the 24ft Luggage and Fruit Vans of 1896 and they were oil lit.

14'0"

24'0"

0   5   10   15 feet

Figure 1.5. 1894 24ft luggage van, drawings 228 and 874.

The underframes were virtually identical to those of the meat vans. Both types had automatic vacuum brakes, and a handbrake lever was provided on one side only, operating the brake shoes on one wheel only, involving slotted links in the rodding, as for the DB97A van. Both the 24ft and the 18ft vans had brakes with diagonally mounted operating levers and outside link rods like those that Mr Panter had introduced for carriages, and referred to in some records as "Allen" brake rigging. The wheels appear to have been 3ft 4in diameter Mansell pattern, but one photograph shows one of them with ordinary spoked wheels.

Virtually all of them seem to have been withdrawn after quite a short life, between about 1900 and 1916, although some that were ciphered might have lasted a little longer. The underframe of

No 136 was re-used in 1904 for a solitary 18ft elliptical roofed van, still with louvred sides. In this form it lasted into Southern days, when it became No 1251, ending up in service use from 1935 until 1965 as No 919s.

A solitary 22ft 6in milk van, No 227, was built to Eastleigh drawing No 186, dated September 1893 and titled "New body for 227 milk van" using the new semi-elliptical roof shape, two double doors each side and with louvres in all upper panels and doors. The underframe was not shown. Since the number 227 follows the previous batch and there was no known earlier 22ft 6in milk van this is a little puzzling. No more were built, though this one survived until 1938. It is listed at Appendix item 1.4 but is not illustrated here.

It was quite quickly followed by a batch of 25

Plate 1.5a. A12 class 0-4-2 at Padstow. The leading van is a 24ft luggage van to drawing 228, followed by two covered carriage trucks, possibly 21ft, then five 18ft covered wagons.　　　*(LSWR Magazine/N Pomfret)*

Plate 1.5b. A class T9 with up milk train nearing Weybridge. The middle van in the left-hand arch is 24ft passenger luggage van to drawing 228.

Plate 1.5c. The leading vehicle is a 24ft passenger luggage van to drawing 228, and it is followed by a 44ft passenger brake van, two 48ft lavatory tri-composites of 1897, a 42ft third, and a 30ft arc-roofed passenger brake van. (B Curl collection)

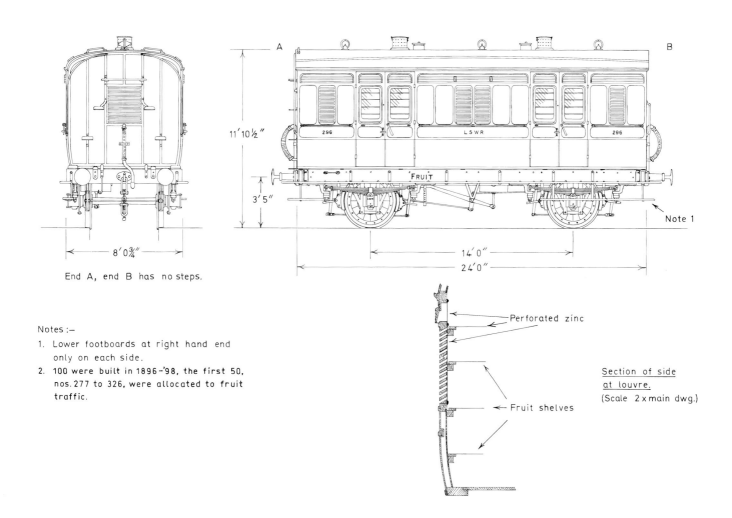

End A, end B has no steps.

Notes :—
1. Lower footboards at right hand end only on each side.
2. 100 were built in 1896 –'98, the first 50, nos. 277 to 326, were allocated to fruit traffic.

Perforated zinc

Fruit shelves

Section of side at louvre.
(Scale 2 x main dwg.)

0   5   10   15 feet

Figure 1.6. 1896 24ft luggage and fruit van, drawing 636.

Plate 1.6a. 24ft luggage van, formerly No 340, drawing 636, at Wimbledon in May 1920. *(HC Casserley)*

Plate 1.6b. 24ft luggage van LSWR No 393, drawing 636. *(Author's Collection)*

new luggage vans between July and September 1894 to drawing 228 (Figure 1.5), which shows a vehicle very similar to DB97A, including the use of "skew" brake rigging, but with the new semi-elliptical roof. Some of these were provided with oil lights and some with gas, the latter being reserved for newspaper traffic. Their capacity was 5 tons, which was increased to 6 tons from about 1918. A lever hand brake was fitted on one side only, again apparently only operating on one wheel.

The drawing was altered by the introduction of waist panels, ventilation louvres in some of the mid panels and in the ends, as well as by the use of vertical brake rigging, and was re-issued as No 636 in 1896. 100 more vans were then built to it, shown here as Figure 1.6. At least the first fifty, built in 1896 and 1897, had the word "Fruit" painted on the solebars. Internally, these fruit vans were fitted with four perforated zinc fruit shelves. It is not clear whether the remaining 50 built in 1898 were also fitted for fruit traffic or not. All were recorded as having oil lamps.

A further 24ft version followed in 1897, built to drawing 874, which is here included in Figure 1.5 with the details shown as Appendix item 1.5(b). The body was virtually identical to drawing 228, but the underframe and brakes were the same as for drawing 636. This time only a dozen were built; they were probably all oil-lit. A curious recording confusion exists about the next to last one, No 379. The 1904 register shows it as a hearse van, as were numbers 377 and 378, however the 1912 renumbering register

shows it being to drawing 874, and the Southern Railway showed it as the same diagram number as the rest of the drawing 636 and 874 vans. Perhaps there was a change of mind between authorisation and completion!

In 1895 a solitary 26ft "combined fruit and brake van" was built, being really a luggage van with a Guard's compartment at one end (Appendix item 1.7). At about the same time a drawing was prepared for a 26ft "combined milk and fruit van", but none of these appears in the registers. They were not mentioned in the minutes so one can only speculate on the reasoning. Certainly, fruit traffic had developed very greatly since the 1850s, but was mainly being catered for by the use of old passenger vehicles fitted with shelves. It is probable that the plan for these new vehicles was overtaken by the rapidly increasing availability of old AVB fitted carriages.

Fruit traffic was, of course, highly seasonal, although quite a lot came in throughout the year from abroad. Some idea of the extent of the home fruit traffic can be gained from the report of a talk given by Mr AC Holmes, Assistant District Superintendent for Central District during the middle of World War I. He said that the season for 1916 had been exceptionally good. Produce at Botley and Fareham had been plentiful and of good quality. The season practically closed on 15th July. In the previous season more than 450 vans had been provided for loose fruit, but this year it had not been possible to find more than 250 vans and they had

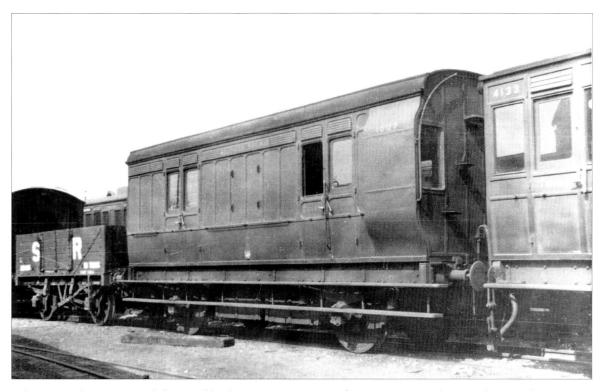

Plate 1.7. The solitary 26ft fruit and brake van, LSWR No 46, drawing 602, seen here on the Isle of Wight.

been obliged to make use of 18 passenger trains to make up the deficiency. This included four First class trains that were fitted up for the traffic, and these had given them a total of 375 vehicles, but as the passenger trains were in blocks of 10, 9, 7 or 6 vehicles each, which could only be used for consignments going to one destination, this showed how heavily the staff were handicapped in dealing with the traffic.

In 1915, the special trains sustained delays in starting to the extent of 2,162 minutes in aggregate, but in this season the total had been 1,482. The 1915 season commenced a few days earlier than this year and for the first 21 days the traffic was heavy, and on five occasions over 100,000 baskets a day were dealt with; on one day 126,000 were sent away. They only sent away more than 100,000 baskets on two occasions this year, which they considered fortunate since, had they been offered 100,000 on three consecutive days, there would have been no vehicles available for the fourth day's traffic. In the aggregate this year they were only just over 45,000 baskets behind the number for the corresponding days last year. They had despatched nearly 1,500,000 baskets of fruit from Swanwick alone and 2,490,000 from the whole district. The use of the passenger trains for the Manchester, Liverpool, London and Kew Bridge specials had enabled them to unload the carts quicker, and had resulted in the last trains getting away to time, which he was quite sure had benefited the staff as it had enabled them to leave work earlier at night.

The origin of the 48ft fruit vans, shown here as Figure 1.8, is somewhat confused. The luggage van register records fifteen built to drawing 791 in 1898, whilst the subsequent entries in the Guard's van register list seven of them as having been built in January and February 1898, with a further three in January 1899. However, the first mention in the minute books is in November 1898 when, following a proposal to build five bogie 44ft Guard's vans, it was also stated that the carriage works had capacity to build ten bogie fruit vans by June 1899. All earlier reference to bogie vans or Guard's vans can be identified with 44ft vans actually built. It therefore seems likely that the register entries should all read January and February 1899, particularly as the drawing, No 791, appears to have been drawn at the beginning of that year.

This drawing shows a Guard's compartment with handbrake column on one side of a fixed central partition, but with no lookouts, windows or doors, the only access being via one of the adjacent main luggage compartments. Thus, apart from the rodding below the solebars, there was no external evidence that it might be a Guard's van. It must be said, however, that from the heaviness of some lines and traces of possible erasures, the partition and Guard's seats might have been drawn in

subsequently. An inference might be that they were originally provided with a Guard's type hand-wheel brake simply as a "parking" brake instead of the external lever brake fitted on 4- and 6-wheeled vans. A note on the drawing states that fifteen were built for fruit traffic, and also that they each had four oil lamps. Only the ventilators are shown on the drawing.

In February 1900, the minutes record that five of the bogie fruit vans were being converted to ambulances for the War Department. In May 1900, approval was given for the construction of five new fruit vans, with Guard's compartments, to replace those converted to Ambulances – this might account for the apparent drawing alteration mentioned above. The luggage van register shows the five sold to the WD and twelve transferred to the Guard's van list in late 1901 and early 1902. The other three were recorded as broken up in mid-1903, although they actually reappear with the others in the Guard's van list. There was no further authorisation, but the 1906 diagram book lists the fifteen of them as Guard's vans, all with a central Guard's compartment, lookouts and doors, as shown in drawing 932. The Guard's van register shows them all as built to drawings 791 and 932, so whether the small "concealed" Guard's compartment was ever actually incorporated is not at all certain. Although drawing 791 shows the first fifteen as having four oil lamps the Guard's van register says they were all gas-lit, whilst photographs show some of them with gas lamps in addition to the oil lamps.

Three vehicles were re-classified as mailbag stowage vans in 1915, and had side gangway connections installed to match up with Post Office vans. Six were converted to aeroplane vans in 1918, these had their ends knocked out and replaced by double doors, as for covered carriage trucks. The Guard's compartment and handbrake on these were stripped out and Westinghouse brakes were fitted, but the lookouts appear to have been left in position until about 1930 or 1931. All of them appear to have been withdrawn by the end of 1938.

Although included in the PLV register, one might prefer to think of hearse vans as in a rather different category! Insufficient is known of the early hearse vans used for the Necropolis trains to permit a drawing, though they can just be seen in some photographs of the London Necropolis station in the fascinating book *The Brookwood Necropolis Railway* (2nd edition) by John M Clarke, published by The Oakwood Press in 1988.

The Deputy Chairman of The London Necropolis Co described the 1854 hearse vans as follows:

"...each (truck) divided transversely with twelve compartments, six above and six below, each compartment being at least seven feet long, that is as long as the interior width of the carriage, the width

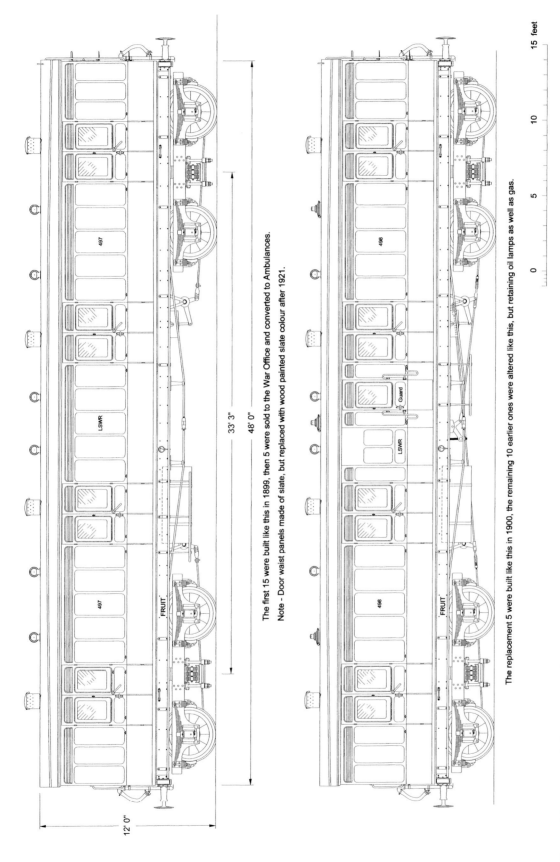

The first 15 were built like this in 1899, then 5 were sold to the War Office and converted to Ambulances.

Note - Door waist panels made of slate, but replaced with wood painted slate colour after 1921.

The replacement 5 were built like this in 1900, the remaining 10 earlier ones were altered like this, but retaining oil lamps as well as gas.

Figure 1.8. 1898 48ft fruit van and fruit brake, drawings 791 and 932. (1 of 2)

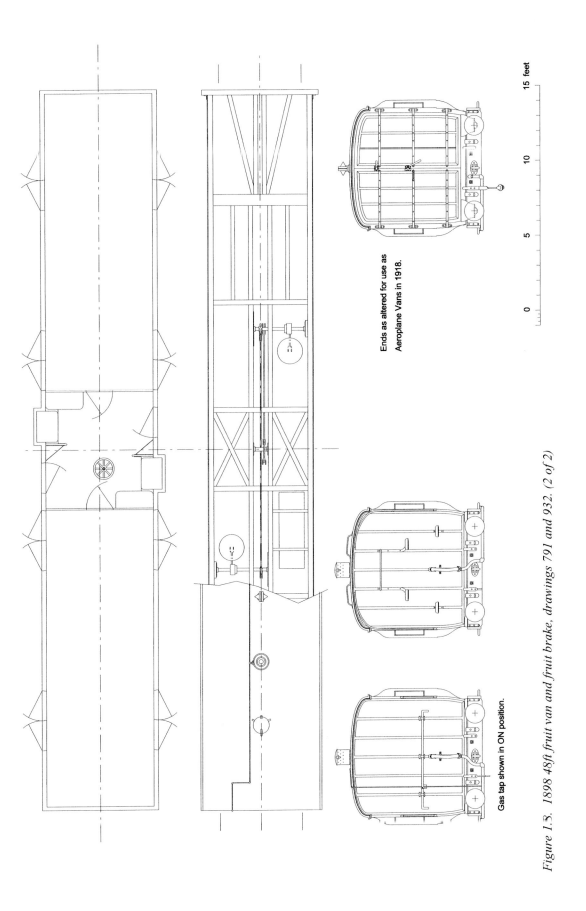

Ends as altered for use as
Aeroplane Vans in 1918.

Gas tap shown in ON position.

Figure 1.3. 1898 48ft fruit van and fruit brake, drawings 791 and 932. (2 of 2)

Plate 1.8a. Loading strawberries at Swanwick circa 1910. Two 48ft fruit vans (brake), drawing 791, are in the further train. Note that both have gas and oil lamps. Also present are 24ft passenger luggage vans, drawing 636, former passenger carriages used as fruit vans, and Midland (or S&DJR) luggage vans.

Plate 1.8b. *More fruit being loaded at Swanwick, but later than the previous view, as a 5-ton crane has been installed. In front of it is a 48ft fruit brake van. Note the gas and oil lamps.*

Plate 1.8c. *Up milk train approaching Wimbledon with 24ft luggage van, drawing 636; 48ft fruit brake van, drawing 932; 44ft brake van, drawing 667; 24ft luggage van, drawing 636; 44ft brake van.* (L&GRP/NRM)

Plate 1.8d. Channel Islands flower train hauled by class T9 No 286 with 48ft fruit brake, eight 24ft passenger luggage vans to drawing 636, and another 48ft fruit brake. (B Curl Collection)

and depth of each compartment to be that of an ordinary hearse."

Two Anglican and two Nonconformist trucks were built to this description at £16 each. This low price suggests that they were conversions of old carriages.

An Instruction to Station Agents in force in 1858 stipulated:

"Corpses conveyed in the Company's hearse carriage: 1/- a mile by ordinary trains. Corpses conveyed in a hearse on a carriage truck: 1/- a mile by ordinary trains. Corpses conveyed in a horse box: 8d a mile by ordinary trains, or in a hearse on a carriage truck by Parliamentary trains, 6d a mile. The charge to be no less than 8/- in any case."

These vans were looking distinctly ancient by the end of the 19th century, so two new ones were built in December 1899 to LSWR drawing 884, shown here as Figure 1.9 and seen in the photo of a double funeral train that was published in *LSWR Carriages, Volume 1* as Plate 4.16. They were 24ft long and broadly similar to the luggage and fruit vans of 1896, though of course they needed no windows or lighting! They had four compartments, if that is the right word, each with double doors. Cards with the names of the deceased could be inserted in card holders fitted to the doors. Originally, they were fitted with rollers on the floor and on the two upper racks for the easy loading and unloading of coffins. From the diagram book it appears that 24 coffins could be carried, but the upper racks were removed around 1910, which presumably reduced the capacity to eight. The original cost was £224 6s 11d each.

Automatic vacuum brakes were fitted, of course, but with a single lever hand brake as well. Steam-heating through-pipes were fitted in 1908 to permit heating in the rest of a Necropolis train. One of them was destroyed in May 1941 when a land mine destroyed the Head Office, the Waterloo Necropolis Station and the company records. The other survived the war but was withdrawn in August 1949.

At the end of 1902, a small batch of five fruit and milk vans (listed as usual in the register as luggage vans) was produced. The first one used the underframe of scrapped six-wheeled First No 434, 31ft 4in long and 7ft 6in wide, built in 1866, presumably at Nine Elms. Two more were built on similar, but unidentified, old underframes, and a further two on new underframes. Two LSWR drawings applied, 1115 for the body and 1131 for the new underframe. The accompanying drawing, Figure 1.10, is based on the latter. It can be seen that they looked very much like a "stretched" version of the 1894/96 24ft luggage and fruit vans. They were provided with movable shelves for seasonal use as fruit vans.

For no obvious reason they do not appear to have found much favour for milk or fruit traffic. No more were built, and two of the five were transferred to departmental use as early as 1913, while two more had end doors fitted to convert them into aeroplane vans in 1918. Structurally, they were sound because three remained in use until between 1939 and 1948.

Between 1907 and 1909, sixteen vehicles described as special milk vans were built to drawing 1598, and seen here as Figure 1.11. Despite the description, they do not appear to have been used solely for that traffic. They were 32ft long and had six wheels. The first three, numbers 163, 198 and 266, took their numbers from the three vans that were destroyed in the milk train that was involved in the Salisbury smash of 1906.

To improve cooling, the roof had an inner lining, but all the roof sticks and the top of the ends had holes to permit a through draught, this was aided by the fact that the torpedo ventilators only ventilated the roof cavity. A photograph of the first van built, No 163, shows only four ventilators, but the official drawings and photos of later vans show six. That photo of 163 also shows the end vents unhooded, as do the drawings; however, as with the 24ft vans, it seems probable that they all had hoods

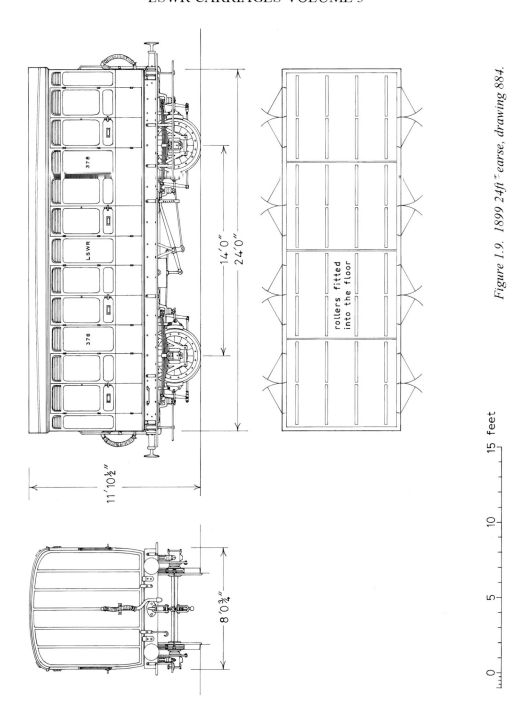

Figure 1.9. 1899 24ft hearse, drawing 884.

rollers fitted
into the floor

14'0"
24'0"

11'10½"

8'0¾"

15 feet

10

5

0

from very early on.

A drawing of the underframe was published in *Modern Railway Working* in 1912. This is fully detailed, but there is a discrepancy when compared with photographs of actual vans. In the drawing the brake handles are both shown as right-handed, needing a reversing link on one of them. However, photographs show one right-hand and one left-hand lever, so the present drawing shows them that way. Both vacuum and Westinghouse brakes were fitted, and a steam-heating through-pipe was also provided. As with the 6-wheeled Guard's vans, they were not permitted to be worked into Southampton Docks,

nor were they allowed on the Lee-on-the-Solent or the Easton and Church Hope branches. They were only permitted on the Lyme Regis branch "when absolutely necessary".

The most obvious feature of one of these vans was that the whole body, including the ends, of the officially photographed one, No 163, was originally painted in LSWR salmon colour, presumably as a further aid to keeping the interior cool. It is not known whether any of the others were painted similarly, but Plate 1.12a shows six of them in normal two-tone livery by 1911.

In 1918/19, nine of these vans were altered to

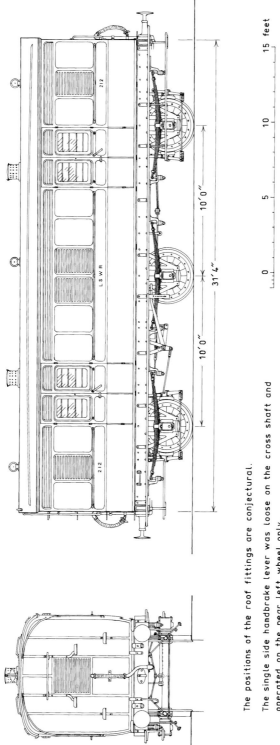

The positions of the roof fittings are conjectural.

The single side handbrake lever was loose on the cross shaft and operated on the near left wheel only.

Five were built in Dec.1902, the first on an old underframe of 1866, the rest on new frames, as shown.

For details of the louvres, see the 24ft. Luggage Van of 1894.

Figure 1.10. 1902 31ft 4in fruit and milk van, drawings 1115 and 1131.

Plate 1.10a. 31ft 4in fruit and milk van, probably LSWR No 195.   *(RC Riley Collection)*

Plate 1.10b. 31ft 4in fruit and milk van No 212, drawings 1115 and 1131, at Exmouth Junction in June 1948.
(JH Aston)

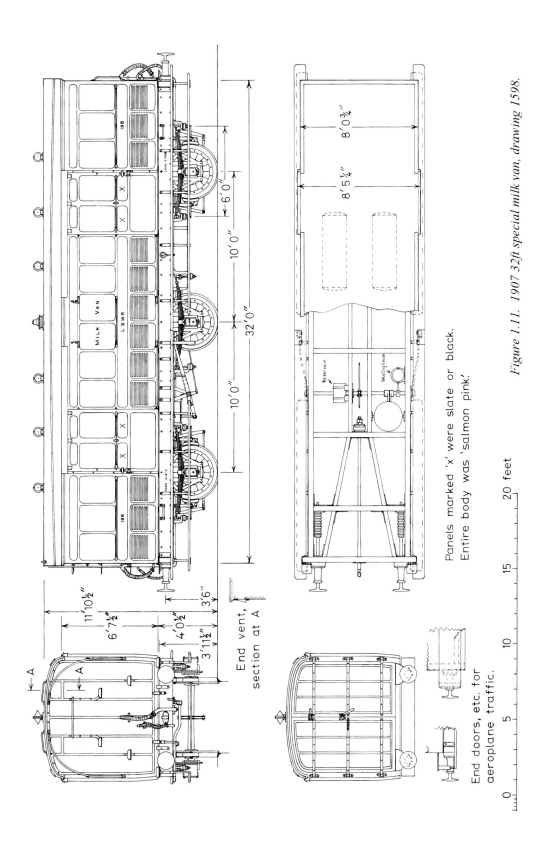

Panels marked 'x' were slate or black.

Entire body was 'salmon pink'.

End doors, etc. for aeroplane traffic.

End vent, section at A

Figure 1.11. 1907 32ft special milk van, drawing 1598.

Plate 1.11a. 32ft special milk van No 163, drawing 1598, in original salmon livery.

(British Railways)

Plate 1.11b. 32ft special milk van, LSWR No 223, drawing 1598, nearing the end of its days at Ashford in June 1958. *(JH Aston)*

carry aeroplanes. This involved fitting double doors in both ends and steel wheel plates along both sides of the floor, extending out over the buffer stocks. These features are shown in Figure 1.8, the 48ft fruit brake vans, of which six were similarly converted. The brake connections had to be altered of course, presumably with headstock level pipes as for corridor carriages.

A new design of luggage van was introduced in 1909 that, with slight variations, was to be the standard such vans right through until Grouping, in fact the final twenty were completed under Southern

ownership, and therefore did not receive LSWR numbers.

Like the 32ft special milk vans, they had sliding doors and louvres in all the bottom panels, also including the doors. The roof was of a noticeably flatter section than on other vans and non-corridor carriages.

There were several different drawings over the years, affecting underframes, brakes, shelving, a change to steel panelling instead of wood, and so on, but they all had the same essential features and dimensions, so all were included on the same

Plate 1.12a. A special train of specie vans from Waterloo, seen at Eastleigh circa 1911. Five 24ft special passenger luggage vans, drawing 1835/6; six 32ft special milk vans, all in two-tone livery; and a 44ft passenger brake van. *(B Curl Collection)*

Southern diagram, No 929. The first fourteen, from March 1909, were to drawings 1835 and 1836, the difference between these drawings and the next ones, 2104 (body) and 2105 (underframe), to which 45 vans were built between October 1912 and December 1913, is not at all obvious. In 1916, drawing 2571 was issued, but it is not certain what this covered, probably shelving, flooring or panelling, since the next batch was built to drawings 2104, 2105 and 2571. There were thirty of these between April and August 1916. The next thirty, from June to December 1917, were to the original body drawing 2104, and 2716, which was therefore presumably the underframe. An example of this batch, No 5025, is preserved at Quainton Road, and it can be seen that the brake gear appears to be based on the Dean-Churchward pattern. The next variation was a reversion to the original underframe, drawing 2105, but the body drawing 3072, had three upper panels in place of every pair on the other vans. The top, waist and bottom panels were unaltered. Twenty were built like this between June and September 1919. Thereafter the appearance reverted to the original style, although the 1923 batch had different floor materials and fruit shelving that were detailed in drawing 3992. Figure 1.12 attempts to depict most of the variations.

The earlier vans were gas-lit but in August 1916 a change was made to oil lighting and this was used for all the later vans. As with all types of so-called luggage vans they were in fact used for all sorts of work. A 1911 picture of a bullion train shows some of these among 32ft milk vans and 48ft fruit brake vans. Many of them are shown in the register as marked for fruit traffic, particularly the early batch, most of those from October 1913 to August 1916, and the "3-panel" batch. Some were also shown as for milk and fruit. Probably those reserved for fruit had the word "FRUIT" painted in 3in white lettering on the solebars. The livery did not repeat that of the first 32ft milk van, but was the normal LSWR livery as for carriages.

At least two were bought by preservation societies. As mentioned, No 5025, SR 1451, which had acted as a parked store at Tisbury for many years, went to Quainton Road in about 1970. No 5498, SR 1584, was condemned in June 1969 and subsequently preserved on the Bluebell Railway.

Several of the van types considered have either been described as milk vans, or batches have been reserved for milk traffic. Certainly they had to be reserved for the work both to avoid contamination of the milk by other goods carried, and so that any spilled milk did not contaminate other goods. Milk had to be carried from country districts to most large towns on the system, but an indication of the traffic to London is given in the *South Western Gazette*. In February 1885, it recorded, "The number of Imperial gallons of milk conveyed to Waterloo in the quarter ending 31st December 1884 was 932,488, and to Vauxhall, Clapham Junction, Chelsea, etc 439,500, a total of 1,370,988 gallons". Again, in May 1886, another statement was, "Vauxhall milk traffic – in the quarter ending 31st March, over 51,000 churns

Plate 1.12b. 24ft luggage van, LSWR No 5368, drawings 2104, 2105 and 2571.   *(F Foote)*

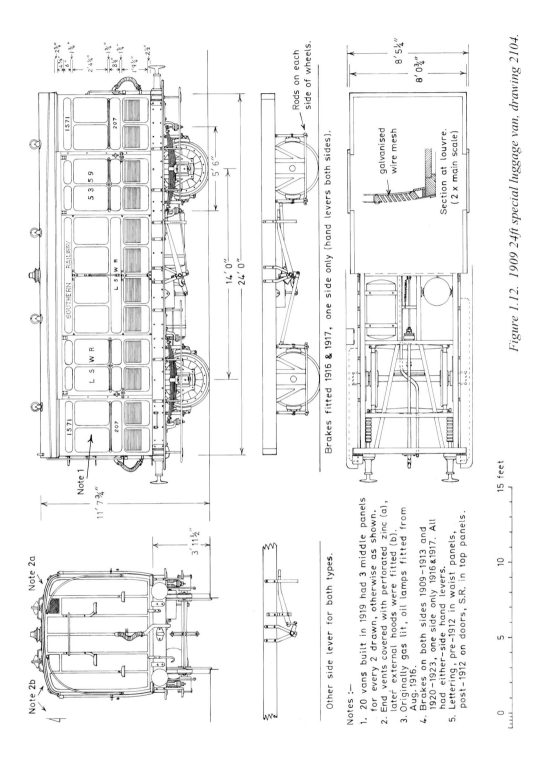

Figure 1.12. 1909 24ft special luggage van, drawing 2104.

Notes :-

1. 20 vans built in 1919 had 3 middle panels for every 2 drawn, otherwise as shown.
2. End vents covered with perforated zinc (a), later external hoods were fitted (b).
3. Originally gas lit, oil lamps fitted from Aug. 1916.
4. Brakes on both sides 1909–1913 and 1920–1923, one side only 1916 & 1917. All had either-side hand levers.
5. Lettering, pre-1912 in waist panels, post-1912 on doors, S.R. in top panels.

Plate 1.12c. 24ft luggage van, SR No 1615, built December 1923 to drawings 2104 and 2105, at Hayling Island in 1948. *(JH Aston)*

Plate 1.12d. 24ft passenger luggage van, No 158 (SR No 1569), built October 1912 to drawing 2104 seen at Fratton in April 1948. *(JH Aston)*

were received[1]. Earlier, in November 1883, there had been official complaints about the condition of the milk arch at Waterloo as a result of which there had been a meeting with the Managing Director of the Aylesbury Dairy Company, who were thus presumably the current tenants.

From quite early times, special vehicles had been required for the carriage of bullion and other high-value goods to and from the ships at Southampton. These had generally been provided

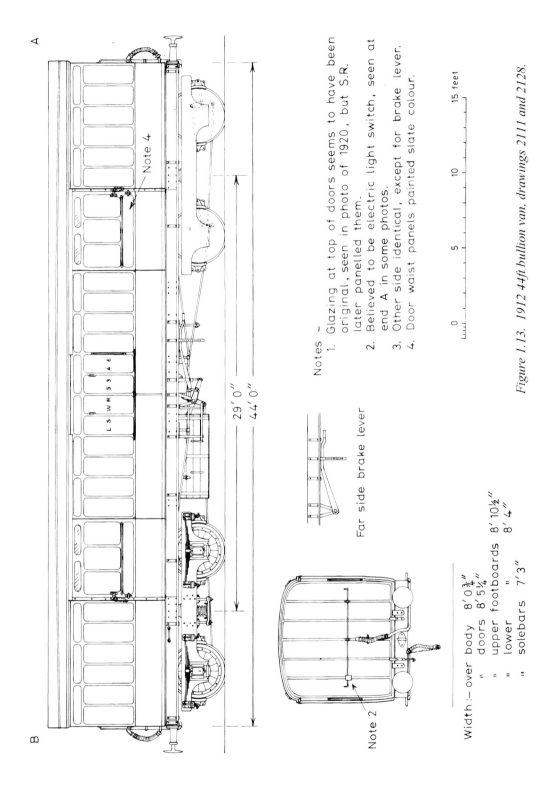

Notes :-
1. Glazing at top of doors seems to have been original, seen in photo of 1920, but S.R. later panelled them.
2. Believed to be electric light switch, seen at end A in some photos.
3. Other side identical, except for brake lever.
4. Door waist panels painted slate colour.

Far side brake lever

Note 2

Width :- over body   8' 0¾"
  "   doors   8' 5¼"
  "   upper footboards   8' 10½"
  "   lower   "   8' 4"
  "   solebars   7' 3"

Figure 1.13. 1912 44ft bullion van, drawings 2111 and 2128.

by strengthening some ordinary vans, and reserving them for the purpose, but in November 1911, it was decided to build twelve special bogie vans for this work. The drawings were No 2111 (body) and 2128 (underframe), shown here as Figure 1.13, and they were completed and put into service during December 1912 and January 1913.

They were entirely steel panelled, both outside and inside, including under the floorboards and inside the roof. There were no windows apart from two glazed lights in the top of each sliding door. It is difficult to see what use these windows served, and they were replaced by panels by the Southern Railway. The underframes were of steel, and were provided with the usual vacuum brakes and steam heating through pipes. Hand brakes with levers on both sides were provided. Electric lighting was fitted, supplied from two battery boxes. This lighting appears to have been controlled by an external switch at one end of the body, using a switch box and operating rods very similar in appearance to the gas switches fitted on earlier vehicles. Tare weight was around 22 tons and the authorised load was 10 tons.

The bullion vans were the last passenger rated vans to be designed by the LSWR.

Although any of the vans described in this chapter could have been seen running in passenger trains, singly or severally, anywhere on the system, the LSWR also ran some trains solely made up of vans or, in a few cases, with just a few passenger vehicles included.

Looking at the Waterloo Trains Summary for 1911/12 several of the early morning and late evening trains are of this sort. For example, those leaving from the Waterloo South and Central Stations are shown in table 1, and those leaving from the North Station are listed in table 2.

No records are available to show the extent to which these vans ran as such substantial trains in the Up direction, though it seems likely that many were attached in small quantities to passenger trains.

The luggage vans that were either built for, or assigned to, fruit traffic have already been discussed. However, to meet the seasonal demand, a lot of old passenger carriages were adapted for this work by having their seats replaced by shelving; these were known as "J" sets.

The set formations shown in the Appendix have been culled from the carriage registers; there is no known official list of the "J" sets. In some cases, only one vehicle can be identified, though it is assumed that all sets were of two carriages. In a few cases there are discrepancies between the registers. The original date of such formations is not recorded, although a few vehicles have dates around 1908-1910 marked against the "J" set entry, but the *Railway Magazine* for August 1907 had the following note:

"The London and South-Western Railway has found a novel use for its old 3rd class coaches. They are being used for fruit traffic, for which work they are adapted with practically no alteration save fixing shelving in them. The exterior lettering remains on the coaches, but the word FRUIT is painted on the solebars."

Vehicles may well have been replaced from time to time, and this seems particularly likely where low number sets have elliptical roofed vehicles. All vehicles listed are believed to have been arc roofed except those marked (E), which almost certainly had elliptical roofs. In all, by 1925, 74 such sets were formed.

Table 1. Early morning and late evening trains leaving from Waterloo South and Central Stations

5.35am   4-coach set and 1 bogie news van to Southampton Pier.
1 Passenger Luggage Van (PLV) to Portsmouth Town.
1 bogie van to Stokes Bay.
1 bogie van to Ascot via Woking.

5.50am   1 bogie van to Wimborne via Bournemouth West.
4-coach set and 1 bogie news van to Weymouth.
1 Post Office van to Dorchester.
1 bogie van to Bournemouth Central.
1 News van to Dorchester via Wimborne.
1 PLV to Lymington Pier.
1 bogie van to Swanage.

6.24am   1 PLV to Wells.
1 PLV to Wincanton.
1 PLV to West Pennard.
1 6-wheel van to Highbridge.
1 PLV to Templecombe.
1 PLV and 1 bogie van to Yeovil.
2 PLVs to Gillingham.
2 M&SW vans to Andover Junction.
3 M&SW vans to Andover Junction, Saturdays only.

9.50pm   1 bogie van to Southampton.
4-coach set and 1 PLV (Mon, Wed & Fri) to Southampton Docks.
1 Post Office van, 2 bogie vans, 2-coach set to Dorchester via Southampton.
1 PLV to Bournemouth Central.
1 Brake Composite (1st & 2nd) to Southampton Docks.
1 bogie van to Portsmouth Town via Eastleigh.

Table 2. Early morning and late evening trains leaving from Waterloo North Stations

3.0am   "Churn Train"
1 bogie van and 1 Westinghouse fitted PLV to Yeovil.
1 PLV (Mon only) to Crewkerne.
1 PLV and 1 Westinghouse PLV to Highbridge.
1 PLV and 1 Westinghouse PLV to Templecombe.
1 PLV to Stalbridge.
1 PLV to Shillingstone.
(Down to here were all loaded in No 16 road, the rest in No 18 road.)
3 6-wheel Westinghouse milk vans to Gillingham.
1 6-wheel van and 1 PLV to Semley.
1 bogie van to Salisbury.
1 bogie van to Wimborne, via Salisbury.
1 M&SW van to Swindon.
2 M&SW vans to Andover Junction.
1 PLV to Southampton.
1 PLV to Wimborne.
1 PLV to Gillingham.
1 PLV to Aldershot.
1 bogie van and 1 PLV to Petersfield.
1 PLV to Southampton via Alton.

7.17am   2 PLVs to Southampton Docks with Cherbourg churns (when required).
1 covered carriage truck, 3 open carriage trucks and 9 horse boxes to various stations.
1 PLV and a covered carriage truck or van, Mondays only, to Eastleigh shops for tail lamps.
1 corridor Third brake to Bournemouth Central.

12.25pm   "Churn Train"
1 PLV to Gillingham.
1 PLV to Semley.
1 bogie van to Bournemouth West via Salisbury.
1 PLV to Salisbury.
2 M&SW vans to Swindon.
1 bogie van to Basingstoke.
1 PLV to Petersfield.
1 new milk van to Midhurst.
1 bogie van to Liss.
1 PLV to Alton.

3.36pm   1 covered carriage truck, 3 open carriage trucks and 12 horse boxes to various stations.
1 corridor Third brake to Eastleigh.
10.12pm 1 bogie van (Sat ex) to Exeter.
1 bogie van (Sat ex) to Plymouth.
1 bogie van to Yeovil
1 PLV to Henstridge.
1 6-wheel van to Stalbridge.
1 PLV to Shillingstone.
1 S&D van to Bridgewater.
1 bogie van to Basonbridge.
1 Westinghouse PLV to Wells.
1 PLV to West Pennard.
1 PLV to Pylle.
1 PLV to Wincanton.
2 PLVs to Bath.
1 bogie van to Templecombe.
1 6-wheel van to Yeovil Junction.
1 PLV to Crewkerne.

*Plate 1.13a.
44ft bullion van,
LSWR No 5345,
drawings, 2111
and 2128.*

Plate 1.13b. 44f specie van built December 1912, seen as DS105 after September 1945, with roof ventilators and a gas cylinder.

POST OFFICE VANS

As with much else about LSWR rolling stock, very little detail is recorded about the actual vehicles used for the carriage of mails, although there are several references in the Minutes to the various requirements of the General Post Office (GPO). Worse, from the present point of view, is the fact that, with one incomplete exception, no builders' drawings seem to have survived. The LSWR and SR diagrams still exist, but even here there are slight discrepancies, and definitely some undated alterations. Also, there are very few photographs, possibly because many of the mail trains ran at night, and the postal carriages probably spent most of the daylight hours tucked away in carriage sidings. Therefore, all the drawings for this section have had to include some degree of conjecture. It is hoped that readers will accept this as better than having no drawings at all.

Fortunately the Post Office has retained in its archives a considerable quantity of Letter Books, which contain copies of outgoing letters, and other documents from which quite a lot can be gleaned. Understandably though, for every letter concerning the actual vehicles on any of the many railways concerned there are dozens relating to new and rerouted bags, complaints of delays, and so on. Particularly regrettable is the fact that although the books are complete until January 1871, after that the volumes for only the first half of every fifth year have been retained. Therefore one is lucky if discussion of vehicles or services occurred just in those periods, but of course even these scraps are extremely helpful. I am very grateful to the staff of the Post Office Archive at Mount Pleasant for their help in explaining their system and getting the various books out for me.

The earliest mention of postal services in the London & Southampton Railway Minutes was in June 1838, when the L&SR joined with several other companies to petition Parliament against a proposal by the Post Office that it should be authorised to run its own trains on all railways in much the same manner as it ran mail coaches on the roads.

At this time, and until after the passing of the Post Office (Parcels) Act in 1882, Post Office mail consisted only of letters; any parcels traffic was handled by the railways. From 1883, the public had the choice for parcels to go *via* either the PO or the railway company.

The next, fairly short-lived scheme, was for the Post Office mail coaches to be carried on the trains, using the earliest form of open carriage truck. The Post Office guard stayed in or on his coach during the journey, and at first the Post Office apparently provided tarpaulin sheets to give their vehicles some protection. The first specific service mentioned, in October 1839, was from London (Nine Elms) to

Farnborough, then a week or so later from Farnborough to Basingstoke. At the beginning of December, the Post Office announced that the Exeter coach would be carried by train between Nine Elms and Basingstoke from 5th December. In another source this is referred to as the Devonport coach, *Quicksilver*. This was followed by the Portsmouth coach from 17th December. It was not mentioned where this latter was transferred to the road, but presumably at Woking.

By May 1840, the Post Office was requiring that accommodation should be provided in or on the railway company vehicles for the mails and the guard, and it was stated that an "Imperial" (a large weatherproof box) on the roof for the mail bags, and an outside seat for the guard, would be adequate. Mr Beattie was then instructed to have some carriages altered for this purpose, but no details specific to the LSWR have come to light. The PO Guards were charged the same fare as an "outside" passenger and mailbags were charged at 1d per mile.

In September 1842 it was recorded that the Post Office would be charged £7 per night for the night mail from Gosport to London. Presumably, this included the mail from Portsmouth, and would have travelled to Bishopstoke for connection with the London train. The following August saw the need to provide substantially more mail accommodation between Southampton and London, since Mail Packet Boats were now terminating at Southampton instead of at Falmouth. This would have needed just wagon or van accommodation.

Nearly three years later, in July 1845, the Post Office ceased sending a coach by Carriage Truck to Andover Road station (Micheldever), thus saving costs. It is clear that by November 1847 mail bags were being carried somewhere other than in Imperials because at the time it was required that Imperials should be used again "pending better arrangements". It seems possible that excess bags were being put into compartments, wagons or vans without any special precautions.

A year later the Post Office had apparently queried the fares for the guards and whether the LSWR would take responsibility for the mails, which the latter firmly declined to do. It may be that it was after this that the "better arrangements" were that the Post Office should have certain compartments of Second class carriages allocated for the mails.

An unsigned and undated paper in the Post Office Archives states that both day and night sorting carriages started running between London and Southampton in April 1850. Unfortunately, there is no information at all about these early sorting carriages. Sorting carriages are only recorded as working four routes on the South

Western: London – Southampton, Southampton – Dorchester, Southampton – Portsmouth, and Exeter – Torrington. The first two were combined at some time after the opening of the Northam curve in 1858, permitting through running between Waterloo and Dorchester.

Mail for North Devon travelled via the Great Western and the Bristol and Exeter Railways. At no time up to Grouping did the LSWR carry London mail to Exeter, but the LSWR carried the mail between Exeter and North Devon. In the reverse direction anything that went through the Exeter Post Office for London travelled up by the GWR.

GPO instructions of 1854 show that bags from the London Inland Sorting Office and from the sorting carriages of the other railways were sorted so that bags could be put down at various stations on the way, and other bags picked up. For example, bags for Guildford and Ripley were left at Woking, and those for Portsmouth, Gosport and Fareham were left at Bishopstoke (later Eastleigh).

At Southampton, the bags for local distribution were handed to PO messengers and all those for what was called the Dorchester Road were transferred to the guard (whether PO or LSWR is not clear) of the Southampton – Dorchester service. The Dorchester service carried bags for Salisbury, Lymington, Ringwood, Wimborne, Poole, Wareham, Dorchester, Bridport, Sherborne and Yeovil. The inclusion of Salisbury on that line seems strange, since the Southampton to Salisbury line via Bishopstoke and Romsey (the GPO spelt it Rumsey) had opened in 1847.

In November 1853, the LSWR agreed to Post Office proposals to place mailbag exchange equipment at various (unnamed) places. Nothing further came of this, and another writer claims that this was because of opposition by the LSWR Directors. This is possibly because there had been some problems on other railways for various reasons, most of which were not overcome until the Post Office developed an improved design of apparatus in 1858. As far as the LSWR was concerned, the matter was not officially raised again until October 1885, when the Post Office wanted to accelerate the Down Mail by having mailbag apparatus installed at Surbiton, Woking, Farnborough, Winchfield and Micheldever. The exchange apparatus was to be fitted in "the two mail vans in regular use". We will return to this later.

The first reference to the construction of a new special vehicle for the mails was in July 1854, when the Locomotive Committee considered Mr Beattie's plan for a "Post Office and Guards Van in one frame". It had been approved by the Superintendent of the GPO, and it was recommended that two should be built for the Dorchester line. In those days carriages were usually built fairly quickly, certainly within four or five months. So it is a little puzzling

that a minute for June 1855 reports that Mr E J Page, Inspector General of Mails, had complained of insufficient accommodation provided by Mail Van No 65 on the Southampton to Dorchester line, and requesting that a proper carriage be substituted. Mr Beattie was then again required to submit a plan for a "Post Office van and Break on one frame". This description sounds rather like a variant of a normal Goods Brake Van, but with the goods area fitted out for the use of the Post Office. The reference to "Mail Van No 65" suggests that they were using a specially-reserved ordinary passenger vehicle.

In discussing luggage vans earlier in the previous Chapter, it was mentioned that in April 1859 it was decided to have built by contract "twelve covered wagons ... for mails, fish, baggage, etc, by the passenger trains". When Mr Beattie submitted plans in the following August, he recommended that they should be fitted with breaks – which presumably implies a guard's compartment. Whether any of the resulting vehicles were actually used as bag tenders, or possibly for what Post Office records refer to as "district sorting duties", is not certain.

A further letter was received from Mr Page in December 1858, suggesting that the LSWR should bear a proportion of the cost of construction of new carriages required by the Post Office. This was referred to the Locomotive, Carriage and Stores Committee to ascertain whether existing Post Office carriages could be adapted for any other purpose, and if so at what cost. On their response, it was agreed in January 1859, that the cost of three new enlarged carriages for sorting on the night mail trains should be shared, the Post Office contributing £60 each towards the shells, and to provide all the internal fittings. The existing carriages were to be used for any purpose the LSWR thought fit. There is no evidence of any immediate action on this.

Around this period, there were several requests from the GPO for quotations for the carriage of day mail bags on various lines. In each case, the reply was that each bag would be charged as for a Second class passenger.

The Post Office wrote at the end of April 1859 to say that the Postmaster General had authorised the payment of £100 towards the cost of the shell of each of the new night mail sorting carriages. The Post Office would also pay for all the internal fittings, but would only require two carriages to be built. They would require their Inspector of Mails to meet the carriage builder to explain the dimensions and specifications. Rather surprisingly, in view of the revised requirement for two carriages, Joseph Wright offered, in October, to construct the "three Sorting Vans agreed with the Post Office" for £391 each, delivered on the line, and this was accepted. Then in January 1860, it was belatedly noted that only two of the three Post Office vans would be

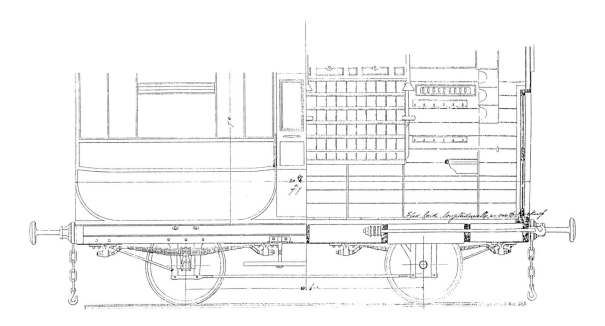

Figure 2.1. Circa 1860 LSWR 20ft 4in sorting van No 1. (Not to scale.)

required, and that Wright had agreed to convert the third one to a First class carriage at the same price; this was accepted.

A month later the Post Office requested unspecified alterations to the painting of the vans, and that they should be fitted with "Moderator" lamps, "as done by the South Eastern Company". In October, Wrights charged £34 8s for the extra roof and sealing wax lamps supplied for the two new PO sorting vans, and it was agreed that the LSWR should pay £20 of it.

Just to confuse matters, the LSWR Register of 1904 shows No 2 as having been built in 1862, and broken up in 1900 (No 1 is not mentioned), whilst the Post Office Roster of TPOs for 1902 lists numbers 1 and 2, both built 1862, as spare at Eastleigh, but with a note that No 2 was formerly shown as No 3, built in 1863. The LSWR Minutes do not mention any postal vehicles either ordered or delivered in 1861 or 1862, although the stock returns for June and December 1862 both record two Post Office sorting vans.

There is a drawing of a 20ft 4in by 7ft 7in Post Office van in the Joseph Wright (Metropolitan) collection (Birmingham Public Library reference 19/45). The drawing is marked L&SW, and appears to date from before the 1862 formation of the Metropolitan Company. Since the Post Office had required that their Inspector of Mails should meet the carriage builder to provide dimensions and specifications, this is almost certainly the one for these two carriages. Unfortunately it is incomplete with nothing above the cornice and cant rail, no end view and no plan. This drawing is shown here as Figure 2.1.

Also shown, at Figure 2.1a, is a conjectural drawing of how it might have looked in its complete form. This drawing was inspired by the efforts of Mr PH Swift of the South Western Circle, who built a convincing model based on photos of similar vans on other lines. Some of the present assumptions are slightly different from his, so any mistakes are entirely my own!

The Wright drawing was originally marked as having a body length of 19ft 6in; the alteration to 20ft 4in for the LSWR doesn't have any obvious reason, unless Joseph Beattie simply wanted to make his own mark on bought-in products, as he seems to have done with several carriages and wagons from outside builders!

This drawing shows that, in common with those of the LNWR and some other railways, they had the main door on one side only. Thus they had to be either turned on turntables (as at Waterloo) or shunted to arrive correctly at platforms. This may seem strange nowadays, but then it was fairly common to move vehicles between platforms by the use of turntables and lines across the station. Goods vans with doors on only one side also featured on many other railways.

By showing only half of the outside and the far half of the inside, the drawing leaves a question over the exact design of the main door. On all the other vans of which pictures have been seen, it appears to be a single, wide sliding door, without turn-under and sliding to the left. This left plenty of space on the right for the bag apparatus installed on many vans, but not of course on the LSWR ones. A detail

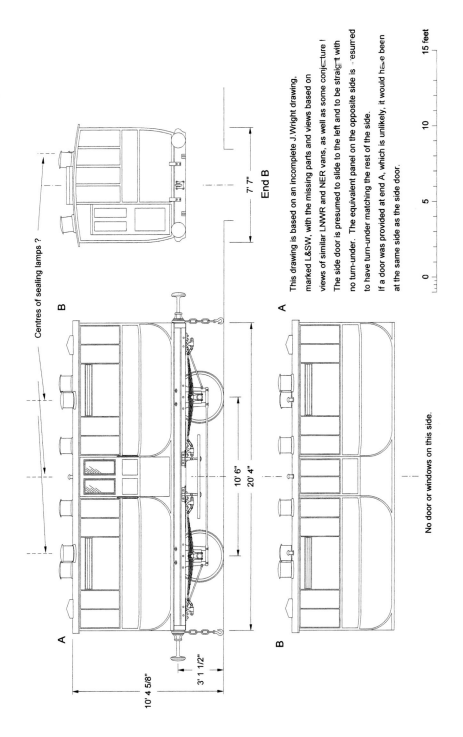

Centres of sealing lamps ?

End B

This drawing is based on an incomplete J.Wright drawing, marked L&SW, with the missing parts and views based on views of similar LNWR and NER vans, as well as some conjecture ! The side door is presumed to slide to the left and to be straight with no turn-under. The equivalent panel on the opposite side is presurred to have turn-under matching the rest of the side.
If a door was provided at end A, which is unlikely, it would have been at the same side as the side door.

No door or windows on this side.

15 feet

Figure 2.1a. Circa 1860 LSWR 20ft 4in postal sorting van No 1. Conjectural complete drawing.

that causes some doubt is what appears to be a horizontal handle on the door shown – if actually fitted to a sliding door it would not pass the door post! Two inward opening hinged doors are possible, but at only about 15in wide seem unlikely.

There is a sliding door shown in one end, but with no indication of whether it was side or central, nor with any sign of a gangway connection. Nor is there any indication of whether one was provided at the other end. This raises the question of how men or mailbags were transferred between vehicles with acceptable safety. It will be seen later that in the 1890s there were requirements to fit gangways – presumably Lansdown type – to these early Sorting Carriages. The end view in Figure 2.1a, showing it as at the main door side, is based, as before, on photos from other lines. If there was a door at the other end it was probably on the same side.

Another unusual feature of the Wright drawing is that it shows the use of an extra set of inside axle guards. This appears to be a variant of Joseph Beattie's patent of April 1859, mentioned in *LSWR Carriages, Volume 1* page 38, designed to minimise the effect of broken axles, of which there had been several reports around that time.

The titles Railway Post Office (RPO), Sorting Carriage (SC) and Travelling Post Office (TPO) are terms used in PO and LSWR records for LSWR services. The term "tender" doesn't crop up until quite late. District Sorting Carriages are mentioned early on, but there is no clear evidence of what the vehicles were like unless they were as mentioned earlier, nor is it clear which district is meant. The

RPOs and TPOs handled mail to and from the London Inland Office and other railway routes.

On 10th May 1862, a new contract was signed between the Postmaster General (PMG), Lord Stanley of Alderley and the LSWR, setting out the details of the postal services to be run and the accommodation required on each. This document is on very large sheets of parchment and is held in the Public Record Office (RAIL 411/348). There are four schedules, the first two of which detail the services.

Schedule 1, to some extent, clarifies the descriptions of the vehicles. The Travelling Post Offices (TPOs) on the London – Southampton Night Mail were clearly numbers 1 and 2 of 1860, with a variety of other vehicles, mainly unidentified Second class carriages and Guards vans loosely described as Mail carriages or vans, but not in any separate numbered postal list. A little more help, though not much, is given by a minute of July 1860, when Mr Scott reported that the Post Office desired increased accommodation in the Post Office carriages used for day mails. It was then agreed, "that a division in the Second class compartment may be removed if the Post Office pays for it". Again, in August 1863, Mr Scott recommended that "the old Post Office vans should be divided so as to give half for mailbags and half for luggage, and that doors should be placed on each side".

In August 1862, the Post Office asked the LSWR to furnish two new sorting carriages for the night mails as quickly as possible. The LSWR clearly prevaricated on the grounds of cost, because

Schedule 1 (all these Day Mails are marked as "Sundays excepted")

Service	Depart	Arrive	Facilities
London – Southampton Night Mail Southampton – London Night Mail	8.30pm 1.30am	11.30pm 4.30am	Travelling Post Office fitted up in such manner as the PMG shall require, also as many extra bag carriages as may be required.
Bishopstoke – Portsmouth Night Portsmouth – Bishopstoke Night	11.20pm 12.45am	12.15am 1.34am	One compartment of a Second class carriage, fitted up as the PMG shall require.
London – Dorchester Night Mail (starts from Southampton) Dorchester – Southampton	12.06am 10.15pm	3.05am 12.57am	The whole or so much as the PMG shall deem necessary of the inside of a Second class carriage fitted up as the PMG shall require.
London – Southampton Day Mail Southampton – London Day Mail	10.15am 8.50am	1.10pm 11.30am	One compartment of a Second class carriage, fitted up as the PMG shall require.
Bishopstoke – Portsmouth Day Mail Portsmouth – Bishopstoke Day Mail	1.12pm 8.0am	2.05pm 8.48am	One compartment of a Second class carriage, fitted up as the PMG shall require.
Fareham – Gosport Day Mail Gosport – Fareham Day Mail	1.38pm 8.10am	1.50pm 8.20am	Company Guard to take charge of the bags.

Overall, the Company to provide sufficient engines, and the travelling Post Offices, carriages, letter bag and other carriages in the foregoing schedule mentioned for the conveyance of the mails, and to convey in such Post Offices and other carriages the clerks of the Post Office attending such despatch, and also the guards employed and appointed by the Post Office.

Schedule 2 (mainly "Sundays excepted")		
Service	**Depart**	**Arrive**
Bishopstoke – Salisbury	1.12pm	2.05pm
Chertsey & Weybridge	11.05am	11.15am (presumably means a service in each direction)
Exeter – Exmouth	10.15am	10.45am
Exmouth – Exeter	12.35pm	1.05pm
Farnham – Woking	9.58am	10.44am
Godalming – Woking	10.15am	10.44am
Godalming – Woking	1.10pm	1.44pm
Godalming – Woking	10.15pm	11.05pm
Gosport – Fareham	11.50am	12.09pm
Guildford – Petersfield	12.20pm	1.17pm
London – Staines	9.45am	10.44am
Poole Junction – Poole	3.00pm	3.12pm
Poole – Poole Junction	9.10am	9.25am
Portsmouth – Bishopstoke	11.40am	12.35pm
Portsmouth – London direct line	12noon	2.55pm
Reading – Bracknell	2.00pm	2.24pm
Salisbury – Bishopstoke	10.35am	11.30am
Salisbury – Bishopstoke	9.50pm	11.20pm
Southampton – London	12.30pm	4.45pm
Southampton – London	11.30am	2.30pm
Southampton – Weymouth	1.24pm	4.00pm
Staines – London	11.38am	12.25pm
Staines – London	3.02pm	3.53pm
Weymouth – Southampton	8.20am	11.20am
Woking – Farnham	11.03am	11.49am
Woking – Godalming	11.03am	11.30am
On all these, the Company's Guard to take charge of the bags forwarded.		

a further Post Office letter pointed out that under the terms of the recent contract, the Company had to bear the full cost of providing postal carriages. This dragged on, and in November, the Post Office served a legal notice calling on the LSWR to comply, but it was only in January 1863, after Mr Scott reported that following discussions only one additional carriage would be needed, that it was agreed to order it from Wright's. Even then, the Post Office complained in March about the continuing delay. It was only at the end of May that the Post Office wrote that, as they had heard that it had just been completed, they proposed that it should start to run on the down night mail on the 16th June. This TPO must have been number 3.

During the same period, one of the existing carriages was to be altered in its internal fittings but there are no details. Also, in November 1862, the Post Office complained that, "The openings of the carriages allotted to the Mail Messengers on the night mail on the North Devon line are so narrow they have great difficulties with mailbags ... also a deficiency of light", and sought improvements. From the description they sound as though they may have been some of the Seconds of the mid-1840s (*LSWR Carriages, Volume 1*, Figure 2.9). What was done is not known, but one might assume that the Post Office would have insisted on something before the next reference in LSWR minutes for November 1884, when the Traffic Committee approved the replacement of "two small Post Office vans now in use on the North Devon line" which were "not strong enough".

By the end of 1863, there were already complaints about the skylights on the TPOs letting in rain onto the sorting desk. One of them stated that, "the rain passes through the skylight as through a sieve". There were also complaints that the lamps, including the sealing lamps, were often either running out of oil, filled with "inferior oil" or leaking onto the desks.

The June 1865 stock return showed the existence of three Post Office sorting vans, but in the same month, the Post Office wrote to say that alterations to the night mail service to and from Portsmouth would require two vans to be fitted up as letter sorting vans; this was agreed to by the Traffic Committee. In December, Mr Beattie reported that two old Third class carriages had been converted to Post Office sorting vans. This was reflected in the stock returns for June and December 1867 showing a total of five. These two conversions seem to have been numbered 4 and 5, and to have lasted until 1892, when new Nos 4 and 5 were built at Eastleigh. There is no indication as to which version of Third they were. The service was between Portsmouth and Southampton via Netley.

Following a request from the War Department, the Traffic and Locomotive Committee agreed, in December 1869, to "an old Post Office van" being altered to convey invalids between Portsmouth and Netley, the work to be paid for by the WD. This is intriguing because it was clearly an elderly six-wheeled carriage, as a month later, the Officers Committee noted that the flanges of the middle wheels were to be turned down sufficiently to give 1½in play when going round sharp curves! It may be recalled that in *LSWR Carriages, Volume 1*, it was mentioned that early six-wheelers were certainly used on the LSWR, and one might conjecture as to whether one or more of the carriages shown there in Figure 2.3 had been converted to a Post Office van. A letter was received from Mr E Lansdown in December 1869, calling attention to his Patent Gangways for Post Office carriages. This was referred to Mr Beattie, but there is no further mention of the matter. Unfortunately, there is no mention in the LSWR records of when the first gangways were fitted to the postal vans, nor of what type. However a Post Office letter mentions the matter, as shown below.

Stock returns still show five Post Office vans up to January 1881, then Mr Benthall of the Post Office wrote stating that the TPOs working on the main line were too small, and requiring the provision of two improved sorting carriages, to run between London and Dorchester, the Post Office bearing half the cost. He also said they should be of the same dimensions as those in use on the LNWR, but with different internal fittings, and without the bag exchanging apparatus. These were ordered from Cravens Railway Carriage and Wagon Co of Darnall at a cost of £501 4s 6d each, and were delivered in the latter half of the year. Numbered 6 and 7, they were 32ft long, and are shown in the Register as being to Drawing DB96 (which has not survived).

As well as requesting the new TPOs, Mr Benthall had suggested that two of the existing carriages should be permanently connected together with a gangway and kept as a reserve. These must have been numbers 2 and 3, since in July, there is a Post Office reference to No 1 being used on its own on the Portsmouth service. Whether this work was carried out, and if so, whether they were of the Lansdown type is not known.

In November 1882, it was noted that the Post Office had stated an intention to require the principle railway companies to provide parcels sorting vans on some trains. It was agreed by the Traffic Committee that if this came about the LSWR should charge an extra 15% on the cost to cover maintenance, and 4d (1.67p) per mile haulage up to 75 miles with 3d (1.25p) per mile thereafter.

The Working Timetable for 1882 includes a note that the 7am Waterloo to Portsmouth direct train must "pass Wimbledon slowly to drop a mailbag" – a trifle alarming for passengers waiting on the platform!

Earlier, it was mentioned that the Post Office renewed its proposal for the installation of mailbag exchange apparatus in 1885. The General Manager reported discussions with the Post Office about accelerating the retimed 9.30pm down mail. The proposal was to run through Surbiton, Woking, Farnborough, Winchfield, and Micheldever without stopping. Mailbag apparatus would be fitted at those stations, and the necessary machinery installed in "the two mail vans in regular use", which probably means the fairly new numbers 6 and 7. A new reserve van would be required "in place of the present one which is not of sufficient size".

This was agreed by the Locomotive Committee in November 1885, but only a couple of weeks later, the General Manager made a fresh proposal. This involved starting the down mail fifteen minutes later, at 9.45pm, and running it non-stop to Basingstoke. An additional train would be started at 9pm, stopping for mail at the necessary intermediate stations to Basingstoke. This would avoid the need for mailbag apparatus and, rather inexplicably, the need for a new reserve van. For the additional service the Post Office would pay £700 commencing on the next 1st January.

Clearly, the Post Office people did not accept the alleged reduction in need for a new reserve van, because they raised the matter again in January

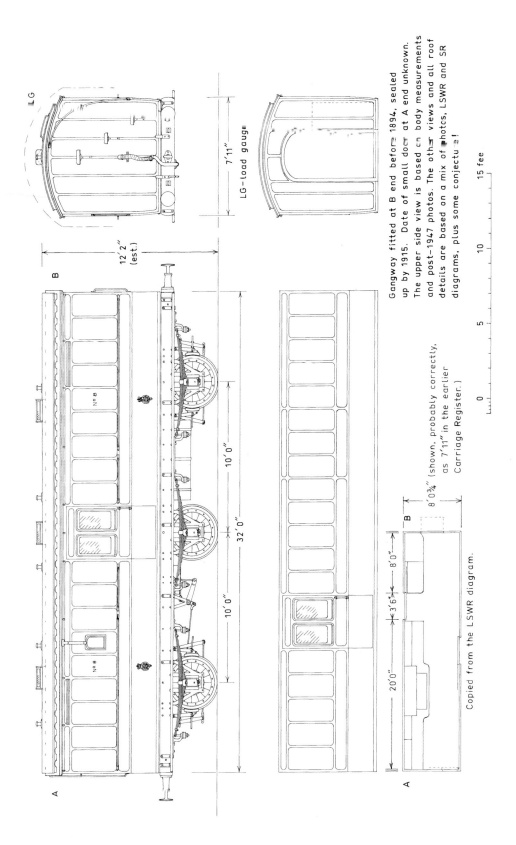

LG-load gauge

12'2" (est.)

10'0"

32'0"

10'0"

7'11"

Gangway fitted at B end before 1894, sealed up by 1915. Date of small door at A end unknown. The upper side view is based on body measurements and post-1947 photos. The other views and all roof details are based on a mix of photos, LSWR and SR diagrams, plus some conjecture!

8'0¾" (shown, probably correctly, as 7'11" in the earlier Carriage Register.)

20'0"

8'0"

3'6"

Copied from the LSWR diagram.

0   5   10   15 feet

Figure 2.2. LSWR 1886 32ft sorting van No 8, drawing DB96.

Plate 2.2a. 32ft sorting van No 8, at Fullerton, June 1955.

(M Rhodes)

Plate 2.2b. 32ft sorting van No 6, 7 or 9 at Eastleigh in 1950.

(D Cullum 0717/Lens of Sutton Association)

1886, when its construction was approved by the Traffic and the Locomotive Committees. This was number 8, once again 32ft long and, described as being to DB96, like numbers 6 and 7, though with the door on the sorting side in a slightly different position from those two. This time it was built at Nine Elms for £432.1s.7d.

In 1894, it was running in the night mail to Dorchester, and was noted as having a gangway at one end. By 1902, it was "permanently joined to numbers 1 and 2 (ex-No 3), available to relieve numbers 12 and 14" and held in reserve at Eastleigh for the Portsmouth – Southampton service. (There is an oddity about that statement regarding No 2, because further down in the same roster there is shown the new 44ft No 2 that was built in 1900.) In 1903, it was separated from the two 20ft vans, and was running with the new 48ft number 1, or 44ft number 12, in the same service. The roster for 1907 showed it still the same, then in 1915 it was noted as still on the same service, but running alone in turns with number 7, but with its gangway "blocked up". Finally taken out of postal use in 1931, it was put into departmental service, first as a mess and tool van No 566s and later as an emergency plant vehicle.

In this guise it was photographed in 1947, and again in 1955. It has therefore been possible to prepare the present drawing, Figure 2.2, using dimensions from the LSWR and the SR diagram books, together with vertical measurements of the side panels from bottom to cornice on one of the other arc-roofed vans, taken by Mr D Cullum in 1950. Because of the lack of photographs of the sorting desk side, the second end, and of the roof before it was covered over all with canvas, there have had to be several points of conjecture in this drawing. A distinct puzzle is the small sliding door at the non-sorting side of one end. This might be a relic of its connection to the 20ft numbers 1 and 2, but unless a photo of around 1902 turns up this cannot be verified. Number 8 was one of three (Nos 8, 9 and 10) all built at Nine Elms, and shown in the Carriage Register as 7ft 11in wide instead of the usual 8ft 0¾in. Both the LSWR and SR diagram books show them the usual width, but it is a strong probability that the Register was right. Numbers 6 and 7, that were built by Cravens, were to the usual dimensions, but were as high at the cornices as it was wise to go within the loading gauge. It can only be conjecture that Nine Elms decided to give a trifle more clearance without making a noticeable difference to the sorting staff.

More interesting is the odd mini-clerestory that can just be detected under the roofing felt on SR 566s (ex-number 8) and on an unidentified grounded body at Eastleigh of one of numbers 6, 7 or 9. On 566s, one can also just make out the existence of

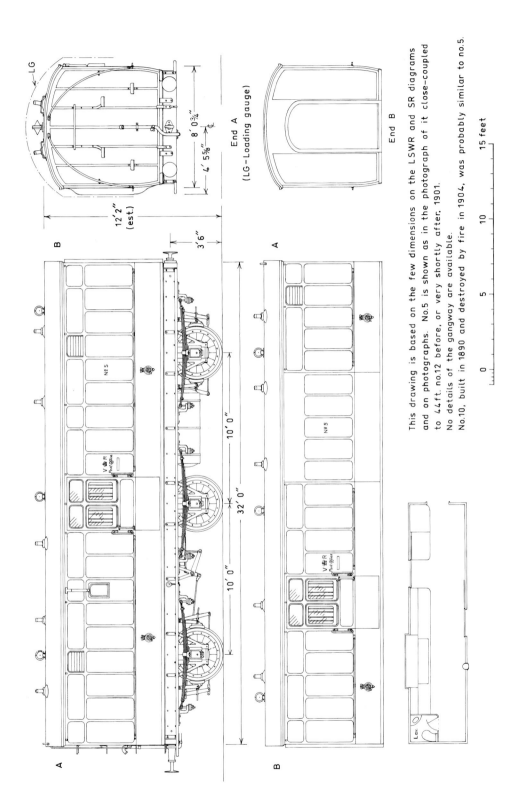

Figure 2.3. LSWR 1892 32ft sorting van No 5, drawings DB96, 619, and 2305.

This drawing is based on the few dimensions on the LSWR and SR diagrams and on photographs. No.5 is shown as in the photograph of it close-coupled to 44ft. no.12 before, or very shortly after, 1901.
No details of the gangway are available.
No.10, built in 1890 and destroyed by fire in 1904, was probably similar to no.5.

Plate 2.3a. 32ft sorting van No 5, SR 4901 at Eastleigh, 25th October 1947.

(D Cullum 0153/Lens of Sutton Association)

three skylights. At this point it may be noted that the height from rail to roof of all the 32ft and longer TPOs is shown as 12ft 1⅞in on the Southern Railway diagrams. Although this seems a rather curious degree of precision, it does, if it is to be believed, imply that all the arc-roofed 32ft vans had the same type of raised roof.

This roof looks very similar to that on a South Eastern Railway 30ft mail van tender of 1881. From the drawing of that vehicle, it is evident that the raised roof above a normal roof was a means of improving ventilation. The holes at the sides allowed free air circulation in the space between the roofs, and the skylights had grilles opening into this space. The lamps were of the "Moderator" type favoured by the Post Office. These were powerful and were suspended well below the roof, allowing the external chimneys to be very small. It is assumed that the roof, skylight and lamp arrangements on numbers 6, 7 and 8 (and possibly 9) were all similar to those on the SER, since it was the Post Office that drew up most of the specification for the bodies and their fittings. Some credence is lent to this assumption by a note in the *South Western Gazette* for 3rd August 1889, which tells that two sparrows had built their nest, and laid four eggs in it, "under the coping on the top" of Travelling Post Office No 8. It goes on to say they must have done so while the van stood at Dorchester during the daytime.

The next van built, in June 1889, followed

approval by the Traffic Committee on 13th February 1889 of the General Manager's recommendation that an additional Post Office mail van should be ordered for use on the North Devon line. This was No 9, which had the same stated dimensions and layout as numbers 6 and 7, but was shown as being to DB96A. There is no evidence to clarify the significance of the A suffix. Like No 8, it was built at Nine Elms, but at the cost of £417 11s 7d.

In May 1890, the Traffic Superintendent recommended the provision of two more sorting vans, probably in view of the proposed extension of the Day TPO to Dorchester via Ringwood, which is understood to have been due to start at the end of June. This was approved but there seems to have been further discussion because the decision was confirmed in August. The details are not recorded but, from what follows, it would appear that the decision was to build one 32ft van, and to prepare plans for a bogie van. The first one, No 10, was completed by the end of the year to the same dimensions and drawing (DB96A) as No 9, and at the same cost of £417 11s 7d.

Number 10 had rather a short life because on 30th May 1904, it was in the carriage sidings at Clapham Junction when a couple of gas fitters were sent to clean the lamps. One of them, Ernest Robert Browning, connected a hose to the gas main. He then started using the jet to pressure clean the lamps. Neither of them had checked the next van connected to No 10, but this still had some lamps alight.

Plate 2.3b. 32ft sorting van No 5 at Eastleigh in 1947.   *(F Foote)*

Browning was killed in the ensuing explosion, his companion and one other were seriously burned and van number 10 was practically destroyed. The connected van, 44ft No 13, was severely damaged. Both were rebuilt, though in the case of No 10 this must have been an "accountancy" rebuild, since there could not have been very much from a 32ft six-wheeler that could be used to "rebuild" into the 44ft bogie vehicle that resulted, shown at Figure 2.7. The Coroner's verdict on Ernest Browning was Accidental Death.

Following the presumed decision mentioned above, a design was discussed in mid-October 1890 for a 44ft sorting van at an estimated cost of £600. This was the first one of this size, and it incorporated the new panel layout and roof shape that had been adopted for No 5 (and possibly 9 and 10 before it). The design was approved by the Loco & Stores Committee, but no order was made. The Post Office wrote to Mr Scotter on 8th January 1891, asking for confirmation of the exact prices in order that special authority could be sought for half the cost of building a new TPO carriage for the day mail and a new TPO for the Portsmouth – Southampton service, also the cost of fitting gangways. It continued, "It is understood that when payment has been made, the Company will place the new bogie carriage on the day mail, and will run the other sorting carriage along with the present sorting carriage, which will be used as a parcel sorting carriage between Portsmouth and Southampton,

these two carriages being connected by gangway".

The Post Office got a reply from the Treasury, dated 16th May 1891, authorising them to accept the terms offered by the LSWR, and to pay half the cost of a carriage for the day mail at £325, half the cost of a new carriage for the Portsmouth service at £225, and £40 for fitting gangways to the two Portsmouth carriages.

On the 15th September, Mr Scotter sent an account for the £590 to the Post Office, and presumably this was settled. Number 11, 44ft long, was completed at Nine Elms in October 1891, at a recorded cost of £629 12s 9d and another one, virtually identical, in May 1892. This became No 4, costing £586 18s 7d, shown here as Figure 2.4. Neither of them had gangways at this stage, both being used for the day mails, one running and one spare. It can be seen that this did not really match what the Treasury had authorised!

That No 4 came about following the agreement, in November 1891, of the Loco & Stores Committee to build two 44ft bogie Post Office vans to replace Nos 4 and 5, the two that had been converted from Third class carriages in 1865, as they were worn out. The Post Office then, in April 1892, asked the LSWR to provide a new parcels sorting van larger than that in use between Portsmouth and Southampton, and when it had been completed to connect the existing two (the original Nos 1 and 2) together by gangways, and keep them as reserve. This seems to have been catching up with the

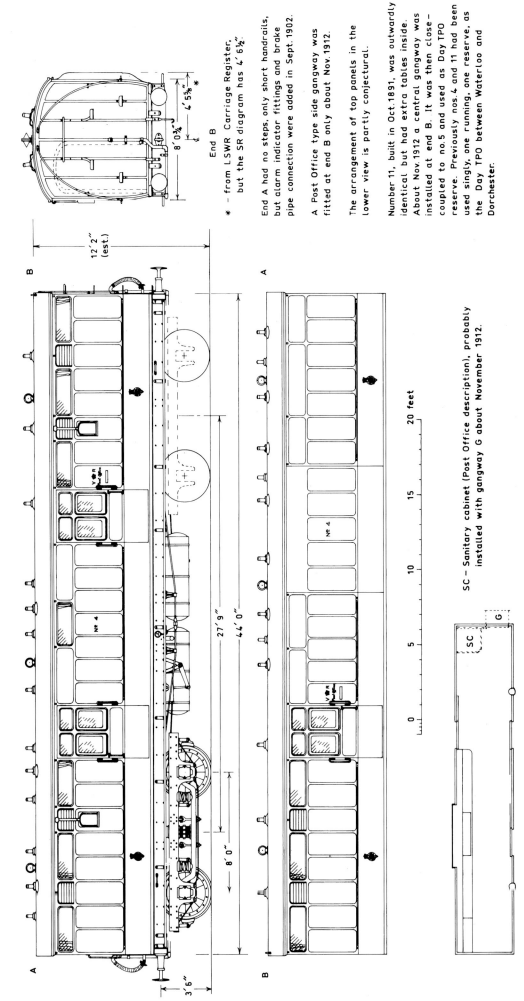

End B

* — from LSWR Carriage Register,
but the SR diagram has 4′ 6½″.

End A had no steps, only short handrails,
but alarm indicator fittings and brake
pipe connection were added in Sept. 1902.

A Post Office type side gangway was
fitted at end B only about Nov. 1912.

The arrangement of top panels in the
lower view is partly conjectural.

Number 11, built in Oct. 1891, was outwardly
identical but had extra tables inside.
About Nov. 1912 a central gangway was
installed at end B. It was then close-
coupled to no. 5 and used as Day TPO
reserve. Previously nos. 4 and 11 had been
used singly, one running, one reserve, as
the Day TPO between Waterloo and
Dorchester.

SC — Sanitary cabinet (Post Office description), probably
installed with gangway G about November 1912.

Figure 2.4. LSWR 44ft postal sorting van No 4 of 1892, drawings 464 and 618.

48

Plate 2.4a. 44ft sorting van No 4.

(National Railway Museum)

Plate 2.4b. 44ft sorting van No 4 at Brockenhurst (undated). Note the bracket, with wear marks, under the EV11R and Post Office lettering, on which a letter box could be hung at a station. (J Tatchell Collection)

Treasury authorisation, but if so the next item is puzzling.

At the beginning of July 1892, the Post Office wrote to the Treasury stating that there were five letter sorting carriages in service, one of 44ft and four of 30ft (*sic*), but only one carriage of 30ft held in reserve. Although there were several others in existence, they were small, only 20ft long, and obsolete. Since there were three distinct services, two more new carriages were needed, one 44ft and one 30ft. The letter continued, "The Company is willing to provide these additional carriages if this department will bear half the cost, which is estimated at £1100. As the Company are only bound to supply new carriages similar to the old, 20ft in length, which are displaced, this offer is fair and reasonable". Then it went on again about the Portsmouth to Southampton service: "The carriage now in use is only 20ft long, and is not nearly large enough for the duty, moreover there is no reserve ... a new carriage 44ft long should be provided for daily use, and one of the old 20ft letter carriages should be fitted for parcel sorting, and connected by gangway to the carriage at present used, and the two then kept in reserve". Finally, authority was sought for half the cost of the new carriages, amounting to £550, together with the cost of alterations to the old 20ft vehicles amounting to £80. The apparent duplication or inconsistency between this request and the authority of the previous year does not seem to have been challenged.

Two vehicles were completed in December 1892, 32ft No 5 letter sorting, and 44ft No 12 parcel sorting vans, and these two were shown in the 1894 roster of TPOs as running in the Portsmouth and Southampton service, connected by gangways. These gangways, at one end only of each, were central ones. A photograph during Queen Victoria's reign (that is, before her death in 1901) shows them to have been close-coupled; from an LSWR diagram the distance between the bodies was about 1ft 6in. They are illustrated here as Figures 2.3 and 2.5. There is no information on the type of close couplings; they were probably the chains and hooks with very short buffers of the type used for the block sets of the 1880s.

Number 5 was fairly similar in layout to the preceding 32ft vans but the door on the sorting side was moved a few inches towards the end. The previous type of two-tier arc roof was replaced with a slightly elliptical single roof (not the normal LSWR shape) that achieved the same height and width of the earlier ones, but with a simpler construction. Much more obvious was a kind of long ducket on the sorting side, a feature common on many railway TPOs and used on some other LSWR ones from then on. The plan views of numbers 6 to 10 show a long sorting desk with letter "pigeon holes" above. Part of this desk widened out to allow deeper pigeon holes along part of it. The deeper ones were required to hold bundles of newspapers (in those days newspapers were not distributed in

Plate 2.4c. 44ft sorting van LSWR No 4, SR No 4907, in June 1937.

(SC Townroe/R Blencowe)

Plate 2.4d. L12 class 4-4-0 with "4½" set near Winchester around 1905. At the rear is 44ft travelling post office No 4 or No 11 and a 44ft brake. *(J Tatchell collection)*

Plate 2.4e. Up travelling post office train, possibly just north of Winchester. The TPO is No 4 or No 11, and the last carriage appears to be an "Eagle" saloon. The use of a caboose passenger brake van on a 4½ set is unusual.   (J Tatchell Collection)

Plate 2.4f. 44ft sorting van No 11, SR 4909 at Eastleigh on 7th September 1949.
(D Cullum 0426/Lens of Sutton Association)

Plate 2.4g. 44ft sorting van No 11, SR 4909 at Eastleigh on 7ᵗʰ September 1949.
(D Cullum 0425/Lens of Sutton Association)

Plate 2.4h. 44ft sorting van No 11, SR 4909 at Eastleigh on 25ᵗʰ June 1950.
(D Cullum 0719/Lens of Sutton Association)

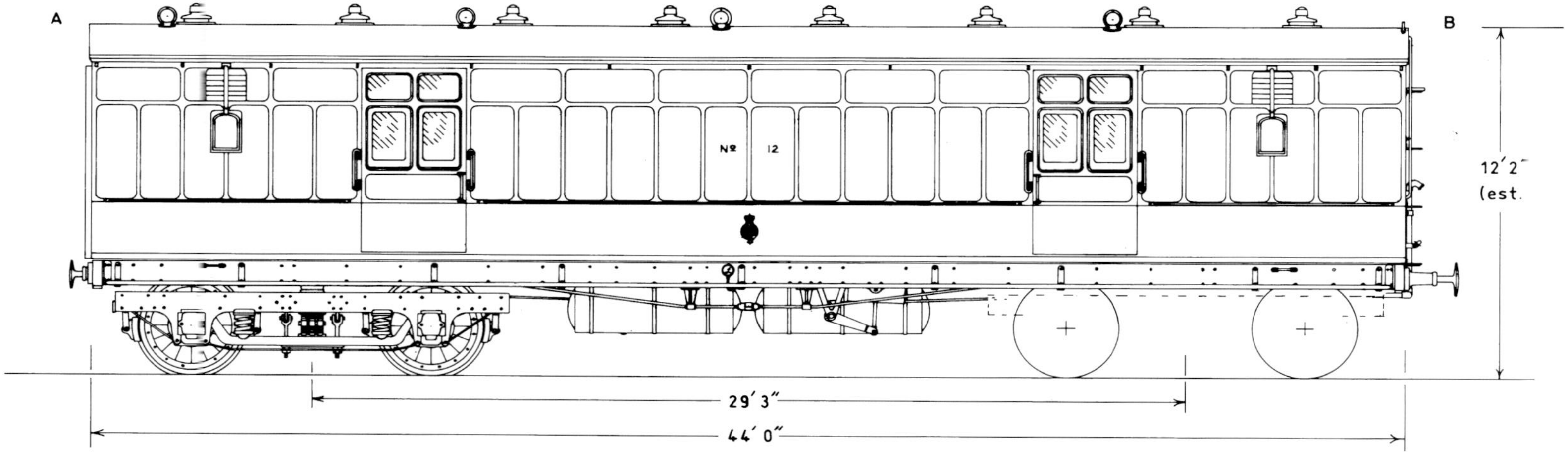

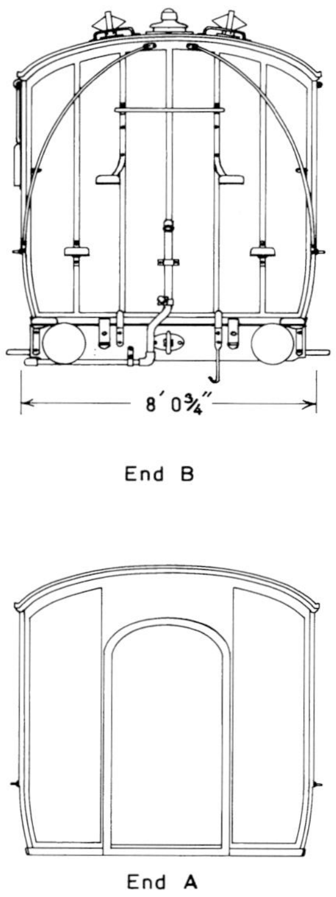

8' 0¾"

End B

End A

12' 2" (est.)

B

N° 12

29' 3"

44' 0"

A

The other side was similar, but without the two sealing lamp chimneys.
No information is available about the gangway, nor about the brake pipe fittings at the A end.

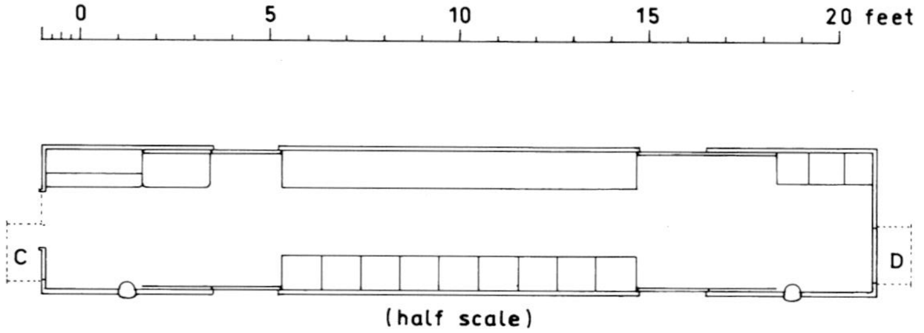

0   5   10   15   20 feet

D

C

(half scale)

No.12 Parcel Sorting Van was completed in December 1892 and put on the Portsmouth – Southampton service, close-coupled with central gangway to Letter Sorting Van no. 5.
The gangway was altered to the side (C) in late 1913. No.12 (re-numbered 5612) then became a reserve for the SW TPO Night Mail. At some time between 1916 and 1923 a second gangway (D) was installed and the vehicle became a Stowage Van.

Figure 2.5. LSWR 44ft parcel sorting van No 12 of 1892, drawing No 146.

Plate 2.5. 32ft letter sorting van No 5 close-coupled to 44ft parcel sorting van No 12 at Portsmouth, circa 1900.

(National Railway Museum)

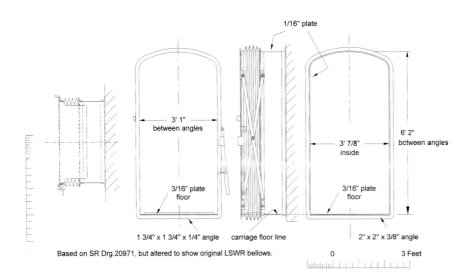

Figure 2.6. SR Western Section Post Office gangway, drawing No 146. (For clarity, this drawing has been reproduced at 7mm scale)

anything like the vast quantities of later years). The two types of pigeon hole were referred to as letter sets and newspaper sets. For the greater convenience of a straight sorting desk, in number 5 and later vans, the front of the newspaper sets were built flush with the letter sets. To do this, the backs of them were enclosed in what looked rather like long Guard's duckets.

Number 12 was a very straightforward vehicle with parcel bins and bag pegs on one side and desks on the other. As with the letter sorting vans, wax-sealing lamps were provided on one side. Following the reduction of parcel sorting duties during and after the First World War, the desks and so on were stripped out at the end of 1923, and the vehicle was described as a stowage van from then on until it was withdrawn at the end of 1939.

Numbers 5 and 12 continued in the Portsmouth – Southampton service at least until 1908, and possibly until November 1912, when LSWR minutes recorded that No 5 was to be permanently connected (still with a central gangway) to No 11, and then used together "as one vehicle" as reserve for the South Western TPO day mail. No 12 had its central gangway replaced with a side gangway at each end after July 1913, and was then used as a reserve for the South Western TPO night mail.

The casings and chimneys for the sealing lamps, shown in several of these illustrations, are worth a mention. Throughout the period under review, mailbags were tied up and sealed with a blob of sealing wax. Therefore all carriages used for sorting and bagging had to have at least one burner to heat the wax. It is not known when the side-mounted casings shown were first introduced but they can be seen in illustrations of postal vehicles on many railways. They were generally fitted on the side opposite the sorting tables.

The evidence regarding the provision of gangways in the 32ft vans is extremely confusing,

and can be interpreted in various ways. It has already been mentioned that two of the 20ft vans might have had gangways fitted about 1882, though from the Metropolitan drawing it seems that they at least had small sliding doors at one end when built.

Rather more positively, in December 1893, Post Office expenditure of between £50 and £60 was authorised for "provision of gangways in the South Western TPO carriages (half gangways to three carriages and gangways at both ends of one carriage, four in all)". Judging from the 1894 roster, these were probably No 6, with gangways at both ends, and three out of Nos 7 to 10, each with a single gangway. No 7 received its second gangway after a Post Office request in October 1895. The 1915 roster shows No 6 with side gangways and Nos 7, 8 and 9 with central ones, but later diagrams show Nos 7 and 9 with side ones.

The gangways had a clear width inside of 3ft. Because of this width, where they were central there was no space remaining on either side for a sliding door, and hinged ones were not used, so when these carriages were uncoupled they were only protected by a heavy curtain or, probably, a gangway end cover. On the LNWR, these end covers had a window in them, but no photos are available to show the LSWR practice.

Figure 2.6 is based on a Southern Railway drawing of the gangways of PO vans on the London – Southampton, etc, route. Since the ex-LSWR vans were still in service, it is a fair assumption that this drawing is substantially as provided in the 1890s, although the SR bellows were reshaped and strengthened; that detail has been altered to match period photos for this figure.

A rather curious letter to the LSWR in the Post Office Archives records an incident on 16th March 1896. It reads, "I have made enquiries as regards the letter box of the TPO which fell off the night mail train on the 16th ultimo. It appears that this box, instead of being taken in before the train left

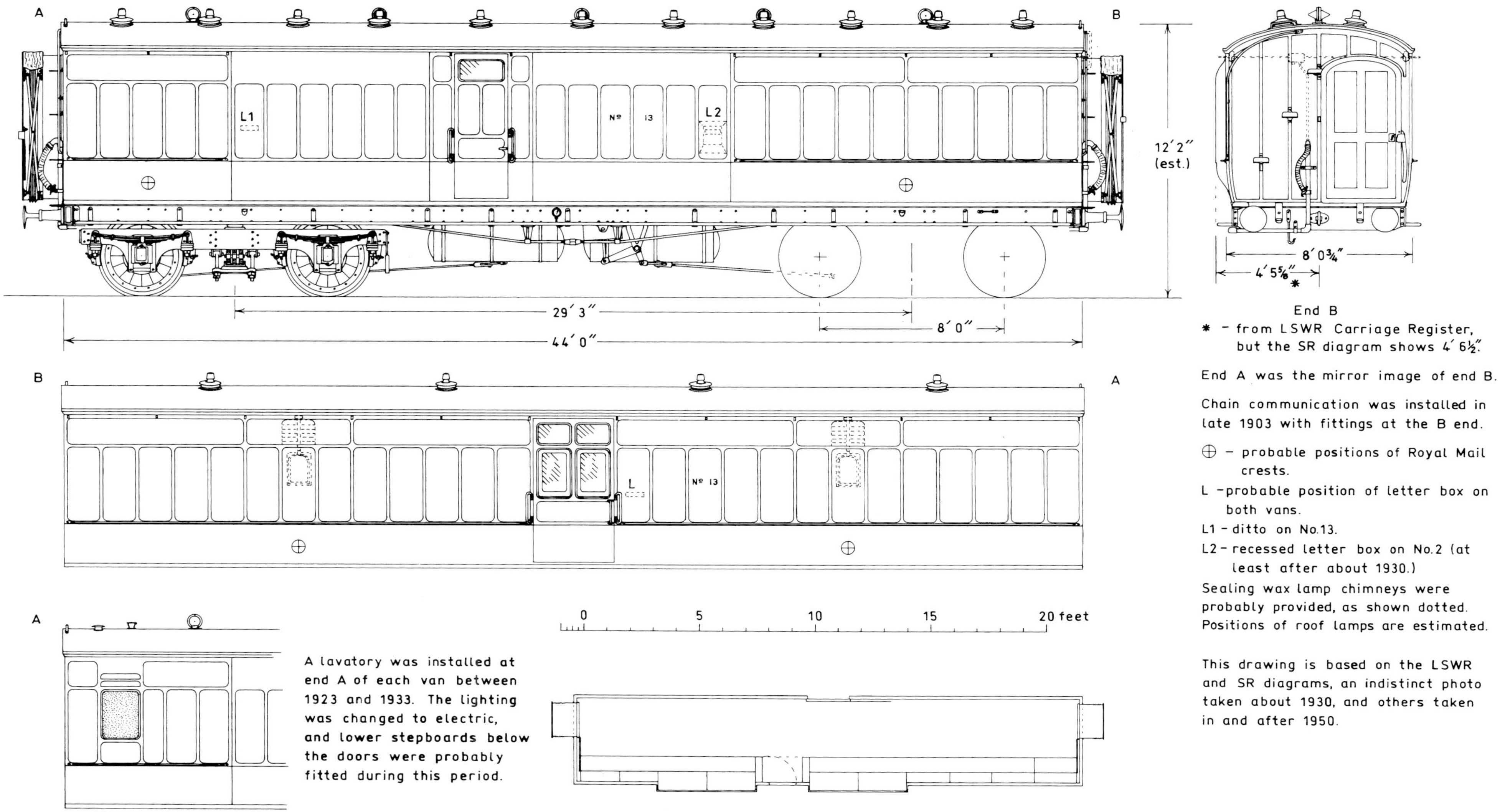

End B

* - from LSWR Carriage Register,
  but the SR diagram shows 4' 6½.

* - A was the mirror image of end B.

Chain communication was installed in
late 1903 with fittings at the B end.

⊕ - probable positions of Royal Mail
  crests.

L - probable position of letter box on
  both vans.

L1 - ditto on No.13.

L2 - recessed letter box on No.2 (at
  least after about 1930.)

Sealing wax lamp chimneys were
probably provided, as shown dotted.
Positions of roof lamps are estimated.

This drawing is based on the LSWR
and SR diagrams, an indistinct photo
taken about 1930, and others taken
in and after 1950.

A lavatory was installed at
end A of each van between
1923 and 1933. The lighting
was changed to electric,
and lower stepboards below
the doors were probably
fitted during this period.

8' 0¾"
4' 5⅝"

12' 2" (est.)

8' 0"

29' 3"

44' 0"

L1   Nº 13   L2

L   Nº 13

0   5   10   15   20 feet

57

Figure 2.7. LSWR 1898 44ft postal sorting van No 13 (1898) and No 2 (1900), drawings 749, 755 and 936.

Plate 2.7a. 44ft sorting van No 13 at Wimbledon in September 1958.

(J H Aston)

Plate 2.7b. 44ft sorting van No 13 at Wimbledon in June 1953.

(J H Aston)

Plate 2.7c. X2 Class No 580 at Bournemouth. To the left is 44ft letter sorting van No 2.

Plate 2.7d. 44ft sorting van No 2 of October 1900, SR 4906, at Eardley sidings on 1st July 1951.
(D Cullum 1034/Lens of Sutton Association)

Surbiton, was left outside and it apparently, when crossing the points near that place, was thrown off on to the line. I have not failed to take notice of the irregularity". This shows that some letter boxes were portable, unlike the built-in ones seen in the photos of Nos 4 and 5, and other later vehicles. In fact a group photo of staff at Brockenhurst, that was clearly taken before the official photo of the same TPO (No 4) shows what appears to be one of a pair of small metal loops, with rubbing marks where the letter box had been put on and off.

The Post Office asked for additional mail van accommodation between Southampton and Dorchester in March 1898. This resulted in the completion, in the following October, of the 44ft sorting van number 13 at a cost of £718 4s 6d. This one certainly had side gangways at both ends by 1902, probably from new, and is shown here as Figure 2.7 which, because of a lack of photographs in LSWR condition, is based on the LSWR and SR diagrams, helped by photos of this and the similar number 2 in their 1950s condition, by which time some alterations had been carried out (omitted from the drawings).

Three old four-wheel postal vans were scheduled for withdrawal in the latter half of 1899; they were to be replaced by two bogie vans. Almost certainly, these were the original numbers 1, 2 and 3. The first replacement, 48ft stowage van No 1, was completed in November 1899, apparently with a central gangway at one end, at a cost of £600. Curiously, the new No 1 is shown in the Post Office roster for 1902 as No 14, the old No 1 being still on the roster at that time. The surviving LSWR register was started in 1904, and showed no number higher than 13, so whether No 14 actually had that number painted on is not certain.

The other new van was 44ft sorting van No 2, built in October 1900, at a cost of £739 6s 2d. It was practically identical to the No 13 mentioned above in Figure 2.7. In September 1936, its body was transferred to the underframe from SECR First No 2360 (SR 7263), and it then continued in service until 1943, when it became departmental No 1887s.

The old 20ft No 3 had latterly been used as a bag tender on the Exeter to Torrington service, which had been extended from Barnstaple from 12th August 1896. It was withdrawn in April 1900, and replaced on the service by the 32ft No 9 sorting van, with its central gangway door space blocked up. With no replacement for No 3 yet built, the stock return for December 1902 stood at twelve Post Office vans.

In October 1903, Surrey Warner reported that on the instructions of the General Manager he had put in hand the construction of a new 44ft sorting carriage for the London to Dorchester night mail service at a cost of £750, which would be wholly paid by the Post Office. This was the replacement

No 3, completed at Eastleigh in the following November. No drawing can be shown here, as no photographs are available, nor of the No 10 mentioned earlier. However, both are shown on the same LSWR and SR diagrams, on which Figure 2.8 is based.

The General Manager again authorised the building of another van to be paid for by the Post Office in October 1912. This was a 56ft by 8ft 6¾in sorting van with side gangways at each end, and a roof shape similar to that of the dining saloons of 1913 (*LSWR Carriages in the 20th Century*, Figure 8.21). At the same time, it was ordered to fit No 4 with a side gangway at one end, also to fit a lavatory in 44ft No 11, and to connect it permanently to 32ft No 5, presumably using the close-coupling that already existed on the latter. The new 56ft van was completed in June 1913, and because of the new 1912 numbering scheme, it received the number 5614. The works drawings have not survived, and no photographs of it in LSWR condition are available, so Figure 2.9 is really only a sketch based on the LSWR and SR diagrams. Dimensions and layout are reliable, but details are lacking, and those shown are not necessarily true to scale.

The lavatory in No 11 was the first instance mentioned of one on an LSWR postal vehicle, although they were noted concerning four LNWR vehicles in February 1896, if not earlier. The Post Office distinguished between "lavatories" and "sanitary cabinets" though the difference is not clear. However, from reported complaints of their smell on the LNWR, perhaps it was that they did not have a proper water supply, and were merely an early form of chemical closet. Anyway, it was "sanitary cabinets" that their records show as installed in LSWR No 11, No 4 and some others.

In July 1913, the Post Office asked for another new van to be built, this time as a parcels sorting van. They also called for side gangways to replace the existing central ones on Nos 1 and 12, the latter work to cost a total of £70. The parcels sorter, again 56ft by 8ft 6¾in, was turned out by Eastleigh in March 1914 as No 5615 at a cost of £900. As with No 5614, because of the lack of works drawings or photographs in LSWR condition, the same reservations apply to Figure 2.10 as to Figure 2.9.

In order to supply additional mail stowage vans quickly in October 1915, it was agreed to take three of the 48ft former fruit and brake vans (illustrated in *LSWR Carriages in the 20th Century* as Figure 9.8) and fit them with side gangways; this would cost £156, which would be paid by the Post Office. The three, former numbers 503, 507 and 508, became stowage vans 5616, 5617 and 5618.

Services were reduced during the First World War. Parcel sorting was suspended from December 1915 on both the Portsmouth and Southampton, and the South Western TPO day mail. In July 1917, the

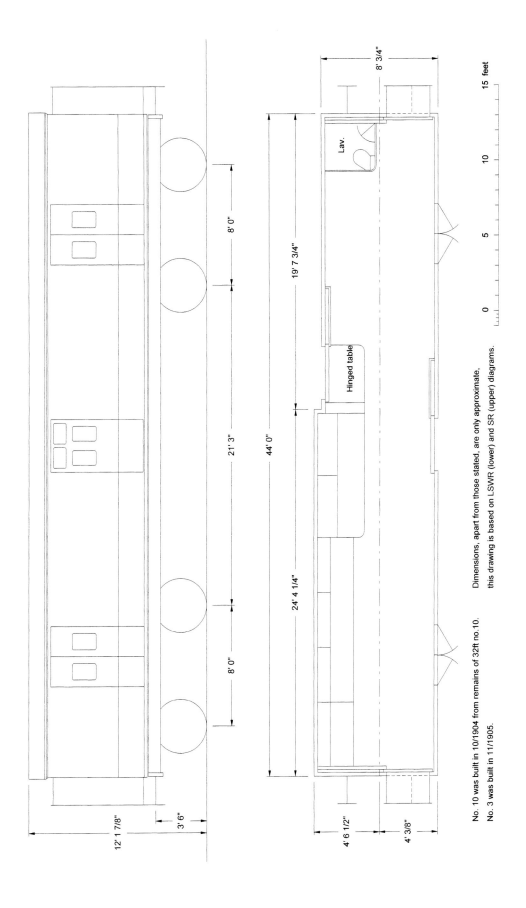

No. 10 was built in 10/1904 from remains of 32ft no.10.

No. 3 was built in 11/1905.

Dimensions, apart from those stated, are only approximate,

this drawing is based on LSWR (lower) and SR (upper) diagrams.

Figure 2.8 LSWR postal sorting vans Nos 3 and 10.

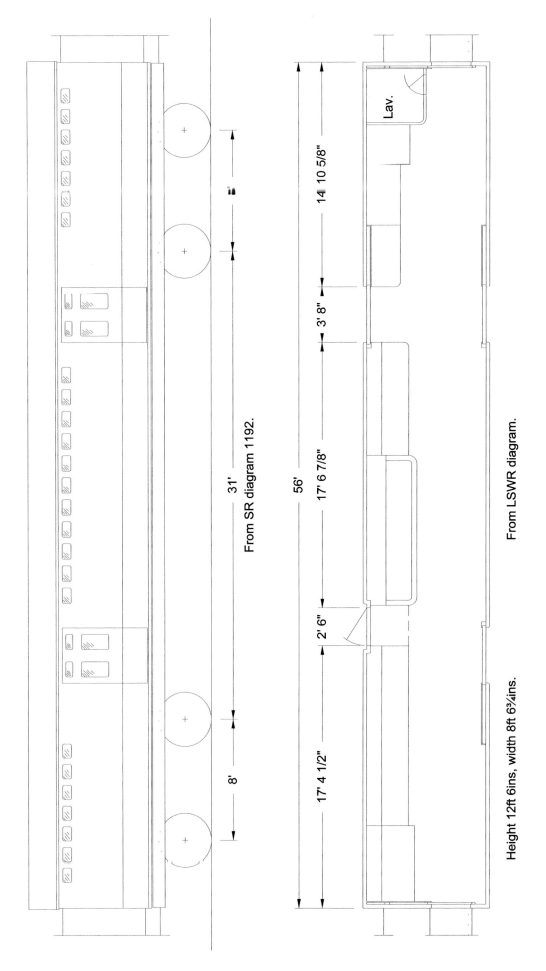

From SR diagram 1192.

From LSWR diagram.

NOT to scale.

Height 12ft 6ins, width 8ft 6¾ins.

Figure 2.9. LSWR 56ft letter sorting van No 5614 of 1913.

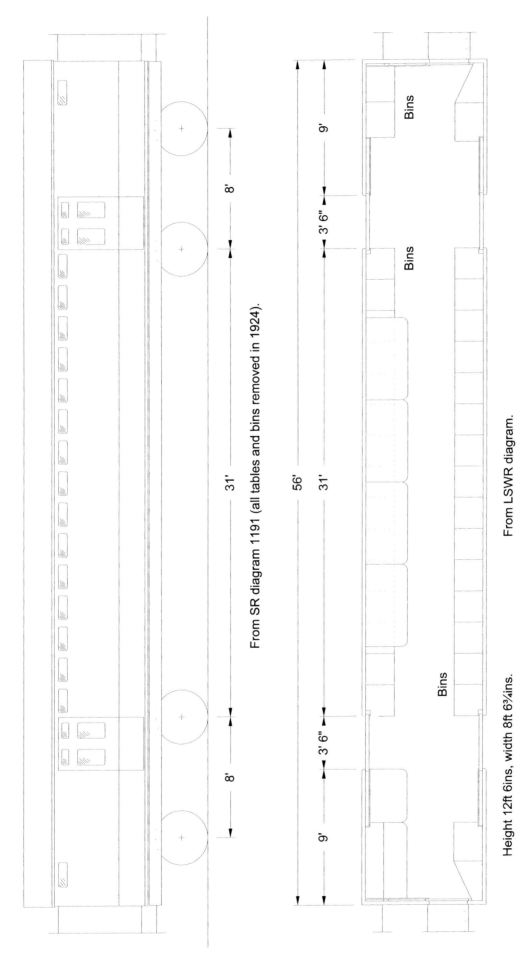

8'

31'

From SR diagram 1191 (all tables and bins removed in 1924).

31'

8'

56'

9'

3' 6"

Bins

Bins

Bins

9'

3' 6"

From LSWR diagram.

Height 12ft 6ins, width 8ft 6¾ins.

NOT to scale.

Figure 2.10. LSWR 56ft parcel sorting van No 5615 of 1914.

Exeter –Torrington service ceased and bag tender No 9 was sent to Clapham Junction to be a reserve. Then, in the following November, the South Western TPO day mail ceased.

The Portsmouth sorting carriage ceased on 6th October 1923, and the first part of the down TPO (formerly the 9pm) also ceased. However, the day TPO was resumed on 26th November 1923, but to and from Bournemouth only.

There have been several references to the Post Office rosters. In the Post Office Archives, there are six books entitled *Roster of Post Office Carriages*. These show, for every railway that had Post Office Carriages, details of the duties, and are for the years 1894, 1902, 1903, 1907, 1915 and 1935. The first five show, not only the carriage numbers, sizes and building dates, but also the services on which they ran. The one for the LSWR for October 1903 is shown in Appendix 2 as an example.

The Southern Railway kept all eighteen postal vehicles officially in use, although the six-wheelers were probably only reserves. These were withdrawn between January 1928 and November 1933, when they either went into departmental use, or were grounded as cabins. The bogie vehicles carried on until the late 1930s and early 1940s, when several were grounded, though the 56ft vans numbers 5614 and 5615, by then extensively rebuilt as SR S4916S and S4918S, were still in postal use in June 1957. Figure 2.11 is based on them in that condition.

A large part of the 1862 contract between the LSWR and the Post Office was described earlier, and there must have been revisions from time to time, but it may be interesting to note that in May 1904, the Traffic Committee recorded that a new contract had been agreed under which the Post Office would increase their annual payment from £35,721 to £55,100 for the current services. They would also pay 3 shillings (15p) per mile for any additional or special trains required for foreign or continental mails, also the cost of any alterations or additions to the existing Post Office sorting carriages, and for any further accommodation at stations. The new contract was to operate for seven years from 1st July 1904, subject thereafter to 6 months notice.

So far, we have considered mainly the recognised postal vehicles and the main line routing of mails to and from London. We should now turn to the local mail services to see how they operated. Fortunately, Mr N Pattenden of the South Western Circle has done a substantial study into the mail arrangements in North Devon around Christmas 1914 for publication in the *South Western Circular* (Volume 13, No 2, April 2004). In writing a very abbreviated version of his work, with some generalisations of my own, I fully accept responsibility for any omissions!

The LSWR North Devon and Cornwall lines really were tree-like, with a short stem that branched again and again. From the Post Office point of view, the stem and main branch was the line from Exeter St David's to Barnstaple, with a spur from the root back to Exeter Queen Street. Mail from London and the rest of the country (other than much of the LSWR area) came down the GWR main line to St David's, being sorted on its way. Mail from most of the LSWR area found its way to Queen Street, but in bags either already sorted at the originating offices, or to be sorted at the Exeter Post Office.

We have already seen that from a very early time some carriages, or compartments of them, were allocated to the Post Office for mails, and it is these that were first mentioned in connection with the service to North Devon, apparently between Exeter and Barnstaple, and the inference is that they were in passenger trains. However late night passenger trains were pretty scarce away from the London area, so much of the postal traffic had to travel by goods trains, presumably in the goods section of goods brake vans, also known as road vans or (when they were available) in passenger type vans attached to goods trains. Working Timetables sometimes described such trains as "Goods and Mail" as distinct from "Passenger and Mail", or simply "Mail".

On the down service from Queen Street, the night goods and mail train, which was limited to 35 wagons, would have to wait at St David's for the arrival of the down GWR Paddington – Penzance TPO service, and the transfer of bags for North Devon. After this, it ran, stopping at all stations, to Barnstaple, dropping off and taking up bags. At Barnstaple, bags were transferred to other trains for South Molton, Ilfracombe, Bideford and Torrington. In the case of Ilfracombe, the service travelled by the down goods and mail, returning in the evening by a passenger and mail. The inclusion of South Molton might seem surprising, as it was a GWR station, but this is what the Post Office requested in 1864, and most of their routings remained unchanged for a very long time. It seems likely that it was in fact the earliest route each day for forwarding mail that had arrived at the Exeter sorting office from South Devon, etc.

Back at Yeoford, a goods train from Exeter to Devonport had waited to pick up the vans containing bags for stations to Tavistock, and the branches to Bude and Padstow. From Yeoford to Tavistock, it became a goods and mail train, limited to 21 wagons as far as Okehampton, and to 25 from there to Tavistock. After pausing at Okehampton, the Devonport train would stop again at Meldon Junction for transfer of vans to a Wadebridge and Padstow train, which in turn stopped at Halwill Junction to pass vans to yet another goods train for Bude. On leaving Tavistock, the Devonport train was no longer goods and mail, just goods only.

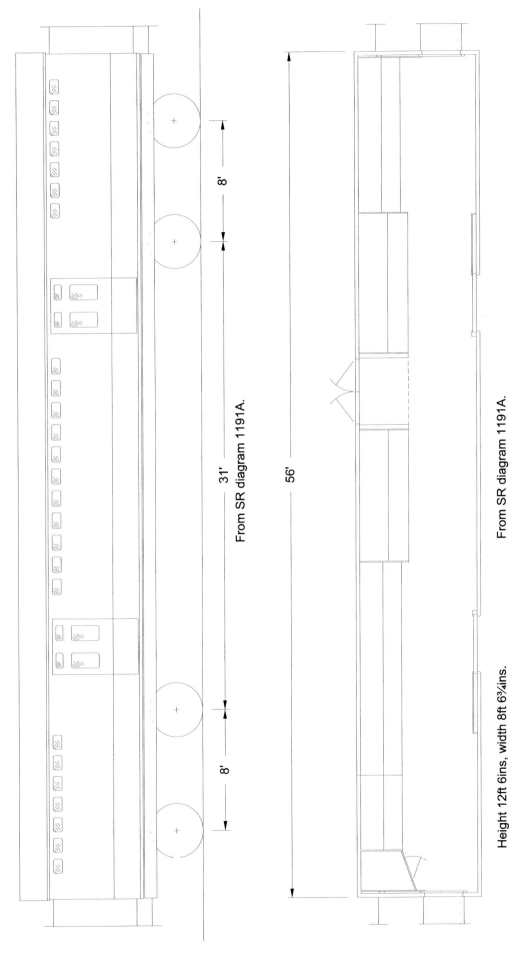

8'

31'

8'

From SR diagram 1191A.

56'

From SR diagram 1191A.

Height 12ft 6ins, width 8ft 6¾ins.

NOT to scale.

Figure 2.11. Sorting vans 5614/5 as rebuilt by SR.

Plate 2.11a. 5⅞ft sorting van No 5614, as altered by the SR. Clapham Junction, 1953. (R H Clarke)

Plate 2.11b. 56ft sorting van No 5615, as altered by the SR.

(R Blencowe)

The restrictions were doubtless to ensure the punctual running, which was vital for Post Office services, and it seems probable that a bogie van counted as two wagons. These trains included vans, both bogie and four-wheeled, as well as goods wagons and goods brake vans. The mails are assumed to have been carried in the brake vans, either bogie or goods.

The Exeter to Barnstaple route was apparently the only part over which a true postal van ran, this was shown in 1894 as No 3, one of the original 20ft 4in TPOs, but as a bag tender, leaving Queen Street at 3.10am. By 1902, this had been replaced by No 9, a 32ft TPO, but again used as a bag tender. In 1903, this service is shown as extended to Torrington, still as a bag tender, but described as "Goods and Mail". The up working from Torrington at 7.40pm is shown as "Passenger and Mail". From August 1906, the bag tender reverted to its original function as a TPO with sorters on board. By 1907 the similar 32ft No 6 was also assigned to the service, one running and one held as spare at Exeter.

In the up direction the Plymouth Devonport through Tavistock line would carry anything for the North Devon area, but naturally nothing for Exeter or anywhere east of Crediton, which would all go on the GWR route. The combining of trains or vehicles from the branches was largely the reverse of the splitting in the Down direction. However, there were a few cases where presumably the mailbags had already gone on an earlier train, so that instead of stopping, the drivers had instructions to go slowly through certain stations, such as Bere Alston and Bridestowe, so that mail and newspaper parcels could be dropped off.

East of Exeter, a similar system applied, sometimes using goods trains because of the scarcity of night-time passenger trains. The 1909 Working Timetable does not give such a clear view of postal services, and it has to be assumed that more use was made of ordinary passenger trains than was possible in North Devon. No study similar to Mr Pattenden's has been done of these services, but from the North Devon case, it was noted that mailbags for Portsmouth and Southampton went from Exeter by the brake van of the 10.25pm limited load goods train, calling at Yeovil Junction, Templecombe and Salisbury, though not shown as "Goods and Mail".

From Salisbury, a passenger and mail left at 2.35am for Yeovil Junction, Mondays excepted; on the Mondays the mail went by a fast goods at 4.05am, stopping at Semley and Gillingham to put out mailbags only, reaching Yeovil Junction at 5.45. Another goods to Yeovil, except on Saturday nights, left Salisbury at 4.50am, and stopped at Tisbury to put out mailbags only at 5.31am.

These rather scrappy notes serve to illustrate how complex the mail circulation network was, and the amount of attention that railway staff had to give to ensure that connections and transfers were correctly and reliably maintained.

Plate 2.11c. 56ft sorting van, LSWR 5614 of June 1913, SR 4918, at Clapham Junction on 5th June 1951.
(D Cullum 1007/Lens of Sutton Association)

AMBULANCE CARRIAGES

In the previous chapter, it was noted that in late 1869, the War Department had requested a vehicle to convey invalids between Portsmouth and Netley, and that it had been agreed to convert "an old Post Office van", apparently an early six-wheeler, at the cost of the WD.

At the LSWR Officers' Committee meeting on 17th January 1871, a letter from Major Close was read concerning an ambulance carriage that had been built (*sic*) to convey invalid soldiers to the Netley Hospital, under which it was ordered that the flanges of the middle wheels were to be turned down sufficiently to give 1½in play when going round sharp curves. The only further mention of (presumably) this vehicle is in the minutes of the Traffic and Locomotive Committee on 12th June 1872, when it was noted that the Metropolitan Carriage & Wagon Co had altered the Government ambulance carriage so that "it is not safe for use on any Railway". It was ordered that they should be remonstrated with.

It is probably this carriage that was referred to in *Hospital Ships and Ambulance Trains*, by Lt Col John H Plumridge (published by Seeley, Service & Co in 1975). He says that Surgeon-General Sir T Longmore drew up a plan in 1870 for an ambulance carriage to carry invalids between Southampton and Netley Hospital. One was built (or converted?) by Metropolitan, having a side entrance and folding doors at each end. It carried eight bunks for patients,

a seat for a medical officer, and folding seats for the orderlies. There were also cupboards, a stove, a sink, and a water closet with a water tank in the roof. He also says the design was so satisfactory that another one was built in about 1885. Unfortunately, no other details are available, but this later vehicle could be one that ended up at Woolwich Arsenal.

In the earlier volume, *LSWR Carriages in the 20th Century*, while discussing corridor carriages, there were several references to the conversion of passenger carriages for use in ambulance trains. Also, in the present Chapter 1 on passenger-rated vans, it was mentioned that five bogie fruit vans were converted to War Department ambulances in 1900 for carrying Boer War casualties from ship to hospital. They are illustrated here as Figure 3.1. The plan for this conversion was prepared by Major WD Macpherson of the Royal Army Medical Corps (later Major-General Sir William Macpherson).

Each carriage was provided with both vacuum and Westinghouse brakes to permit unrestricted use. They had twelve Fieldhouse patent portable beds fitted in six double-tier berths. There were also fixed seats for twelve sitting cases and two first class seats in a curtained-off compartment for either officers or medical staff. Two lavatories, a small cooking stove, linen and crockery cupboards were also provided.

The panels below the waist and all the raised fascias were painted khaki, while the upper panels

Plate 3.1a. 48ft Army ambulance.

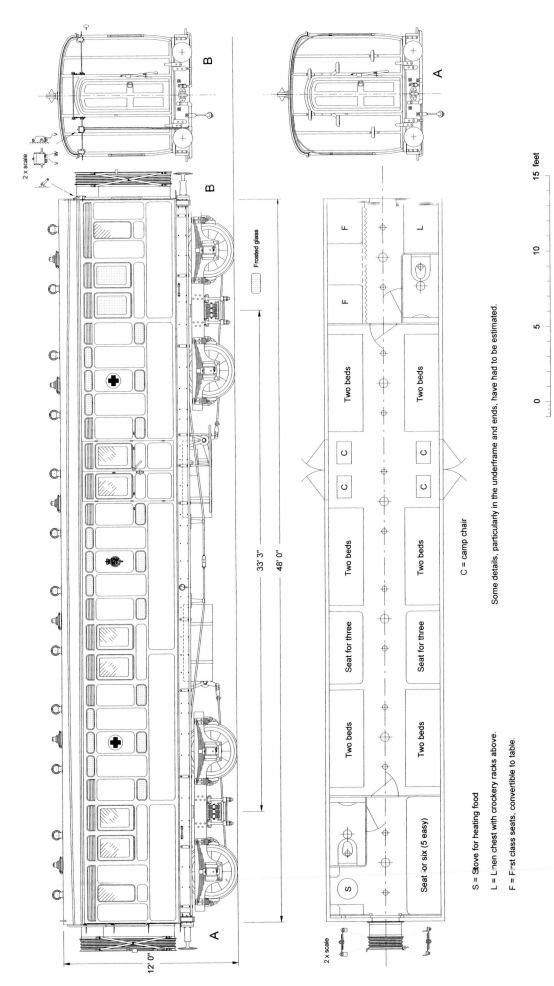

2 x scale

Frosted glass

33' 3"

48' 0"

12' 0"

2 x scale

S = Stove for heating food

L = Linen chest with crockery racks above.

F = First class seats, convertible to table.

C = camp chair

Some details, particularly in the underframe and ends, have had to be estimated.

Seat for six (5 easy)

Two beds

Seat for three

Two beds

F

F

Two beds

Seat for three

Two beds

L

0   5   10   15 feet

Figure 3.1. 48ft War Office ambulance, converted from fruit vans.

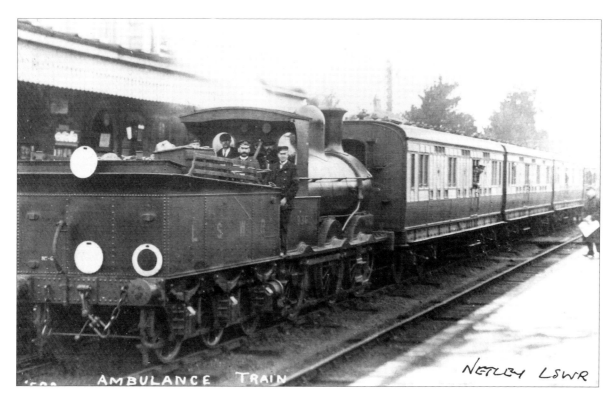

Plate 3.1b. Beyer Goods 0-6-0 No 336 hauling ambulance carriages into Netley Hospital station.

were French grey. The fascias were picked out in yellow, and fine-lined with red. On each side, there were two red crosses on white discs, while the Royal Arms in full colours appeared in the central upper panel. "War Department Ambulance Coach" was originally painted on the khaki panel immediately below the Royal Arms, and Army numbers 1 to 5 were painted in the waist panels at each end under the double windows. This lettering appears to have been omitted at some later stage; the total effect must have been very impressive. Inside, they were enamelled white with mahogany trimmings, the upholstery was dark maroon leather and the floor was covered with Corticine.

These ambulances were normally berthed at the Royal Victoria Hospital, Netley, and were frequently used between Southampton Docks and Netley, although they probably occasionally travelled quite far afield. The *South Western Gazette* records that their first use was on Sunday 8th April 1900, when they carried about 160 sick and wounded from the Union Line ship *SS Greek*, from Southampton to Well Hall (SECR) for treatment at the Royal Herbert Hospital, Woolwich. An indistinct photograph also shows two of them in a train unloading casualties at Sandgate, Kent. It was also noted that they carried the first casualties from France in August 1914 from Southampton to Netley. At the beginning of the Second World War they were still at Netley, and Mr Sedgwick noted that they were soon repainted

overall khaki, with red crosses on the roofs. It has been reported that in 1943 or early 1944, they were assigned to the United States Army and later left Netley. What happened to Nos 1 and 5 is not known, but 2, 3 and 4 were transferred to the Longmoor Military Railway, where Mr D Barnard noted that they were converted into ordinary passenger vehicles by replacing the beds with tram type seats along the sides. They were made into a three-car set, each end being provided with a guard's compartment with a handbrake. At this time, Mr Barnard observed that the colour was not the usual khaki, but a kind of teak colour. The date of final withdrawal is not known.

In both World Wars the Government called upon the major railway companies to provide carriages for use as ambulances, either as "loose" vehicles or as complete trains. Some were for use in this country, and others for use on the Continent. The subject is scantily documented in LSWR records and elsewhere. So far as the LSWR is concerned, there is some disparity between what was recorded in the minutes, other accounts, and what was shown in the Carriage Register.

Accounts of some vehicles and trains have appeared in various journals and books, but probably the only work devoted to the subject is *Hospital Ships and Ambulance Trains*, mentioned earlier. This book deals with the subject in general, but does not go into much detail of the actual rolling stock

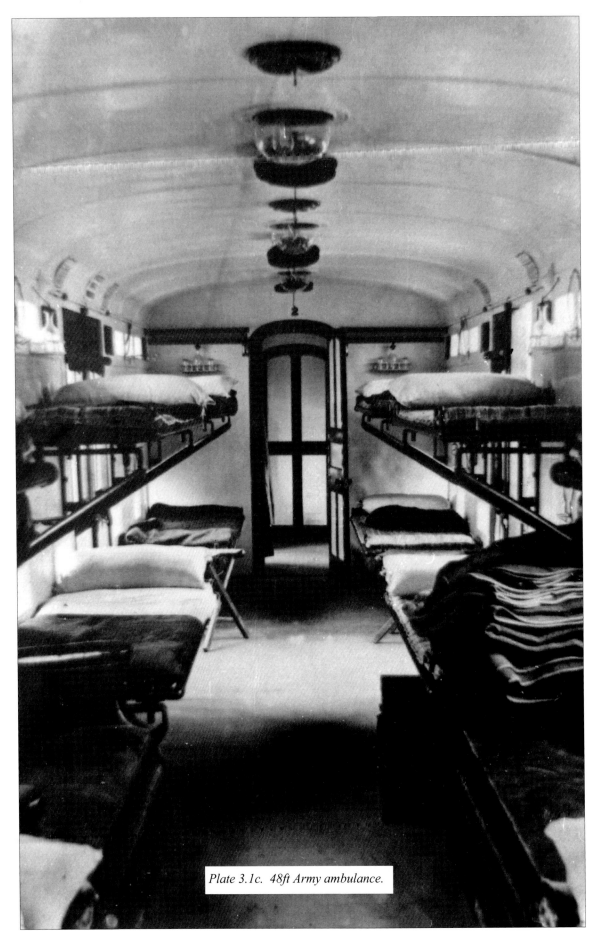

Plate 3.1c. 48ft Army ambulance.

Plate 3.1d. Netley postcard.

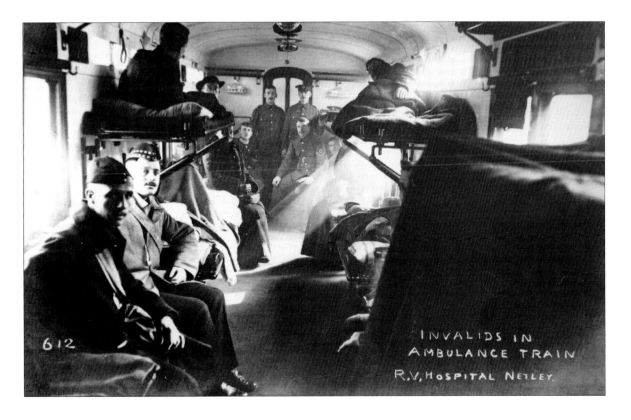

Plate 3.1e. Netley postcard.

Plate 3.1f. 48ft ex-Army ambulance, ex-fruit van, at Longmoor Military Railway in 1948.

(D P Callender)

used.

During and after the Boer War, the War Office had been discussing the provision of ambulance trains in a war emergency with various railway companies, particularly the LNWR. Thus, by the time of the outbreak of the First World War in August 1914, complete drawings and specifications were in existence, both for the conversion of existing stock and also for the construction of new stock.

According to Mr Plumridge, twelve ambulance trains from various railways, including one of nine carriages from the LSWR, were marshalled at Southampton in the early days of the war. This is not mentioned anywhere in LSWR records, but he states that the first sick and wounded arrived at Southampton on 24th August 1914, and were taken to Netley Hospital in the War Department train, the 1900 one described above, strengthened with some additional ordinary carriages. Thereafter, the WD train was mainly used to take officer casualties to London, as the first train away from each hospital shipload. He goes on to state that later, four emergency trains were provided for sitting patients,

consisting of ordinary corridor stock, including dining cars.

LSWR Special Notice No P60 SL, of early 1918, on the working of ambulance trains, which lists 28 trains numbered 1 to 23, then 26, 31, and 37 to 39, records the trains numbered 10 and 21 as each consisting of ten dual-braked LSWR vehicles, train No 26 having seven LSWR carriages, including a diner. Train No 37 was formed of six LNWR carriages and four from the LSWR (from other records this included a diner and two "emigrant" brake thirds, Nos 1449 and 1488). Train No 38 again had six from the LNWR and two (diner No 7842 and "emigrant" third No 92) from the LSWR. Train No 39 consisted of ten carriages, including a diner, from the LSWR. These latter four were just vacuum braked. Trains 23, 26, 31 and 37 to 39 were described as "emergency trains", that is, they were not converted to ambulances like the rest but could be used mainly for sitting cases.

The first reference in the LSWR minutes was, rather surprisingly, in October 1915, when it was stated that the company was to provide an

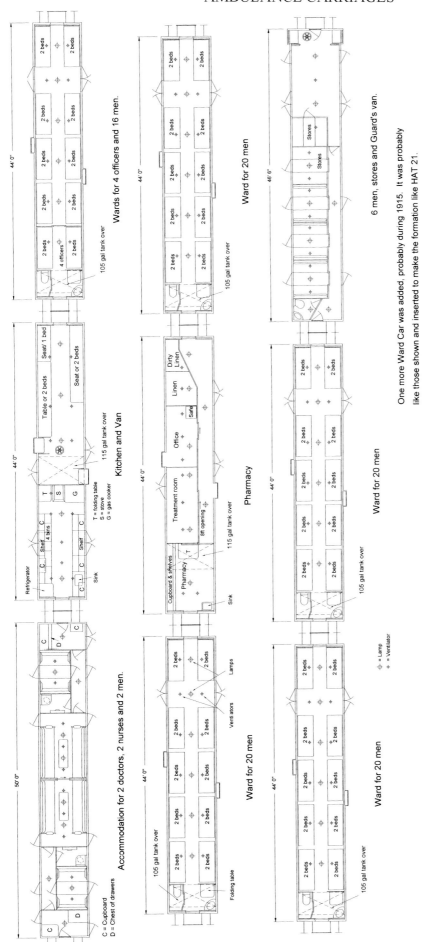

Figure 3.2. *Arrangement of Ambulance Train No 10, in 1914. (Not to scale.)*

ambulance train for use in the United Kingdom by converting existing stock. Surprising, because in the Autumn of 1914, *The Railway News* published a description of the "South Western train converted for ambulance purposes". This train, Home Ambulance Train No 10, is shown here as Figure 3.2. Livery was the standard LSWR, with the addition of a red cross on a white square of 2ft 6in sides near the centre of each vehicle, lined up with the windows. The floors were covered with linoleum, all angles and corners filleted to be water and dust tight. The wards and pharmacy were painted with white enamel, and steam heaters with regulators were provided throughout.

The LSWR Carriage Register records two vehicles running in a "War Department ambulance train" in September 1914, clearly dating No 10. These are a 50ft saloon and an "emigrant" 46ft 6in brake third shown as Figures 6.1 and 9.6 respectively in *LSWR Carriages in the 20th Century*. The 44ft vehicles were converted from 44ft passenger guards vans, shown as Figure 5.12 in *LSWR Carriages, Volume 1*.

The 1915 minutes reference was to the train described in *The Railway News* for December 1915. Then it said that the LSWR had built two ambulance trains, the second generally similar to the first, but with ten vehicles. The original diagram showed five ward cars with a capacity of 100 patients, whereas the 1915 article and diagram show six, which raised the capacity to 120. At some stage, train No 10 was augmented with an additional ward car, but its origin is not certain. The 1915 article goes on to say that the ward cars were converted from guard's vans, and were lettered A to F, and that the officers' and nurses' carriage was converted from an emigrant corridor composite. This train was also illustrated in *The South Western Railway Magazine* (formerly the *South Western Gazette*) for December 1st 1915, and is shown here as Figure 3.3.

In both trains, the beds were arranged in two tiers, the lower ones on pillars from the floor, the upper ones hinged to the side pillars, so that they could fold down to act as backs to the lower ones for sitting patients. Each bed had a mattress and two hair pillows. Hanging straps were provided to help patients to sit up and there were wire racks for ashtrays and other oddments.

One significant improvement in train No 21 was the provision of a bath in the officers' and nurses' carriage and another in the pharmacy car. The office of the pharmacy car had a telephone that connected to the two staff cars at the ends of the train, and could probably be connected to the GPO system at stations. As with train No 10, this one was dual-braked and steam-heated throughout. The *South Western Railway Magazine* states that, as well

as being painted with the normal LSWR livery, the Geneva cross in red on a white ground was painted prominently on both sides and the roof of every vehicle, the latter no doubt in recognition of the increasing risk of air attacks.

It is interesting that the diagram of train No 10 shows the kitchen and van with apparently no access between the kitchen and the van end, unless a small hatch was cut into the bulkhead. Possibly, this small kitchen was not originally intended to provide catering for the whole train, but just for the permanent staff, who probably lived on the train for several days at a time. If this is so, presumably station stops were arranged for the longer journeys to permit refreshments for the wounded passengers. However, in the diagram of train No 21 there is a definite door shown behind the folding table.

In the LSWR Carriage Register, it is noted that the Royal Train cooking car, LSWR No 73/4384, was used in ambulance train No 10. However, it has been stated elsewhere that it was used in Continental ambulance train No 10, otherwise provided by the Etat company. The layout of the kitchen and van shown by *The Railway News* is a lot more elaborate than the pre-1912 LSWR diagram of No 73/4384, though that is not necessarily of any significance.

At this point, the train numbering schemes must be mentioned. The trains shown on the LSWR special notice were Home Ambulance Trains (HATs). Plumridge lists thirty train numbers between 1 and 43 as Continental Ambulance Trains (CATs) serving in France. The first eleven of these were formed of French stock. The rest came from British companies but only one, number 35, was from the LSWR.

Reverting to 1915, and the lack of LSWR records, the Imperial War Museum has a large and excellent model, with opening roof to show the fully fitted interior, of an ambulance car bearing the number 33-C. It is described as an LSWR vehicle, although it bears no resemblance to any LSWR design. This model was given to the museum by the Southern Railway in May 1936, accompanied by a statement that thirty of them were built by the LSWR in 1915 for the conveyance of wounded soldiers from the Channel ports to the hospitals of Great Britain.

The War Museum also makes the statement that the model is of ward car C in train No 33. According to the official records, this was a CAT of sixteen carriages provided by the Great Western, and made its first loaded journey from Etaples to Calais on 30th August 1917. The Southern Railway statement implies that the thirty were built to contract for the Government, and were therefore not recorded as LSWR vehicles, and that they were used on both HATs and CATs. Doubtless there would

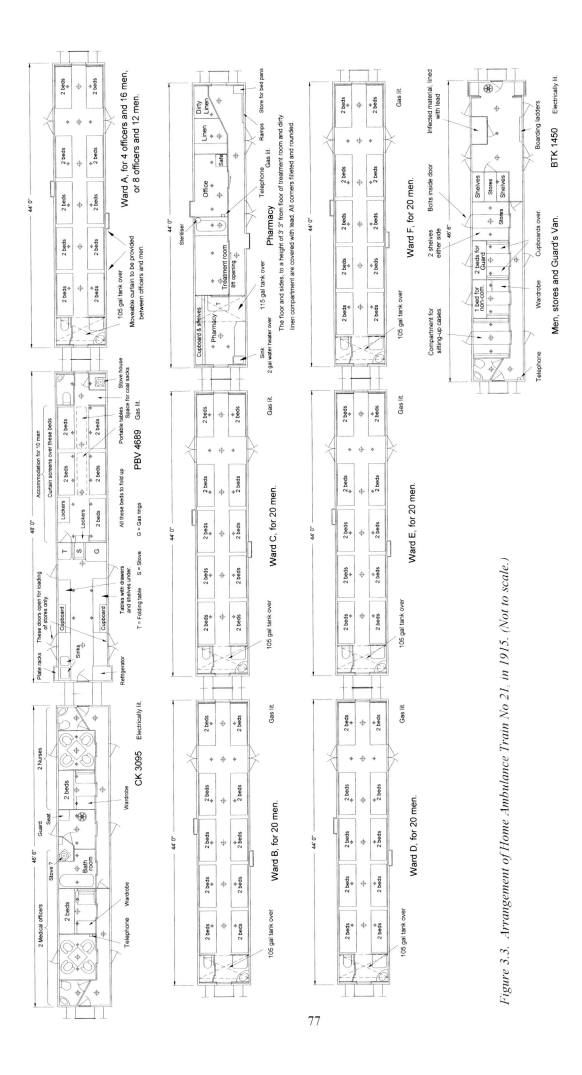

Ward A, for 4 officers and 16 men, or 8 officers and 12 men.

Moveable curtain to be provided between officers and men.

105 gal tank over

CK 3095   Electrically lit.

2 Medical officers   2 Nurses

Guard   Seat   Wardrobe

Stove ?

Telephone   Bath room   Wardrobe   2 beds

Accommodation for 10 men

Curtain screens over these beds

Lockers   2 beds

Lockers   2 beds   2 beds

Portable tables   Gas lit.

Stove house   Space for coal sacks

All these beds to fold up

G = Gas rings   T = Folding table   S = Stove

These doors open for loading of stores only

Plate racks   Sinks   Cupboard   Cupboard   Tables with drawers and shelves under.   Refrigerator

PBV 4689

Pharmacy

Office   Linen   Dirty Linen   Safe

Sterliser   Treatment room   8ft opening

Ramps   Store for bed pans

Telephone   Gas lit.

115 gal tank over

Sink   2 gal water heater over   Cupboard & shelves   Pharmacy   X T

The floor and sides, to a height of 3' 3" from floor of treatment room and dirty linen compartment are covered with lead. All corners filleted and rounded.

Ward F, for 20 men.   Gas lit.

105 gal tank over

Ward C, for 20 men.   Gas lit.

105 gal tank over

Ward E, for 20 men.   Gas lit.

105 gal tank over

Ward B, for 20 men.   Gas lit.

105 gal tank over

Ward D, for 20 men.   Gas lit.

105 gal tank over

Men, stores and Guard's Van.

BTK 1450   Electrically lit.

Infected material, lined with lead

Bolts inside door

2 shelves either side

Compartment for sitting-up cases.

Telephone

Wardrobe   Cupboards over.

1 bed for non-com.   2 beds for Guard   Stores   Shelves   Stores   Shelves

Boarding ladders

Figure 3.3. *Arrangement of Home Ambulance Train No 21, in 1915. (Not to scale.)*

77

have been records at Eastleigh, but it seems that all of these were got rid of during the BR clear-out of "old rubbish".

The next LSWR reference was in May 1917, when it was minuted that the Government had asked for another ambulance train (CAT No 35, mentioned above), one of six that were to be sent to the Continent. It was then agreed to convert seven brake thirds, six thirds, one brake composite, a 48ft van and a 44ft van. In fact, the train was reported as complete in October 1917, entering service in France on December 17th. It was actually formed of twelve brake thirds, three thirds, and one 44ft brake van. They are listed in the Appendix to Chapter 3 (part 3.4), but they were fully illustrated in their original form in Chapter 9 of *LSWR Carriages in the 20th Century*. Although many of the CATs were well described and illustrated in various railway journals of the time, this one only seems to have had brief mentions, so the actual function of the various vehicles and their positions in the train cannot be described. However it seems likely that the conversion work was extensive and very similar to that shown for US train No 62 in Figure 3.5.

In April 1918, it was reported that another train that had been asked for in the previous September, consisting of twelve brake thirds, three thirds and a bogie van (just as the previous one), had been sold to the Government, and converted for the use of the United States Army on the Continent as ambulance train No 62, at the price of £22,233. According to the register, this train actually consisted of eight brake thirds and eight thirds, the vehicles being numbered from 6201 to 6216. Before being handed over, some of the carriages had been on view in the week commencing 6th May at Waterloo, Kingston and Bournemouth West, a charge of 8d being made to the public and 4d to members of HM Forces; total receipts had been £1080 6s 6d, after deduction of expenses. The nett profit of £952 went to the L&SW Servants Orphanage, St. John's Ambulance, St. Dunstan's Hostel and comforts for railway troops.

The LSWR also printed descriptive pamphlets showing the layout, on which Figure 3.5 is based, with descriptions and interior photos of the various carriages. These pamphlets sold for 4d (1.67p) each. Copies of the photos in the pamphlet are shown here and on the following pages.

An odd point about the exterior views of the

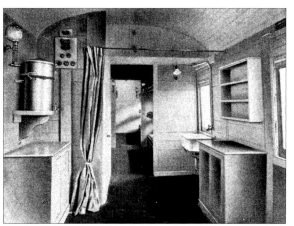

Interior photos of the various carriages of the United States Army Continental Ambulance Train No 62, taken from an LSWR pamphlet of 1918.

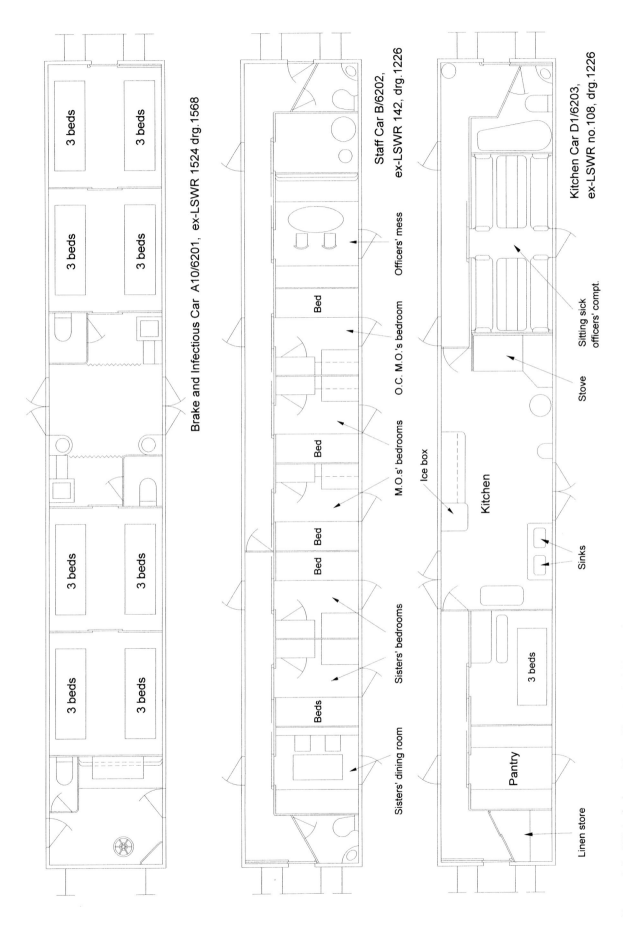

Figure 3.5. *US Ambulance Train No 62 of 1918. (1 of 3)*

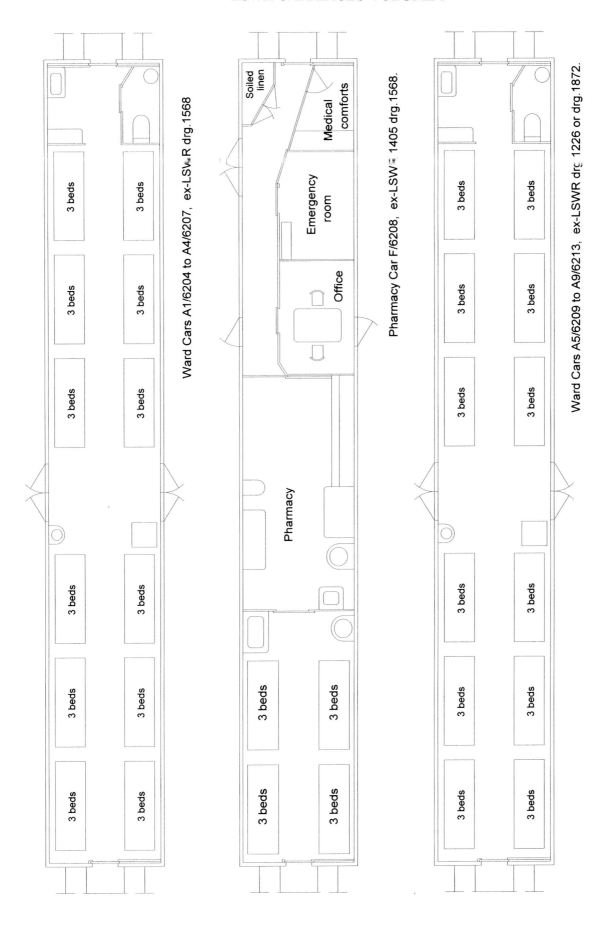

Ward Cars A1/6204 to A4/6207, ex-LSWR drg.1568

Pharmacy Car F/6208, ex-LSWR 1405 drg.1568.

Ward Cars A5/6209 to A9/6213, ex-LSWR drg 1226 or drg.1872.

Figure 3.5. US Ambulance Train No 62 of 1918. (2 of 3)

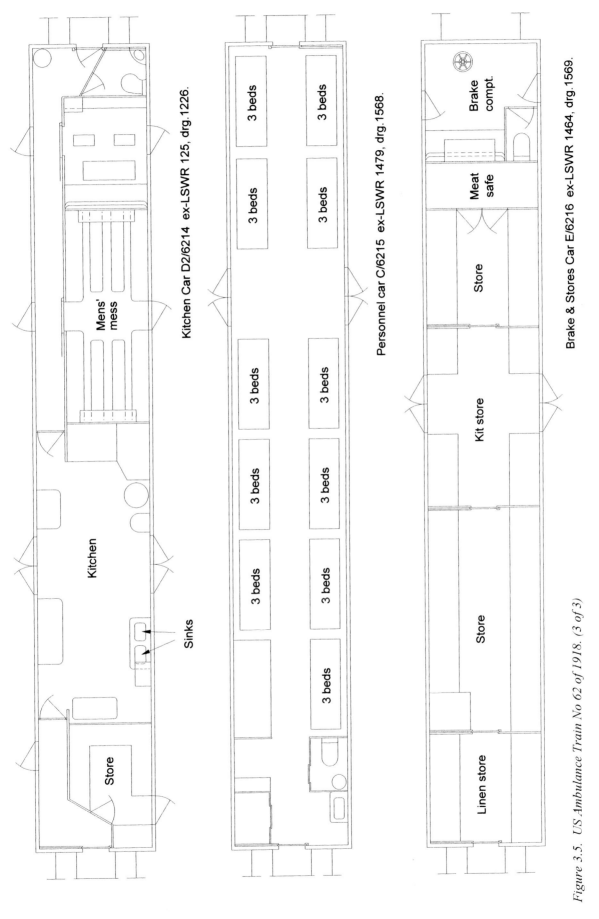

Kitchen Car D2/6214 ex-LSWR 125, drg.1226.

Personnel car C/6215 ex-LSWR 1479, drg.1568.

Brake & Stores Car E/6216 ex-LSWR 1464, drg.1569.

Figure 3.5. US Ambulance Train No 62 of 1918. (3 of 3)

Interior photos of the various carriages of the United States Army Continental Ambulance Train No 62, taken from an LSWR pamphlet of 1918.

cars is that the water tanks that were fitted to the roofs have been blanked out. The pamphlet includes a small view of the whole train, on which white patches clearly show where the tanks have been blotted out. Such censorship seems very strange. Copies of the photos published at the time, such as the one at page 83 of *Southern Reflections* by RC Riley show those tanks quite clearly. They were not in the same position on every vehicle, probably those on the ward cars were in the same places, but for example on car 1201 (Brake and Infectious Car) which was at one end of the train, the tank was over the ward section, clear of the brake compartment.

Immediately after the show week, the complete train was despatched to France. The vehicles are listed in the Appendix to Chapter 3 (part 3.5), and their layout is shown in Figure 3.5. There were: a Staff Car providing dining and sleeping accommodation for the medical officers, two Kitchen Cars, a Pharmacy Car with treatment facilities and ten Ward Cars, one of which was reserved for infectious cases. Each ward car had 36 beds, and there was a personnel car that could carry

38 orderlies – a relatively higher proportion of medical staff than on the HATs. The publicity stated that the train could carry 480 patients, or 680 if all were sitting; the tare weight was 440 tons. The whole train was painted in khaki-green with very large red Geneva crosses on sides and roof, also very large letters "US" on each carriage.

After the war, the vehicles from the two HATs were returned to service without much difficulty, the 44ft vans merely needed removal of the ward equipment and restoration of the brake compartments, but whether the gangways were removed or replaced with the later wider type is not clear. The other vehicles needed relatively little restoration.

In July 1919, the sixteen carriages of train No 62 were offered back to the LSWR for £800 each, and this was accepted. Of course, the original sale price included the conversion, and as returned they had to be reconverted, though in fact, because of the structural alterations on all except the staff car, this was done fairly cheaply by turning fifteen of them into passenger brake vans. It seems likely from the

AMBULANCE CARRIAGES

Interior photos of the various carriages of the United States Army Continental Ambulance Train No 62, taken from an LSWR pamphlet of 1918.

register entries that the staff car No 6202, which had not been much altered from its original form, was used for a short time in a Naval ambulance train. It was returned to the SR who restored it as third No 744.

In December 1920, it was agreed to buy back ambulance train No 35, now reported as 13 vehicles, together with two additional vehicles, again at £800 apiece. All fifteen of these carriages went back into service as vans. The 44ft brake van did not return, or at least it is not shown in the records. The conversions to vans are described later.

Naturally, the HATs could not run to any schedules so a system of "speed tables" was drawn up covering all the likely routes between ports and hospitals within the LSWR area, and junctions with other railway companies. For each route, there was

a service number with detailed timings based on zero minutes at the start point and showing arrival and departure, or passing, times in minutes and hours from that zero at the major points on the way. For every route, there was also a list of all the stations that had to be notified by telephone or telegraph. Thus, as soon as an ambulance train was ordered, the service number could be called through to all affected stations so that staff could immediately calculate the arrival or passing time. There was a separate set of tables for returning empty trains, including stops for recharging the gas cylinders and cleaning.

Most of the services were naturally starting from Southampton Dock Gates at zero minutes. Some examples, omitting all the intermediate timings, are shown below.

Service	Description
1	Netley Hospital 34min.
4	Epsom (for hospitals at Horton Park) via Havant at 0hr 52min, attach assisting engine if necessary, via Guildford at 1hr 58min, detach assisting engine, arriving at Epsom at 2hr 33min.
13	M&SWJR or Midland Railway. Arrive at Andover Junction at 0hr 55min, depart at 1hr 0min. The LSWR engine will work through to Cheltenham in charge of the M&SWJR pilotman.
14	GWR. Arrive Salisbury at 0hr 53min, depart at 0hr 58min. The LSWR engine will work through to Trowbridge or Bristol as required in charge of the GWR pilotman.
24	Basingstoke for Park Prewett or to GWR, GCR, or L&NWR. Arrive Basingstoke at 0hr 55min, depart at 1hr 0min. The LSWR engine will work through to Oxford or Banbury as required in charge of the GWR pilotman. (Includes special details for working over the Park Prewett line.)
32	GNR. Via Woking, stopping at Staines at 1hr 50min for water, Acton Wells Junction at 2hr 28min to take up the North London Co pilotman, hand over train to GNR at Canonbury at 2hr 57min.
33	GER. Same as service 32 as far as Acton Wells Junction to pick up North London Co pilotman, then Victoria Park at 3hr 5min to pick up GER pilotman, hand over train to GER at Channelsea Junction at 3hr 9min, then proceed light engine to Stratford and wait to pick up return empties at Gunnersbury.
85	Ambulance trains from Dover (SECR) for the Midland Railway will be worked by MR engine, Clapham Junction at 0min, take up LSWR pilotman and guard, Kew East Junction at 15min to set down the LSWR pilotman, Brent at 32min to set down the LSWR guard.
118	Naval Ambulance Train. From Plymouth North Road at 0min, Exeter St David's arrive at 1hr 54min, depart at 1hr 57min, Exeter (Queen St.) arrive at 2hr 0min, depart at 2hr 10min, Eastleigh at 5hr 11min. May stop there for gas and water. From Eastleigh to Gosport at 30min. On arrival at Gosport the train may be required to run to Gillingham or Chatham SECR stopping at Catford or Greenwich, via various routes, services 120 to 124.

General View of American Ambulance Train No. 62.

Exterior photos of the United States Army Continental Ambulance Train No 62, taken from an LSWR pamphlet of 1918.

COMPOSITION OF TRAIN No. 62

No. of Car	Medical Designation	Description	Accommodation for
6201	A 10	Brake Van with 4 Infectious Wards	1 Train Guard. 24 Infectious lying-down cases
6202	B.	Staff Car	3 Medical Officers 3 Nurses
6203	D 1.	Kitchen Car, with sitting room for sick officers ...	3 Cooks 12 Officers (sitting)
6204	A 1.	Ward Cars, each 36 berths ...	144 lying-down cases
6205	A 2.		
6206	A 3.		
6207	A 4.		
6208	F.	Pharmacy Car ...	12 lying-down serious cases
6209	A 5.	Ward Cars, each 36 berths ...	180 lying-down cases
6210	A 6.		
6211	A 7.		
6212	A 8.		
6213	A 9.		
6214	D 2.	Kitchen Car, with 2 Mess Rooms	2 N'n-Com. Offic'r
6215	C.	Personnel Car ...	33 Orderlies
6216	E.	Brake and Stores Car	1 Train Guard
Sixteen Cars with accommodation for ...			418 Persons, or with a maximum of sitting-up cases a total of 680

In *LSWR Carriages, Volume 1*, Chapter 5, it was recorded that twelve of the former "Eagle" saloons were sold to the War Department in 1916. Mr RW Kidner has found a little more information about them. The first two arrived in Egypt on the *SS Arum* on 27th October 1916, and four more on the 31st on the *SS Priestfield*. They were immediately ordered to be converted to ambulances and first ran as ambulance train No 6 in December 1916, first crossing the Suez Canal on 5th December.

The other six were similarly formed into train No 9 in June 1917. These were presumably local numbers as they were renumbered 48 and 51 respectively in 1918 (and later shown as 48/51, presumably combined), which might fit in with the theory that there was by then a single train number series covering all spheres of operation. Further details are recorded in the magazine *Harakavet* for June 1990.

Most of the September 1919 issue of the *South Western Railway Magazine* was devoted to the South Western War Record, a very large part of which was the Roll of Honour listing all the employees who had died, and those who had received bravery awards during the war. There was also a substantial section giving masses of statistics of the company's contribution. Among these, were the facts that during the war, Southampton had unloaded 2,632 hospital ships, 57,123 sick or wounded officers, 1,177,125 other ranks, and had handled 10,173 ambulance trains.

During the Second World War, there was a need for many types of vehicle to be used in connection with Civil Defence as well as for military ambulances. In Chapter 9 of *LSWR Carriages in the 20th Century*, mention was made of the former dining saloons that were converted to ambulances for the Army, Admiralty, United States Transportation Corps and Civil Defence use. The appendix to that chapter shows some of the details for these but the full story is yet to be unravelled.

Reverting to the corridor thirds and brake thirds that were converted for use in the CATs (Nos 35 and 62) during the 1914-18 war, it was not until about 1919 or 1920 that they were returned, and by then the LSWR was developing the new generation of 57ft "Ironclad" stock. Consequently, most of the ambulance vehicles were not reconverted for passenger carrying but were turned into passenger brake vans.

Whilst it might be considered appropriate to have described them in Chapter 1 with the vans, it was felt preferable to mention them here after dealing with their ambulance use. The actual date of the conversions is not recorded, but most of those from CAT No 35 were at least allocated LSWR

Plate 3.6a. Former 56ft Brake Third, LSWR No 1401, drawing No 1487, altered for Continental Ambulance Train in 1917, on return altered to passenger brake van No 4354, drawing No 3499.

(F Foote)

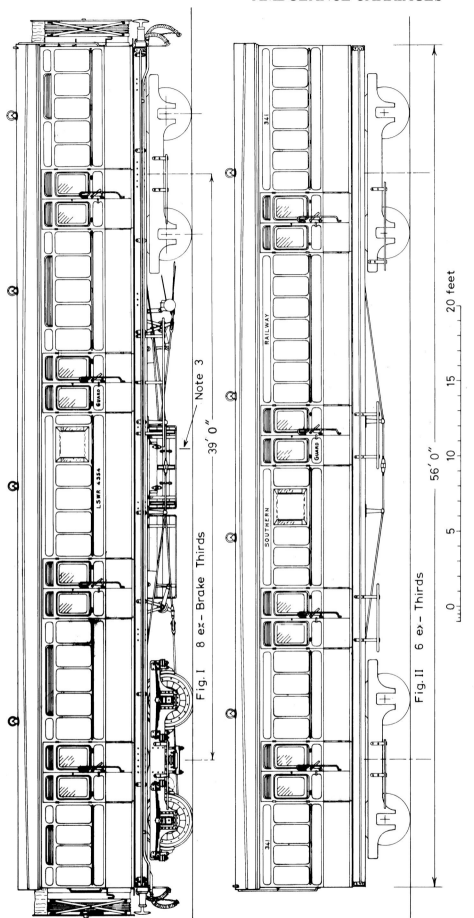

Fig. I 8 ex- Brake Thirds

39' 0"

Note 3

Fig. II 6 ex- Thirds

56' 0"

0   5   10   15   20 feet

Fig 3.6. 1921 56ft LSWR and SR passenger brake van, drawing 3499. (1 of 3)

1. The other side of all vehicles is the mirror image of the side drawn, apart from door handles, etc.

2. All these vans were converted from ambulance vehicles, originally built as Thirds or Brake Thirds.

3. Position of brake wheel spindle.

4. Photographs show variations in positions of roof ventilators, in lower footboards, and in which end had steps and handrails to the roof.

5. Vehicles rebuilt as figures I and II were all recorded as Southern diagram 869. Those as shown at figure III were SR diagram 870, and those at figure IV were SR diagram 871.

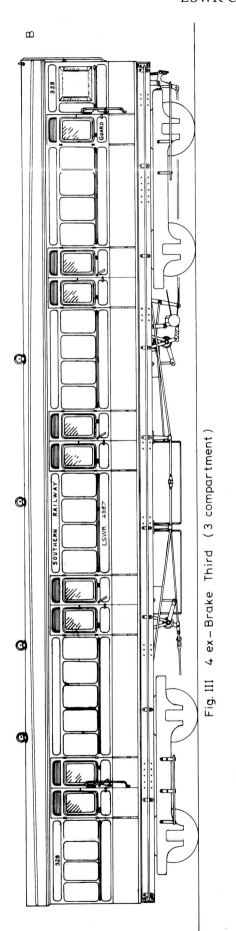

Fig. III 4 ex-Brake Third (3 compartment)

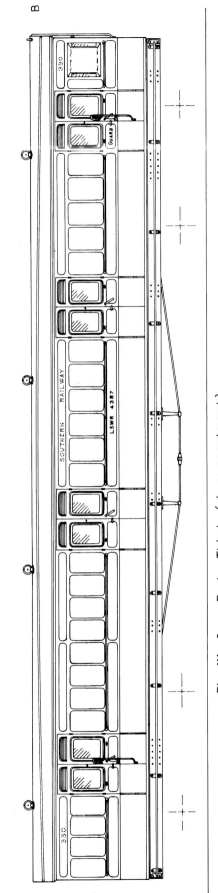

Fig. IV 9 ex-Brake Third (4 compartment)

0   5   10   15   20 feet

Fig 3.6. 1921 56ft LSWR and SR passenger brake van, drawing 3499. (2 of 3)

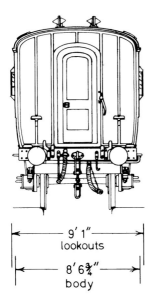

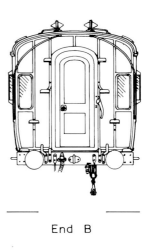

End B

Fig 3.6. 1921 56ft LSWR and SR passenger brake van, drawing 3499. (3 of 3)

numbers in the passenger brake van series, whilst those that had been used for the United States Ambulance Train No 62 only received Southern Railway numbers.

There were four distinct variants. The first batch, which had been built in 1906/07 as four-compartment brake thirds to drawing 1487, and which still retained their guard's brake gear near the centre, were rebuilt to LSWR drawing 3499 as shown at Figure 3.6 (I) and Plate 3.6a. On the LSWR diagram, the portion that had been the original luggage section has a note "126 small or 56 large churns" and the other, former compartment section is marked "138 small or 64 large churns".

Later, probably after Grouping, some former thirds to drawings 1226 and 1872 that had been used in the US train No 62, were converted to a fairly similar layout shown in Figure 3.6 (II). Two other types of brake third, one with three compartments and end lookouts, to drawing 1569, the other with four compartments, to drawing 1568, were also dealt with in a similar way, but with their guard's positions at the ends, Figures 3.6 (III) (Plate 3.6b & c) and (IV) (Plate 3.6d). There are a few discrepancies between the LSWR and SR records concerning some of these vehicles, so the numbering information in the Appendix to Chapter 3 might contain some transpositions.

Plate 3.6b. Former 56 ft brake-third LSWR No 1466, drawing No 1569. Altered to Ward Car T in Continental Ambulance Train 35, and on return, altered to passenger brake van LSWR No 4366. Seen at Topsham in 1949.
(J H Aston)

Plate 3.6c. Former brake third 1465, drawing No 1569, altered to Infectious Car P in CAT 35. On return, altered to passenger brake van 4367 (SR 328), drawing No 3510. Finally becoming DS 3177.

(J H Aston)

Plate 3.6d. Former 56ft brake third LSWR No 1405, drawing No 1568. Altered to US Ambulance Car No 6208 in 1918, and rebuilt in 1924 to passenger brake van SR No 337.

(Hemingway collection, HMRS)

L11 class No 406 on a London-Alton-Southampton special. At least 24 horse boxes are marshalled behind a 48ft brake tri-composite and four 48ft thirds. (*Lens of Sutton*)

CHAPTER 4

HORSE BOXES and CARRIAGE TRUCKS

It has already been said that there is even less known about early non-passenger carriage stock than there is about early passenger carriages. In the first few years, there were occasional mentions in minutes, accident reports and so on, of horse boxes and carriage trucks. However, there are no descriptions, dimensions or illustrations of any value for the present purpose prior to about 1860, the date of the first such LSWR vehicle (a horse box) in the Metropolitan (ex-Joseph Wright) collection of drawings. Similarly, there is no information anywhere about the livery, although from photos later than about 1880, they all look to have been painted carriage brown (though probably without the usual many coats of varnish) and all lettering looks to have been white. However, there is one photo of part of a horse box in which it looks as though the LSWR is shaded black; whether the letters were white or gold is arguable.

There was a massive clear-out of old stock around the end of the 19th century, leaving very little that was built earlier than the mid-1880s surviving to be recorded in the registers or diagram books now held in the Public Record Office. Therefore most of the drawings of earlier vehicles shown here are based on builders' drawings (mostly Metropolitan). Regrettably, they are mainly unsupported by either photographs or documentary evidence other than minutes notes which appear to tie in with the drawing dates and descriptions. Therefore, there is inevitably the chance that they were not built precisely as illustrated, but at least the drawings show the style of things at that particular date. It must be emphasised, as it was in *LSWR Carriages, Volume 1*, that the descriptions and illustrations in this chapter cannot be expected to tell the whole story.

The purpose of horse boxes and carriage trucks seems fairly obvious, though it must be mentioned that while carriage trucks were intended for private carriages and mail coaches, there also grew up a need for very similar trucks for carrying other types of wheeled vehicles. These were not for normal use in passenger trains, were not normally vacuum braked, and were included in goods stock, generally with the description of road vehicle trucks or van trucks. They will therefore be mentioned in the chapter on goods vehicles in the next volume.

One of the few early references to these vehicles is in a *Notice to Enginemen, Firemen and Others* of July 1855. This tells of an engine driver having been dismissed because he allowed a train of horse boxes and carriage trucks to run down the incline to the Queen's station at Nine Elms, and through the wall into Wandsworth Road, knowing that the vehicles were not provided with breaks.

The London & Southampton Railway timetable from 9th November 1840 includes the statement "Private carriages, horses, &c should be at the station a quarter of an hour before the departure of the trains. Horse boxes and carriage trucks are kept at the principal stations on the line, but in order to prevent disappointment, a day's notice should be given." The charges are also listed, ranging from 7 shillings (35p) for one horse from Nine Elms to Kingston, to 50 shillings (£2.50) for three horses from Nine Elms to Southampton, or for a carriage 10 shillings (50p) to Kingston up to 42 shillings (£2 10p) to Southampton.

As early as August 1839, it was decided to order "six trucks to carry heavier road vehicles", but whether this referred to the weight of such things as heavy mail coaches that would go by the passenger trains, or to goods road vehicles that would go by the goods trains, is not clear. Then, on 8th October 1839, the Traffic and General Purposes Committee decided that the charge for horses in owners' vans (presumably loaded on carriage trucks) was to be the same as if they were carried in the Company's horse boxes, the private vans to be charged half the price of a private carriage. Sam Fay mentions in his *Royal Road* that two horse boxes were smashed in an accident at Farnborough on 13th June 1840. On 31st December 1840, according to the ledger, Joseph Wright was paid £164 5s 0d for one horse box, but there is no way of telling whether this was rather late payment for an original, or for an additional vehicle.

In May 1841, the same committee recommended the ordering of an additional seven horse boxes. There was a report in February 1847 that a tyre on horse box number 34 had broken, and by July 1848 the total stock of horse boxes was forty-seven. At the same time there were sixty-one carriage trucks. It was then ordered that passengers in their own carriages were to be charged the First class fare.

The Commercial and Traffic Committee of 29th September 1853 approved a recommendation from the Traffic Manager "that in addition to the stock of forty-seven horse boxes other (*sic*) twenty boxes should be provided as soon as they can be made at Nine Elms Works". In the following July, the Traffic Committee called attention to the non-completion of thirteen horse boxes and six Guard's vans ordered to be built at Nine Elms. Mr Beattie reported that the delay resulted from the lack of room in the workshops and delays in the supply of timber.

Between 1854 and 1859, the stock of horse boxes grew from 47 to 65 while that of carriage trucks remained at 61. In July 1859, another twenty of each were ordered to be built at Nine Elms. However, by January 1860, it became obvious that there were delays, and it was decided to look elsewhere. Wrights tendered at £156 each for the horse boxes and £112 each for the carriage trucks.

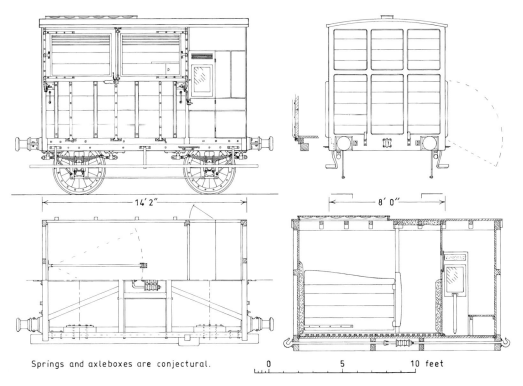

Springs and axleboxes are conjectural.

0   5   10 feet

Figure 4.2. 1861, 14ft 2in horse box, drawing BM39/7.

At first, half of the order was placed with them, then the rest in March 1860, and then for a further ten horse boxes in August 1860. It is at this point that we can get a first look at the type of horse box built, though the carriage trucks are still shrouded in mystery.

Wright's drawing, illustrated here as Figure 4.2, shows an arc-roofed vehicle with a body 14ft 2in long and 8ft 0in wide, giving accommodation for three horses and a compartment for grooms and equipment. With various improvements, this remained the style until the addition of a separate compartment for fodder, etc, in the substantially longer 21ft vehicles of 1905 onwards.

In the Metropolitan index book, there is a date of "23-11-1861" against this drawing, but there is no date on the drawing itself. It is the writer's personal view that the main batch was built with numbers in the range 66 to 95 in response to the 1859 and 1860 orders, with another small batch in 1861/2 as replacements for some worn out original vehicles.

The Metropolitan Company index book was created long after most of the drawings were – possibly well into the 20th century. The identity numbers used in the book, and written on the drawings, bear little, if any, relation to the chronological order of the drawings. Even the dates quoted differ widely in some cases from those shown on drawings, and their significance is something of a mystery. They might sometimes refer to drawing dates or to some particular order,

not necessarily the first. Even dates on drawings cannot necessarily be relied upon, since sometimes they seem to be the dates of alterations applied to later batches. To sum this up, there are several drawings where one has to treat the apparent dates with some reservations.

Horses, for all their size, are relatively delicate animals, particularly as regards their legs, and it is vitally important to prevent them from falling down in an enclosed space. Thus any road or rail horse box has to be designed to substantially restrict their movement, even if the vehicle is bumping or lurching about. In practical terms, this means that railway horse boxes had to be designed for three horses abreast across the vehicle in stalls separated by moveable partitions. The length had to be no more than barely sufficient to minimise backward and forward movement. A fair amount of padding was needed all round, and there had to be ample ventilation. Because horses are generally nervous creatures, whilst some light is desirable it must not be possible for them to actually see anything frightening outside, such as a passing steam engine. It is also desirable for grooms to be able to travel where they can keep an eye on their charges. It can easily be seen from these requirements why, apart from technical improvements, the design of horse boxes changed so little right from the earliest days up until the time when British Railways ceased the traffic.

The War Office did not see the need for such

care of military horses, or perhaps was not prepared to pay for it. Only officers' chargers were authorised to travel in horse boxes, the rest went in cattle wagons, and this will be mentioned again in the chapter on goods vehicles in the next volume.

An instruction to staff in force in 1858 stated that "Entire horses (ie, stallions) must be loaded into horse boxes by themselves and charged as for three horses. This does not apply to horses of military officers".

Unlike some types of goods wagons, horse boxes seem to have always been designed for loading from either side. The loading doors on each side had to act as ramps when open so they had to be solidly constructed. If they had been in one piece they would have been far too heavy to be opened and closed safely, so they were normally divided into upper and lower portions, the upper ones usually being in the form of two side-hinged doors, though in the next drawing we will see a different form. The partitions between the stalls had to be removable or hinged like a door to allow loading the far side from the ramp first. Between the head end of each stall and the groom's compartment there was usually some kind of hatch to allow limited access for checking on the horses.

In this first horse box drawing, it can be seen that the ventilation provided by louvres in the top doors was augmented by a kind of small narrow clerestory with small curved openings on each side. This was not repeated on any later LSWR vehicles. No provision appears to have been made for any oil lamp for the groom's compartment and, in common with Third class carriages, the seat had no padding or backrest at all. Padding for the horses was much less substantial than was provided later, and forward movement was not prevented by anything other than a horse's head coming up against the bulkhead! The partitions each consisted of a padded removable pole and a padded hinged gate. The underframe was typical of early carriages in that the solebars were each made up of two longitudinal timbers, the upper one set partially outside the lower one, as shown in the part section. No handbrake was provided.

In August 1864, it was agreed to order 40 more horse boxes, still at £156 each, and 20 more carriage trucks, two of them being covered, also still at £112 each, from Wrights, or more strictly from Metropolitan by that date. Unfortunately, the open carriage truck drawing does not seem to have survived. The covered ones will be referred to again later. This order for horse boxes, probably those numbered 96 to 135, seems to relate to two virtually identical drawings in the Metropolitan collection. One of these carries the Joseph Wright & Sons label, indicating that it was drawn in 1863 or earlier. The other, which lacks a handbrake but includes internal details, is recorded in the Metropolitan index book with the date "18-6-77", although this date appears

to practically coincide with the dates written on a drawing for a 15ft 6in horse box that we shall come to later!

Although still 14ft 2in long, there were several differences including a reduction in width to 7ft 9½in. Externally, as can be seen in Figure 4.3, they were provided with a single wooden shoe brake, the groom's compartment was entered through narrow double doors and was fitted for an oil lamp, and the horse doors were arranged so that the lowering of the lower section to form a ramp also automatically opened the top door. Internally, there was much better provision for the protection of the horses - partition doors were fitted forward of the pole as well as behind it, and probably the most important improvement was that mangers were provided (though at first they were boarded over) which prevented the horses from surging forward against the bulkhead due to movements of the vehicle.

Instead of the loose poles between the stalls, which could possibly get mislaid, on this version and later ones, they became known as swing poles since they were hinge jointed to the rear partition doors. To get a horse in or out, it was necessary to first lift the head end partition an inch or two and swing it to one side. This released the swing pole, which could then pivot to clear the roof and floor chocks, allowing it, complete with the rear partition, to be swung to one side, upon which the horse could be taken in or brought out.

The arrangement of levers linking the upper and lower flaps, which was used by several railway companies, was ingenious in that there was initially a few inches of free movement for the lower flap, and then the weight of the lower flap became partially counterbalanced by that of the upper one until the former was within a few inches of the ground. In addition to the obvious set of rods on the outside of the end, there was another set at the bulkhead end of the horse compartment, working partially in a casing.

Having two narrow doors for the groom's compartment looks a little retrograde but in fact was probably an improvement. The door of the earlier version had an opening of just less than 21in. Saddles are rather cumbersome items, particularly when a person is climbing up or down through a narrow doorway, and so it may well be that owners objected to the occasional damage when their quite valuable property got scraped. The extra width of double doors was doubtless much more convenient.

The underframe was outwardly similar to the earlier ones, that is, with two-piece solebars, but was braced differently and the drawbar was no longer continuous. As with carriages of the time the coupling hooks did not have a chain or screw coupling permanently fitted, they had to be drawn from, and returned to, the stock at the terminating stations.

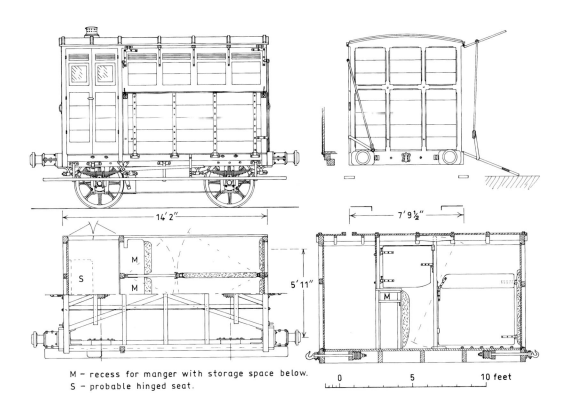

M – recess for manger with storage space below.
S – probable hinged seat.

Figure 4.3. 14ft 2in horse box, circa 1863, drawings BM23/52 and 496/20.

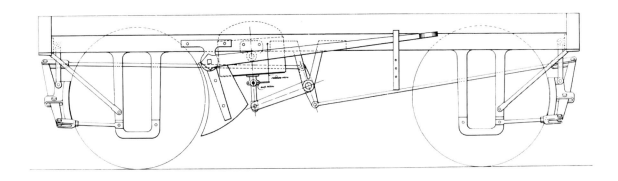

Figure 4.3a. Sketch of brake gear on No 99 horse box, drawing No 635 (not to scale).

At least some of these vehicles were provided with Automatic Vacuum Brake (AVB) in the late 1880s as shown in LSWR drawing 635, reproduced here as Figure 4.3a. From the way it is drawn, it is not clear whether the brakes were fitted on one side of the vehicle only (like the hand brake) or on both.

The diagram book of 1909 includes a vehicle that does not fit into any of the ordinary categories, although it is shown among the cattle trucks and carriage trucks. In fact it probably fits in best here among the horse boxes. It was hounds van No 1, the only one recorded. Built in 1865 at a stated cost of £278 6s 0d, it was ciphered at the end of 1908. There is nothing about it in the minutes, but fortunately there is a drawing, though not very detailed, that seems to have been prepared around 1893. The body appears to be the original of 1865, although it has rather a curious mixture of panelling styles, but the underframe, although only in outline, is certainly in the style of about 1893. The inference is that the old body was still sound but that the original underframe with its low buffer height and weaker structure had to be replaced.

It is the author's belief that the underframe was originally very much in the style of the 20ft passenger brake of 1864 and the 19ft Third of 1865, shown in *LSWR Carriages, Volume 1* as Figures 3.7 and 3.14. However that is only conjecture, and

therefore Figure 4.4 shows it as on the surviving LSWR drawing No 370, with an underframe that was probably similar to that of the 24ft passenger luggage vans of 1894, including AVB.

The louvred panel at one end is curious. The strips either side suggest that it might have been some kind of hatch or door, but there is no obvious reason for such. One possibility is that it was a hatch to make it easier to wash out the van because of the obstruction created at the double doors by the hinged ramps. These appear to have formed a step inside the van, presumably to prevent the risk of hounds catching their paws in the gap that might have formed if it was attempted to make a ramp level with the floor. The plan view merely shows a 3ft 1in high shelf across the width at this point with no indication that it was an enclosed space, the only spaces of that sort being the two under the hinged seats in the whippers-in compartment, these being marked as used for terriers.

Another quite unusual feature is the barring of the windows in the latter compartment, presumably because of the possibility of hounds getting loose through the sliding door. The roof ventilators appear to be quite crude open-ended covers over holes in the roof, but in 1865 there were no better ventilators on the LSWR, indeed not until the adoption of Laycock's pattern in the mid-1880s.

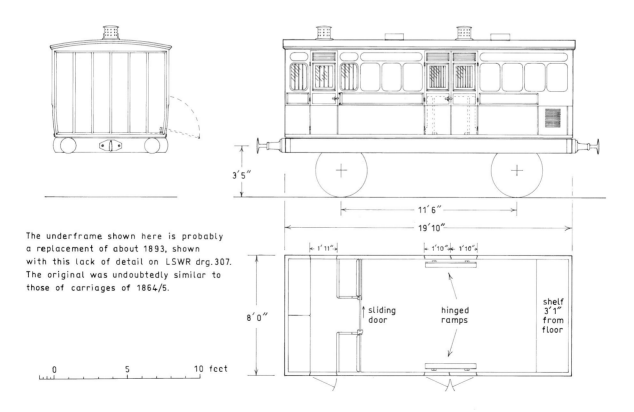

The underframe shown here is probably a replacement of about 1893, shown with this lack of detail on LSWR drg. 307. The original was undoubtedly similar to those of carriages of 1864/5.

Figure 4.4. 19ft 10in hounds van of 1865, drawing 307.

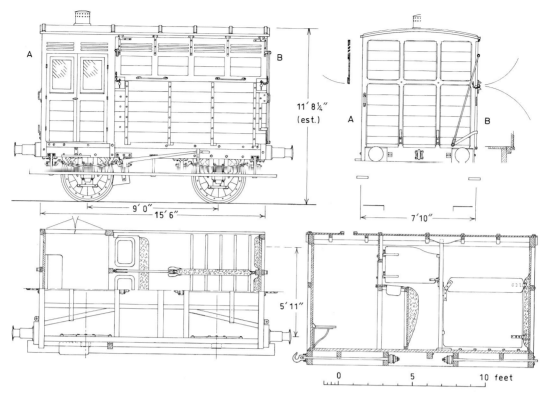

11′ 8¼″
(est.)

9′ 0″
15′ 6″

7′10″

5′ 11″

0   5   10 feet

Figure 4.5. 15ft 6in horse box of 1877, drawings BM16/117 LSW 2218.

Numbers 154 – 186

In those days, before the development of motor transport, it was not very practicable to move hounds long distances for a few days sport, or to help farmers in remote areas who had a problem with foxes. Certainly, some horsemen were quite prepared to hire a horse box from their local station to take their horses considerable distances to a hunt or a point-to-point, as Siegfried Sassoon mentions in his *Memoirs of a Fox-Hunting Man*, but transporting hounds was a very different matter. No doubt cattle trucks could be used but cannot have been very satisfactory since no hunt staff could ride with them, while the spaces above the planked sides were an obvious hazard. Therefore this hounds van must have been a very useful vehicle in the days when management put meeting the needs of its (influential?) customers at a considerably higher priority than is the modern custom. In this connection, it should be borne in mind that the hunting season only runs from November to March, so this van would stand in a siding somewhere for the rest of the year – although this may have contributed to its relatively long life.

A public notice was issued in May 1867 stating that, in future, the charge for horses and carriages would be the same by all trains; the reduction when carried by Parliamentary trains would be discontinued.

The Locomotive Committee received a letter in September 1868 from Mr Pendray, the agent at Exeter, suggesting that all horse boxes and carriage trucks should be provided with "breaks", this was referred to Mr Beattie but was not mentioned again. This clearly implies that many, presumably most of the earlier ones, did not have brakes. This was potentially more of a dangerous problem with passenger class vehicles being parked and shunted around stations than with goods vehicles that were usually kept more remote from the passenger areas.

By the end of 1872, the stock of horse boxes and carriage trucks (both kinds) had risen to 142 and 92 respectively. Twelve more horse boxes were ordered from Oldbury at the end of 1873, and delivered by the end of 1874. The design of these is not known.

The next two orders were placed with Metropolitan, for 20 in mid-1876 and 12 in mid-1877. These were 15ft 6in long, probably numbered 154 to 186, and shown here as Figure 4.5. They were broadly very similar to the previous type, but with a few more inches of space in the groom's compartment. From the records it appears that a few more were built as renewals of some of the earliest vehicles, such as numbers 12, 19 and 20.

Also in 1877, and again in 1881, some 16ft horse boxes were built, but to what design, where and by whom is not recorded, they are noted as Appendix item 4.6.

In August 1883 it was decided to order 24 more horse boxes with a length of 16ft, shown here in Figure 4.7. The Metropolitan tender was preferred, but Metropolitan refused to accept some penalty clauses. After some correspondence, Metropolitan offered to supply them by the following March at the

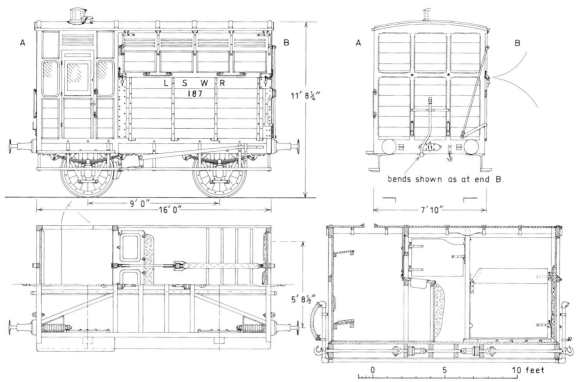

11′ 8¼″

L S W R
187

bends shown as at end B.

9′ 0″
16′ 0″

7′ 10″

5′ 8½″

0   5   10 feet

Figure 4.7. 16ft horse box of 1884, drawings BM 8/104 (DB86 and LSW 4214?).

Numbers 187 − 210

price of £173 10s, but without any penalties. This was accepted, and they were all delivered during 1884 and numbered 187 to 210. The register shows them as drawing 4214. A copy of an undated, undimensioned and unnumbered Nine Elms drawing has survived, this is virtually identical to the Metropolitan drawing, and is thus presumably No 4214. It might also be alternatively identified as DB86.

The increased length allowed a trifle more space for the grooms, who now had the luxury of padded squabs on the seat and backrest, as well as a rudimentary luggage rack. In this compartment, the floor was covered with diagonal boarding to stop the draughts whipping through. The underframe now had one-piece solebars of 11in x 4in timber and screw couplings were permanently fitted. For parking, the brake still consisted of a single wooden block, but through piping was provided for the automatic vacuum brake so that the horse boxes could continue to run in passenger trains. As with carriages, most, if not all, were fitted with full AVB by mid-1894.

At least another six of the same size were built at Nine Elms as renewals during 1885. They were probably to the same design but this is not recorded.

Things become a bit more murky for a while, because the LSWR ceased buying by contract and built their own; unfortunately, not all of the drawings for the next few years have survived. One batch that was built in 1887 was recorded as being to drawing DB86A, which was presumably a

modification of DB86 that has just been mentioned as possibly the same as LSWR drawing 4214. Because of the uncertainty, they are listed here as Appendix item 4.8.

It must be noted that photographs of some vehicles at various dates show slight differences from the respective drawings, particularly in respect to beadings and grab handles. There are not sufficient of these photographs to establish whether the differences were common to particular batches, or due to alterations and repairs in service.

There were at least four drawings for 16ft horse boxes with side-hinged top doors, all with very similar bodies. The differences were mainly in the size, planking and strapping of the bottom horse doors though there were also some internal detail changes. The first one, illustrated here as Figure 4.9, to LSWR drawing No 314, is dated "9-3-1894", although the curious fact is that all the vans recorded as being to this drawing were shown as being built between September 1892 and June 1893. This drawing shows an underframe with a single shoe handbrake and through piping for AVB – although in June 1894, it was reported that no vehicles used in passenger trains were without AVB. Following earlier practice, the top doors had to be closed first, then held in place by a rebate in the ramp door and a vertical bolt operated by a handle. On the later boxes, the top doors closed last and were held in place by pins on chains like the ramp doors themselves.

The other three drawings, Nos 637, 892 and

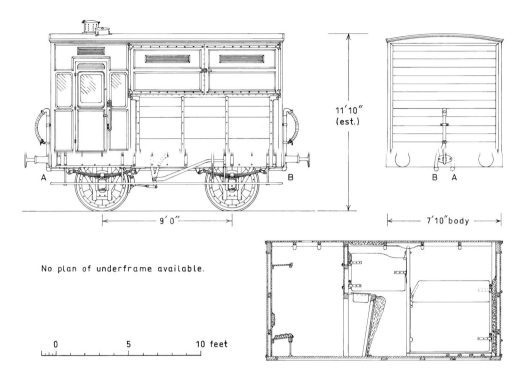

11'10"
(est.)

9'0"

7'10"body

No plan of underframe available.

0   5   10 feet

Figure 4.9. 16ft horse box of 1892, drawing 314.

1085, are combined here in Figure 4.10; these only show the bodies, including side elevations of the underframes. Drawing 892 is titled to show Bartrum's patent tethering apparatus. However, drawing 637 refers to underframe drawings 730 and 780 for those vehicles fitted with skew and straight brakes respectively, whilst in the register they are shown as drawings 637/730, 637/780, 892/780 or 1085/780. On the present drawings, everything below the solebars has had to be based on photographs and comparison with other vehicle drawings.

As might be expected, the earlier drawing 637 vehicles had skew brakes and the later batches straight brakes, but in the midst of the straight braked ones were some more with skew brakes, possibly a case of using up existing stocks of components. The skew brakes were the type that Mr Panter installed on some other types of vans and carriages between 1886 and about 1891. Some vehicles were provided with through piping for the Westinghouse system whilst a few, mainly from the last batches, were fully provided with both AVB and Westinghouse brakes.

When built, all these vehicles had only a single handbrake lever. On those fitted with skew brakes, this was pivoted on the vacuum brake cross shaft, but independent of it, and was linked to one shoe on one wheel only. When vertical brakes were provided, there was a dog clutch between the lever and the main brake cross shaft so that the handbrake operated on all wheels. Many, but not all, of the

horse boxes were later fitted with a second lever. A photograph taken by HC Casserley in September 1932 shows a drawing 637/780 vehicle still without a second lever.

In all cases, this alteration required the shortening of the upper footboard and replacement of a footboard support bracket. For the skew brake type, the lever and its new V-hanger replicated the originals, but whether this was a single hanger, or whether a short cross-shaft to an inner hanger was provided, is not known. The lever crank was again connected to just one shoe only. In the case of the vertical brakes, the cross-shaft was extended across to a new V-hanger, and a lifting link connection was made to the new brake lever.

By a minute of May 1899, all new horse boxes were to be fitted with Bartrum's patent tethering apparatus at the cost of £12 12s per vehicle. From drawing 1085, it can be seen that this consisted of a rope that could be attached to the top of the nose part of a horse's headcollar, this passed up over a pulley on the partition and down in the groom's compartment to a heavy weight loosely retained in a kind of bucket on the floor. This gave sufficient slack for a horse to move its head about and to feed in the manger, but if he tried to rear or snatch away suddenly he would be prevented more gently by the weight than by a fixed tethering ring. The advantage seems to have been fairly small and the system appears to have been dropped from some later batches. One thing though, was that in order to have the ropes fairly near to the centre line of each stall,

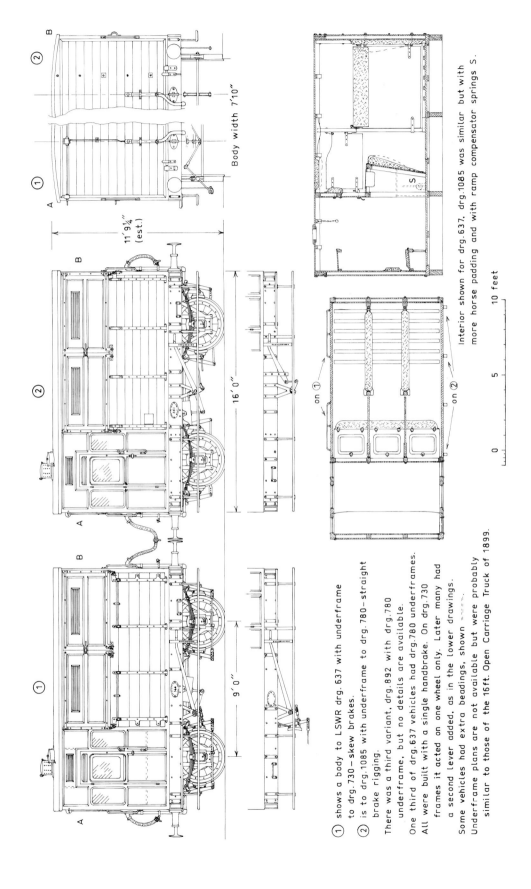

① shows a body to LSWR drg. 637 with underframe to drg.730—skew brakes.

② is to drg.1085 with underframe to drg.780—straight brake rigging.

There was a third variant, drg.892 with drg.780 underframe, but no details are available.

One third of drg.637 vehicles had drg.780 underframes. All were built with a single handbrake. On drg.730 frames it acted on one wheel only. Later many had a second lever added, as in the lower drawings.

Some vehicles had extra beadings, shown ----.

Underframe plans are not available but were probably similar to those of the 16ft. Open Carriage Truck of 1899.

Interior shown for drg.637, drg.1085 was similar but with more horse padding and with ramp compensator springs S.

Body width 7'10"

11'9¼" (est.)

16'0"

9'0"

0   5   10 feet

on ①

on ②

Figure 4.10. 16ft horse boxes after 1896, drawings 637 (underframe 730 and 780) and others.

Plate 4.10a. 16ft horse box, LSWR No 122, drawings 637 and 730, as altered by the SR, becoming No 2607, at Eastleigh in May 1949. *(AE West)*

Plate 4.10b. 16ft horse box, LSWR No 132, drawings 637 and 730, as altered by the SR, becoming No S2616, at Ashford in June 1951. *(AE West)*

Plate 4.10c. 16ft horse box, LSWR No 316, drawings 637 and 780, in original condition at Bromley in September 1932.

(H C Casserley)

Plate 4.10d. 16ft horse box, LSWR No 298, drawings 637 and 780, as altered by the SR at Ashford in June 1951.
(AE West)

Plate 4.10e. 16ft horse box, LSWR No 369, drawings 637 and 780, as altered by the SR, becoming 2797.
(L&GRP/NRM)

the hatches, through which the grooms could view and attend to their charges, had to be narrower and placed asymmetrically so as to be clear of the ropes. Despite the minute the only mention in the register of this system is for vehicles built in 1902.

A hidden, but important, improvement on the batches built to drawing 1085 from March 1902 onwards was the provision of balance springs for the bottom horse doors. The springs were concealed under the manger space, and connected by levers and short chains to the bottom doors.

The practical differences between all these variants from drawing 4214 onwards were so small that when the Southern Railway took over, they grouped them all together under diagram 1000. Those that survived after 1936 were altered by having steel sheeting fastened over much of the outside, including blanking off the groom's compartment window nearest to the horse compartment, and inserting a reinforcing post behind its aperture.

This lengthy series of 16ft vehicles was followed in 1905 by an improved horse box design to drawings 1364, 1371 and 1401 (Figure 4.11). This type was an improvement on the existing ones by virtue of providing full Third class style seating in the groom's compartment and a separate storage compartment for luggage, tack and forage. Naturally, this required an increase in length, so these were 21ft long, though still 7ft 10in wide.

This is another case where the works drawings are misleading. They show the horse boxes with gas lighting, although an oil lamp is superimposed in one drawing. Also shown, are end steps and right-handed brake levers on each side. In fact, the 1912 register shows that they were all originally lit with oil lamps, whilst the only known official photograph shows no end steps fitted.

The drawings show right-handed hand brake levers on each side on the Morton principle, using simple snail-shaped dog clutches outside the V-hangers. However, the official photo of No 193, built in December 1905, shows a left-handed lever on the side remote from the vacuum and Westinghouse cylinders, with both levers inside the V-hangers using drum type clutches. Close examination of the underframe drawing, No 1371, shows traces of the latter type of brake levers and clutches having been erased and redrawn, and Surrey Warner states in his notes in *Modern Railway Working* of 1912 that the levers were both right-handed "to conform to the proposed new regulations of the Board of Trade". So it seems highly likely that all except the three built in 1913 originally had left- and right-handed levers like No 193. Reverting to the lighting, two were converted to gas lighting in November 1912, which probably accounts for what is shown on the drawings; another was converted in July 1914. One, No 232, had the Westinghouse

brake removed at the end of 1915, when it was taken into use as an Army hearse or ambulance (though why is not clear) but then had it refitted in July 1916.

Like the batches of 16ft vehicles to Drawing 1085, the drop-flap horse doors were fitted with counterbalance springs installed in the space under the manger. Also, according to the drawings, at least some of those built from 1905 onwards had Bartrum's tethering system, needing a similar asymmetric arrangement of the hatches, but the 1910 drawings show a reversion to simple tethering rings and uniform hatches. These drawings also show sliding plates to cover the mangers, but why this was done is not at all clear. There was also slightly altered padding for the horses and the added comfort of steam heating for the grooms. Whether the steam heat pipe shown on No 193 was through piping or for a retrofitted heater is not known.

Earlier, the use of the solitary hounds van was mentioned, apparently the proprietors of hunts had acquired some privileges, perhaps not surprisingly. By the early 1900s, this was coming under pressure and the Brighton and the South Eastern & Chatham companies had been in discussion with the LSWR to end the practice. Accordingly, it was agreed by the Traffic Committee in January 1905 to end the free conveyance between certain stations of three members of the Hampshire Hunt and their horses, also of the hunt horses and hounds of the West Surrey Stag Hounds after the end of the current hunt season. After this, special rates would be arranged based on the Railway Clearing House rates. The other two companies were doing likewise.

Turning back now to carriage trucks, the LSWR numbered both Open Carriage Trucks (OCTs) and Covered Carriage Trucks (CCTs) in one list, often without positively distinguishing which they were. Also in minutes they were often referred to simply as carriage trucks, again without distinction. There are therefore doubts at some points as to what was being ordered or mentioned.

There is a drawing in the Metropolitan C&W Co collection that is almost certainly by Joseph Wright, and made around 1840 to 1843, showing an undimensioned side elevation of an OCT. Like some others of his at this time, it seems to be a sample that he could offer to potential customers, incorporating any particular alterations that they required. An example is in the very similar, but partly dimensioned, drawing of an OCT for the South Eastern Railway showing a virtually identical structure but with a 16ft 3in body and a detachable framework of "Railings for Truck when intended to carry Hops, etc." Unlike later LSWR OCTs, this one seems to have had the floor planked longitudinally. The axleguards appear very flimsy, but the combined buffer and drawbar springing was far ahead of what was provided for many other railway vehicles at that time. Figure 4.12 is based

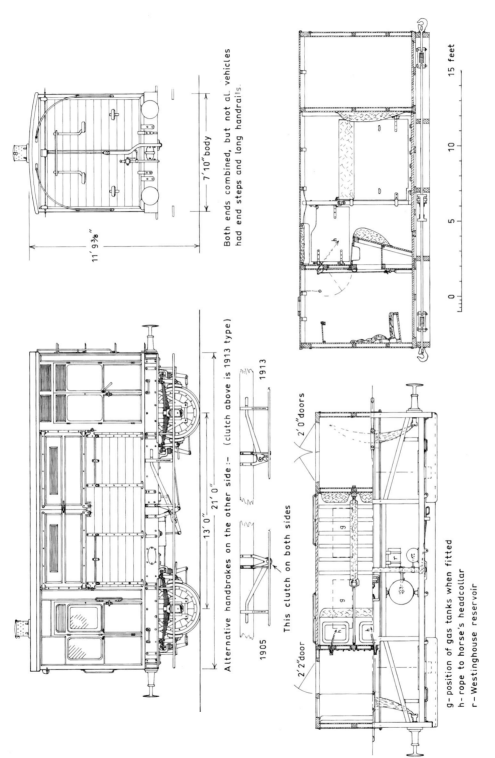

11' 9 3/8"

7' 10" body

Both ends combined, but not al. vehicles had end steps and long handrails

13' 0"

21' 0"

Alternative handbrakes on the other side :- (clutch above is 1913 type)

1913

1905

This clutch on both sides

2' 0" doors

2' 2" door

g - position of gas tanks when fitted
h - rope to horse's headcollar
r - Westinghouse reservoir

0   5   10   15 feet

Figure 4.11. 21ft horse box of 1905, drawings 1364, 1371 and 1953.

Plate 4.11a. 21ft horse box, drawings 1364 and 1371.   (National Railway Museum)

Plate 4.11b. 21ft horse box, LSWR No 5, drawings 1364 and 1371, as SR No 2821 at Stewarts Lane in 1947.

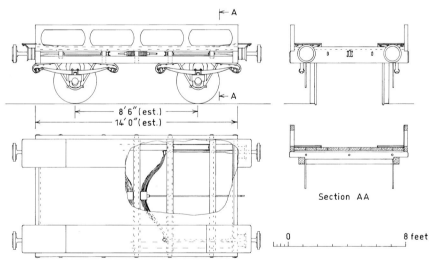

8'6"(est.)
14'0"(est.)

Section AA

0   8 feet

Copied from an undimensioned side elevation in the Metropolitan RC&W Co. collection, probably by Joseph Wright of London in about 1840, possibly as a stock design to offer to potential customers. The other views have been developed from it and by reference to other Wright drawings.

Figure 4.12. Open carriage truck of about 1840.

on the original, but dimensioned and developed with reference to the SER vehicle and to some later drawings. It is thus simply an illustration of the type being built at that time. There is no evidence as to whether LSWR vehicles were exactly like this or not.

By 1847, there were 61 carriage trucks in stock, and still the same number in 1859, although some had been renewed in the meantime. From what follows, they were almost certainly all of the open variety up to this time.

Nothing is known of the twenty carriage trucks ordered from Wrights in 1860, mentioned earlier, except that one of them, No 69, was 26ft long (Appendix item 4.13), and survived to be broken up in 1900. One might have expected them to be numbered 62 to 81, but either there were two types or some were numbered as renewals, since Appendix item 4.14 shows numbers 76 and 78, as well as some earlier numbers, all at a length of 14ft 6in, built in 1861 and later. Nothing more is known about them.

In 1863, the Traffic Committee approved a proposal that two of the existing carriage trucks should be covered, and instructed Mr Beattie to report on the cost of doing this. The result is not recorded but, as mentioned earlier in connection with an August 1864 order to Wrights for horse boxes and carriage trucks, it was stipulated that two of the new carriage trucks should be covered but without any note of a price difference. Wright was

still frequently mentioned in the minutes since Joseph Wright Junior was still managing much of the business in person.

In general the underframes of LSWR OCTs were quite conventional for their period, floors were usually transversely planked on top of the solebars and packing pieces, the plank ends protected by the crib rails, which supported the sides. Longitudinal steel plates were usually laid to cover the wood where the carriage wheels would go. These plates often extended part way over the buffers to simplify loading at an end loading dock.

Plate 4.14x does not necessarily relate to Appendix item 4.14 but is shown here for convenience as it depicts an interesting group of vehicles. The photo was taken at Clapham Junction in about 1898, but the OCT is clearly of a rather earlier design with quite substantial side rails and supports. The PLV is 22ft long, the horse box 16ft and the brake third 28ft, so the OCT could be one of the many that figured in the stock returns but without any details having survived.

Side rails were provided, internally for CCTs, about a foot above the floor level. These rails were pierced with many vertical holes to receive the locating pins of wheel bars, made of wood with metal ends, which were used as chocks to prevent fore and aft movement of the carriage, whilst the rails provided convenient tying down points for straps or ropes. In some cases, mainly in later years,

Plate 4.14x. Clapham Junction circa 1898. 22ft passenger luggage van (see Fig 1.1), 16ft horse box (see Figure 4.10, drawing 1) and an open carriage truck of similar size, but showing early style sides. Next is a 28ft brake third (block) of 1879. (Photomatic/RAS Marketing)

the sides of OCTs were made to hinge outwards to allow sideways loading at ordinary platforms.

There is no information about the 18 OCTs authorised in August 1864, apart from a register entry showing one of 22ft built in 1864 and withdrawn in 1900 (Appendix item 4.15). The two CCTs in that order are shown here as Figure 4.16. Unfortunately, the Metropolitan drawing is of the body only and lacks any indication of the end door locking arrangements, nor does it show any wheel plates. It is possible, though doubtful, that what appear to be the bottoms of the end doors were in fact an end flap; the Metropolitan drawing is unclear on this point. Also, contrary to the statement earlier about OCT underframes, the bottoms of the headstocks are an inch or two above the bottoms of the solebars, suggesting a slight variation in the structure. In order to make the present drawing look more like a vehicle than just a hut, a conjectural underframe has been drawn in, based on designs of the period. Obviously it cannot be taken as anything better than a representation.

The total stock, including both open and covered types, was reported to be 105 in June 1865, but at the end of 1867, it was recorded as 90. Presumably, some early ones had been withdrawn and not yet replaced. In August 1869, it was reported that number 101 CCT admitted dust, and Mr Beattie was instructed to remedy this, and similarly in "the other covered carriage truck", which seems to tie up with the two mentioned above.

Two more CCTs were ordered from Metropolitan in August 1870. These were to be 18in longer, 10in higher and 4in wider than the previous ones and with improvements to the side doors. With these changes they were to cost £132 each. They were delivered a year later. The Metropolitan drawing is not very detailed, possibly the ironwork, such as wheels, axleboxes, springs, buffers and so on, was to be provided by the LSWR. On the other hand, it does show that rollers were set into the floor to make it easier to slide the pole of a carriage in without snagging on the floorboards. The disconcerting feature is a note written across it, "Side elevation of body incorrect", and initialled JR, which is probably J Rawlings, a name that crops up elsewhere as a senior official of Metropolitan. Regrettably there is not the slightest indication of what is wrong with it! It is a fact that the depth of the headstocks has been altered from some obliterated figure to 12 inches without any corresponding alteration to the side elevation, but this seems an insufficient amendment to justify the written comment. The accompanying Figure 4.17 must therefore be regarded with this in mind.

Also built in 1870 were some replacement OCTs of both 19ft and 19ft 6in length, but nothing is known of them except the entries shown as Appendix items 4.18 and 4.19 respectively.

In mid-1872 two open trucks were ordered to be converted to CCTs, but there is no more information at all about them, not even whether the order was carried out. In June 1873, it was ordered that 20 horse boxes and 20 carriage trucks should be constructed "if possible and cheaper at Nine Elms". There is no further mention of the 20 carriage trucks

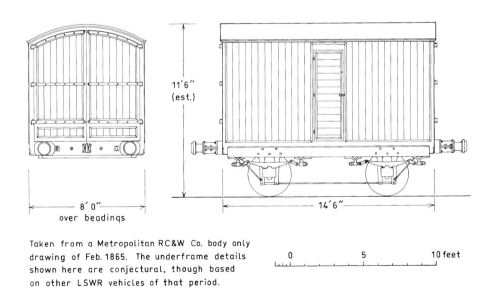

11′6″ (est.)

8′0″
over beadings

14′6″

Taken from a Metropolitan RC&W Co. body only drawing of Feb. 1865. The underframe details shown here are conjectural, though based on other LSWR vehicles of that period.

0   5   10 feet

Figure 4.16. 14ft 6in covered carriage truck of 1865, drawing 17.2.1965 BM 19/19.

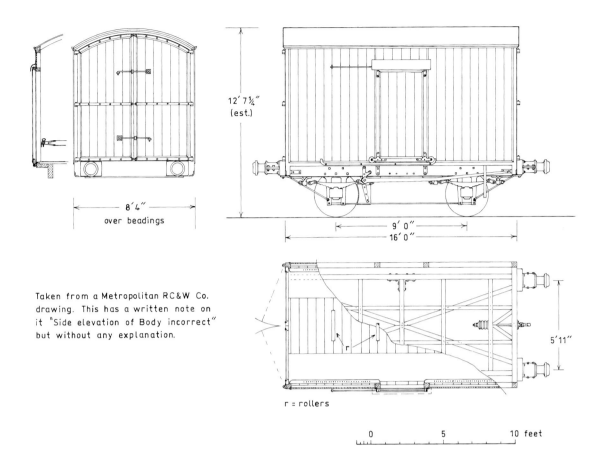

8′ 4″
over beadings

12′ 7¼″
(est.)

9′ 0″

16′ 0″

5′11″

Taken from a Metropolitan RC&W Co.
drawing. This has a written note on
it "Side elevation of Body incorrect"
but without any explanation.

r = rollers

0   5   10 feet

Figure 4.17. 16ft covered carriage truck of 1870, drawing 8.10.1970 BM 19/22.

but they may have been built and largely offset by withdrawals. In December 1873, Metropolitan's tender for constructing four CCTs was accepted, but the July 1874 half-year report only recorded the existence of two CCTs, presumably No 101 and one other.

In the following January report, it was stated that the four had been delivered from contractors since the previous July. These must have been 17ft trucks to LSWR drawing 1894, shown here as Figure 4.20. Two of them, numbers 28 and 39 survived until 1902, though their width is quoted in the register as 7ft 6in compared with 7ft 7in on the drawing. They had a hand brake with a single elm brake shoe on one side only and, like the earlier ones, had a small sliding door in each side with its sill level with the pin rails. Rollers were again set into the floor.

In November 1882, the Traffic Committee, noting that there were only seven CCTs (one more than has been identified so far), recommended the Engineering Committee to order ten new ones. Nothing was done in a hurry, and in the following April, Mr Adams was urging that tenders should be

invited for ten. A fortnight later, he supplied drawings and specifications (which regrettably have not survived). These were then referred to the Traffic Committee, who presumably approved them, since the Engineering and Stores Committee invited tenders on the 23rd of May 1883 for these and for 25 road van trucks.

Each of the tenders quoted two prices, suggesting that there were two different specifications. This appears to be borne out by the Register entries which show eight 16ft and two 19ft 6in CCTs, though all were later valued equally at £167 18s 6d. The tenders are shown in Table 3, and the tender of Birmingham C&W Co was accepted,

Table 3. Tenders for covered carriage trucks ordered in May 1883.		
	Two @	Eight @
Brown Marshall	£164	£157
Midland C&W Co	£146 5s	£138 10s
Birmingham C&W Co	£147	£137 5s
Metropolitan C&W Co	£131 5s	£123 5s

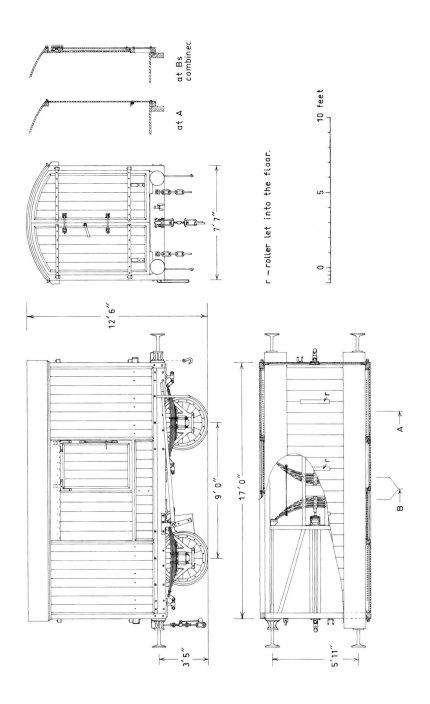

Figure 4.20. 17ft covered carriage truck of 1894.

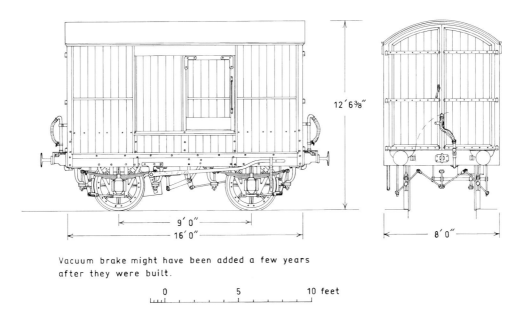

Vacuum brake might have been added a few years
after they were built.

0   5   10 feet

Figure 4.21. 16ft covered carriage truck of 1863.

*Plate 4.21. 16ft covered carriage truck No 98, as converted to vacuum cleaner truck No 24s, circa 1904, later
SR No V3.   (Brousson/RW Kidner)*

although no reason was given.

The eight were numbered consecutively from 97 to 104, so clearly the earlier two, shown as Figure 4.17, or the two doubtful conversions from OCTs, must have already been withdrawn.

Apart from photographs of one of the 16ft version as converted to a vacuum cleaner van around 1904, no structural details are known. From these photographs, they appear to have been very similar to the previous 17ft ones, except that their width was increased to 8ft, and more modern axleguards were used with J-hangers for the springs. Again, a single-sided handbrake was fitted. AVB was provided, but this was probably a few years later, since a note of November 1889 recorded that the automatic vacuum brake would have to be fitted to 106 carriage trucks.

The brake gear can just be detected in photographs, and is very similar to that provided on some of the 1864 type of 14ft 2in horse box, illustrated at Figure 4.3a. At the ends, the vacuum pipes were made to swing down to clear the doors. The present drawing, Figure 4.21, is therefore based on those photographs and the SR diagram book, together with some guesswork regarding the underframe details.

Five of them were converted to vacuum cleaner vans around 1904 or 1905. A petrol motor driven vacuum cleaner with three long hoses was installed. These vans were then used alongside carriages for cleaning the upholstery. As they wore out, the equipment was later transferred to other withdrawn vans.

There was a slightly messy tale about this equipment. Apparently, the British Vacuum Cleaner Co Ltd (BVCCL) took out patent No 17433 in 1901 for this invention, but the LSWR bought some similar machinery from The Consolidated Pneumatic Tool Co Ltd (TCPTCL) so the BVCCL took out injunctions against both of them for infringement of patent. In April 1909, TCPTCL provided the LSWR with a contract of indemnity against actions by BVCCL in respect of the trial of the two machines supplied by them. Eventually, in 1912, the LSWR was granted a licence by the BVCCL, subject to fixing suitable nameplates to the equipment.

There is no information at all about the 19ft 6in version, apart from their numbers, 105 and 106, shown as Appendix items 4.22.

Some renewal OCTs are recorded around 1889 (Appendix item 4.23) with the same length as the more or less standard open wagons, 15ft 4in, but whether that implies that they actually used open wagon underframes is open to conjecture.

The next mention of carriage trucks in minutes was in mid-1890 and mid-1891, when it was agreed to replace three and five respectively; whether the replacements were to be open or covered was not stated. They can only be tentatively identified in the registers as those shown as Appendix items 4.24 and 4.25. However, it does seem likely that three of the latter were 16ft opens, very similar to those shown as built to LSWR drawings 317 and 790, which will be mentioned shortly, and which are listed with them in Appendix item 4.26. As to the covered variety, some partially complete drawings have survived from about this time, for both 19ft 6in and 21ft 10in vehicles, two of the former having hinged side doors and turn-under sides, but there is considerable doubt

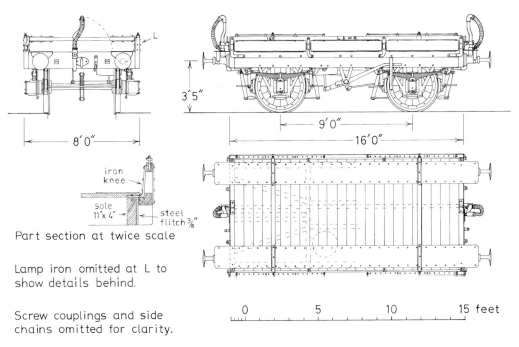

3′5″

8′0″

9′0″

16′0″

iron
knee

sole
11″x 4″

steel
flitch 3/8″

Part section at twice scale

Lamp iron omitted at L to
show details behind.

Screw couplings and side
chains omitted for clarity.

0   5   10   15 feet

Figure 4.26. 16ft open carriage truck of 1899, drawings 317 and 790.

Plate 4.26. Exeter Fire Brigade attending a fire at Honiton in 1911. The steam fire engine is on a 16ft open carriage truck (skew brakes), next is a 16ft horse box, and then a 30ft passenger brake van.
(Allhallows Museum, Honiton)

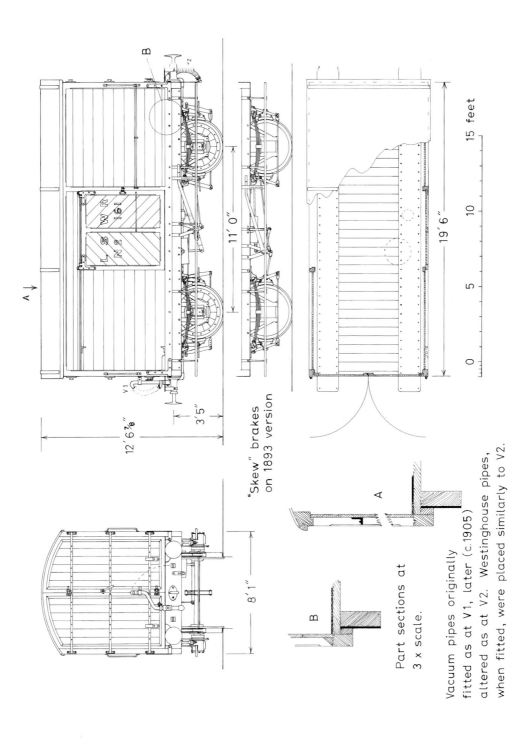

"Skew" brakes
on 1893 version

11' 0"

12' 6⅞"

3' 5"

8' 1"

19' 6"

0   5   10   15 feet

Part sections at
3 × scale.

Vacuum pipes originally
fitted as at V1, later (c.1905)
altered as at V2. Westinghouse pipes,
when fitted, were placed similarly to V2.

Figure 4.28. 1893/9 19ft 6in covered carriage truck, drawings 611 and 786.

Plate 4.28. 19ft 6in covered carriage truck, No 161, drawing 786.

(Colour Rail)

as to whether they were actually built.

To allow through working to the London, Brighton and South Coast Railway and others, it was decided in October 1891 that 50 horse boxes, 10 CCTs and 20 OCTs would be fitted with Westinghouse brakes.

A minute of 13th April 1892 authorised the construction of 15 OCTs and 15 CCTs; the 15 OCTs were delivered from November 1892 to May 1893. The register records them as being to drawing 317, which has not survived, but which logically would have been prepared at some time around 1889 or 1890, when the five mentioned earlier were built. The CCTs can be identified as 19ft 6in vehicles to drawing 611. Seventeen more OCTs were built, probably as renewals, until the end of 1896. Then, in January 1898, 20 more were ordered as additional stock, and this time a fresh drawing was prepared – No 790. What the differences were is not known for certain, though it may well have been just the brake arrangement, but an interesting photograph of the Exeter Fire Brigade attending a fire at St Michael's Church, Honiton in March 1911, shows the steam fire engine on what is almost certainly one of the earlier ones with skewed brake rigging. The fire train consists of this OCT, a 16ft horse box and a 30ft passenger brake van. Because drawing 790 is the only one available, it is this version that is shown here as Figure 4.26. These were delivered in May and June 1899, to be followed by four more on renewals.

The CCTs to drawing 611 were a clear development of the 17ft and 16ft ones. They were provided with AVB, of course, with skewed brake rigging that was similar to that on the 18ft luggage vans of 1887. The brake cylinder was on the centre line with the cross-shaft hangers offset towards one end; a lever handbrake was fitted on one side, working on one wheel only. Most of them had Westinghouse through pipes added at some later date. Three more, probably to the same design, were built on renewals in 1897, then in January 1898 it was decided to build another five. This time, the same body design was used, but dual braking systems were fitted using vertical brake rigging. Drawing 786 was issued for these, and is illustrated here at Figure 4.28, which also includes the earlier skew brakes. Two more were then built on renewals in each of 1902 and 1904.

There are few records of the LSWR catering for fish traffic. The earliest is an instruction from the Traffic and General Purposes Committee in 1840 that one luggage van was to be suitably fitted according to Mr Beattie's plan, but there are no details. Next is an instruction from the Officers' Committee in 1870 that the floors of Guard's vans should be supplied with wooden ribs to drain the water running from parcels of fish and ice, this to be done as the vehicles came into the shops.

Then there is a mention in South Eastern Railway records of that company asking the LSWR in 1877 how they handled fish traffic. The response was that they used ordinary open or covered goods wagons. Also, there is at least one reference in LSWR minutes to complaints from passenger Guards of the smell when fish were carried in the

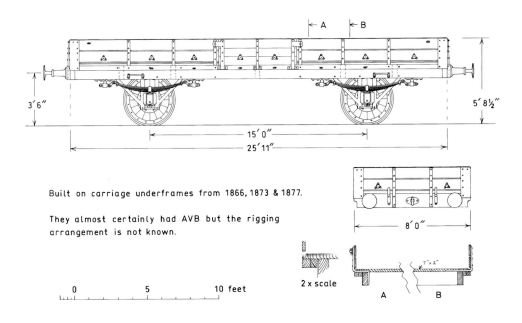

Built on carriage underframes from 1866, 1873 & 1877.

They almost certainly had AVB but the rigging arrangement is not known.

Figure 4.33. 25ft 11in fish truck of 1900, drawing 921.

passenger luggage (brake) vans.

In Chapter 1, it was mentioned that many of the new luggage vans of 1882 were well ventilated and had drainage holes in the floor. It might be assumed that some were used for fish traffic, since there was quite an amount of this from Plymouth, the *South Western Gazette* having reported in September 1885, that the company drew 2,000 of its total 4,446 tons of fish traffic from that port; within the next nine years they had rented a fish vault, storage pens and an office in the new fish market.

There was also a developing fish traffic from Padstow, after the line there opened in 1899. By 1910, it was recorded that 1,735 tons had been carried, increasing to 3,074 tons in 1911. In an 11-week period around May 1922, 2,500 tons went away from 52 trawlers in the port. Some of this traffic naturally went to London, but much also went to Birmingham, Liverpool, Manchester and, perhaps surprisingly, to Lowestoft and Grimsby – both famous fishing ports. The reason for this is that the fishing fleets followed the migration of fish stocks round the coast, so much of their catch had to go back to their home markets.

Following the opening of the line, a Fish Market was established at Padstow, for which Mr Panter reported to the Locomotive, Carriage and Stores Committee in March 1900 that he was providing an old carriage body to be used as an office for it on the quay. The Committee also considered the provision of vehicles for fish. It was agreed that the underframes of a number of old carriages were to be adapted for the carriage of fish or other perishables by passenger train. The cost was to be about £20 each, and they were to be treated as additional stock.

In the event, 12 fish wagons were built. Four were on old 25ft 11in underframes from carriages of 1866, 1873 and 1877. No record exists of this length

in 1866, but the others were probably block set carriages illustrated at Figure 3.20 in *LSWR Carriages, Volume 1*. The other eight were 23ft 11in long, but the frames were to the recent design for the 24ft fruit vans of 1896, not refurbished old ones. Their appearance was much like common two-plank open wagons with bodies 8ft wide. However, they had gaps between the planks and between the bottom plank and the floor.

The Eastleigh drawings show both types provided with small staple-like fittings for tying tarpaulin cords, but they must have been inconvenient, as they appear to have needed the cords to be threaded through them. In addition, and from the marks, they look to be amendments; there are several disc type jamming cleats of the pattern that first appear on a drawing of 1898, and that became standard on open wagons at least until the end of the LSWR. Tarpaulins probably had to be used to keep dust and smuts off the fish boxes, but ordinary wagon ones would have been too wide, and would have draped down nearly to the axle boxes. Doubtless the provision and maintenance of special ones for this small group of vehicles added to arguments against their retention.

The 26ft ones, Nos 162-5, had a drop door on each side 5ft 4½in wide, and are sketched here as Figure 4.33. The 24ft ones, Nos 166-73, had two doors on each side 4ft 6in wide; they are illustrated at Figure 4.34. The doors were made of three planks, not gapped. The first version almost certainly had AVB to permit running in passenger trains, but there is no information on the type or arrangement. The carriages from which they were converted must have had AVB installed in the mid-1880s, and so it is quite possible that the rigging was of the skew type. The later ones had the straight type and a single side hand lever. The only known photo is of one at Padstow, but this is almost end on

*Plate 4.34.
23ft 11in fish truck,
drawing 931, at
Padstow. (A tiny detail
from much larger view.)*

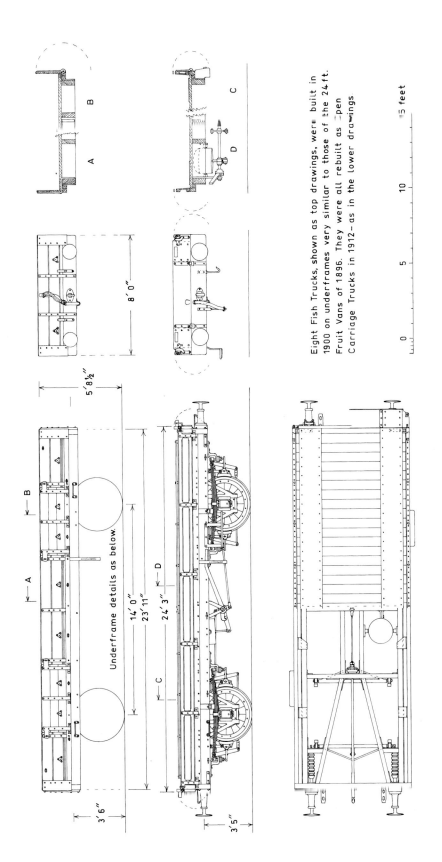

Eight Fish Trucks, shown as top drawings, were built in 1900 on underframes very similar to those of the 24 ft. Fruit Vans of 1896. They were all rebuilt as Open Carriage Trucks in 1912 – as in the lower drawings.

Figure 4.34. 23ft 11in fish truck of 1900, and rebuilt to open carriage truck, drawings 931 and 2087.

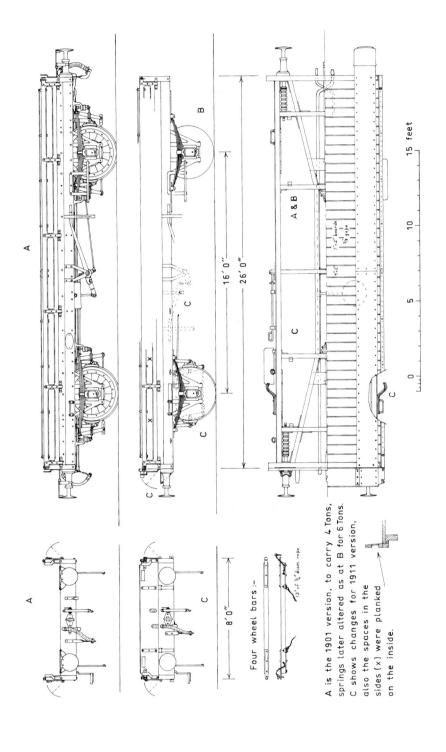

Figure 4.35. 26ft open carriage truck of 1901 and 1911, drawings 1034 and 2066.

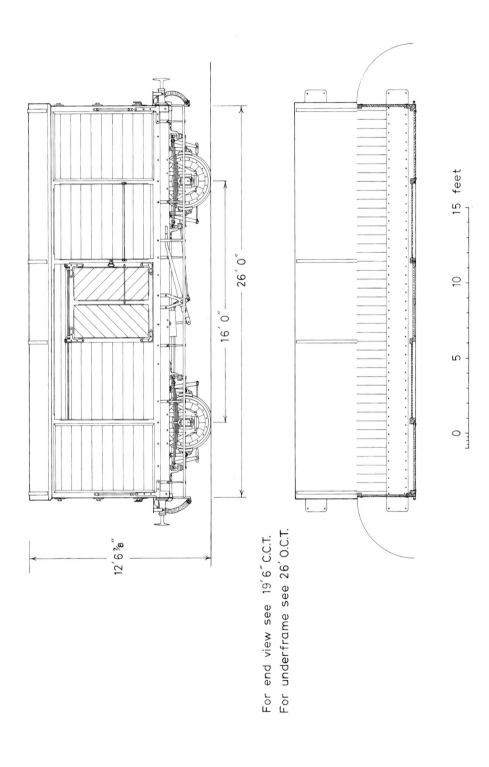

12' 6⅞"

26' 0"

16' 0"

For end view see 19'6" C.C.T.
For underframe see 26' O.C.T.

0   5   10   15   feet

Figure 4.36. 26ft open carriage truck of 1901, drawing 1035.

Plate 4.36a. 26ft covered carriage truck, LSWR No 219, drawing 1035.   *(F Foote)*

Plate 4.36b. 26ft covered carriage truck at Shoreham (Kent) in 1952, showing the end doors and ventilation holes in the side.   *(D Cullum 1280/Lens of Sutton Association)*

and is a very tiny part of the picture.

Towards the end of 1911, the War Office requested that some OCTs should be altered to have both the ends and the sides hinged. This was to allow the convenience of loading military traffic alongside ordinary platforms. These 12 fish trucks were the first to be considered for conversion. Presumably the first four were thought to be too old for further alteration, and so they were broken up in the latter part of 1912. Replacements were then added to the batches of 26ft OCTs that will be described shortly. The remaining eight were converted into OCTs with drop sides and ends as requested. The conversion was fairly extensive, even including new 13in deep headstocks in place of the original 11in ones. If the works drawing is to be believed, the pin rack for the handbrake lever was moved a few inches nearer to the brake cross-shaft, apparently to permit the fitting of a short footboard, though why this could not have been placed somewhere else is something of a puzzle. As with the others that were altered to comply with the War Office request, the side frames were panelled in on their inner sides so as to provide a smooth ramp surface. The War Office request can be clearly understood on looking at Plate 4.43a, taken in 1911, where a wheeled machine gun is having to be lifted over the side rail, clearly not possible with anything much heavier. By comparison, the OCT just seen on the left does have a side dropped onto the platform.

When some new OCTs were ordered in May 1901, they were 26ft long, as were the CCTs ordered at the same time, 25 of each, all with dual braking systems. The bodies of the covered ones were really only an extension of the 19ft 6in ones. Photographs

of one or two of them taken after 1923 show ventilation holes low down in the recessed sections of the sides to the left and right of the sliding door, presumably to clear motor car fumes, but when these holes were bored is not known. Both types had a handbrake on one side only, and were provided with Westinghouse through piping. The open ones had four wheel bars, were rated to carry 4 tons, and had sliding extension pieces to carry the wheel plates over the buffer heads. They were built to LSWR drawings 1034 (open) and 1035 (covered), shown here as Figures 4.35 and 4.36, respectively.

These 25 OCTs were included in the decision, mentioned above, to provide a quantity with drop ends and sides for increased convenience in loading military vehicles, in this case, at the cost of £6 2s per truck. In order to retain the standard heights of the vacuum and Westinghouse pipes, the end doors had to have grooves gouged out to clear the pipes.

From mid-1911, further batches of 26ft OCTs were ordered, including the four replacements for the 1900 fish trucks, being delivered from August 1912 until July 1920. They were closely similar to the earlier ones, but were built to a fresh drawing, No 2066. Following the alteration to the earlier ones, they were provided with falling down sides and ends from the start. Either-side hand brakes were fitted, using the lifting link method. Like the earlier ones, they had Westinghouse through pipes. Unlike any others, they were fitted with "door banger" springs on each side rather like those on most open wagons, but in this case fitted horizontally. The sides of OCTs were not expected to be dropped right down, but to provide something of a bridge when side loading at a platform; in any

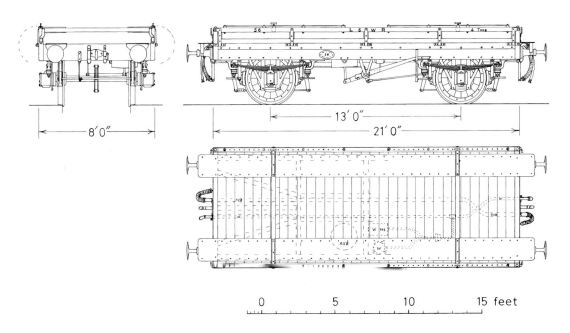

Figure 4.38. 21ft open carriage truck of 1904, drawings 1301 and 1384.

Plate 4.38. T14 class No 447 on down Bournemouth West express at Surbiton. On the right is an open carriage truck on which the wheel bars and wheel plates can be seen.

(ESC Betteley/N Pomfret)

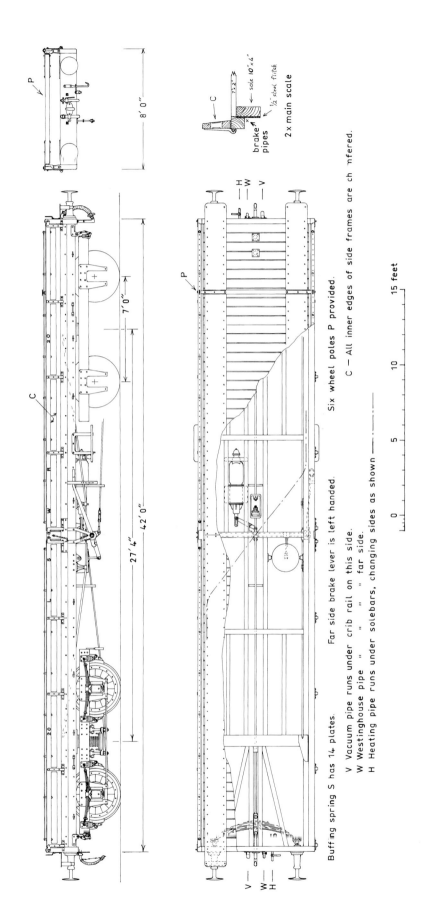

Buffing spring S has 14 plates.   Far side brake lever is left handed.   Six wheel poles P provided.

V Vacuum pipe runs under crib rail on this side.   C — All inner edges of side frames are chamfered.
W Westinghouse pipe "   "   " far side.
H Heating pipe runs under solebars, changing sides as shown ———·———

brake pipes

sole 10" x 4"
7 x 2"
½" steel flitch
2 x main scale

8' 0"
7' 0"
27' 4"
42' 0"

0   5   10   15 feet

Figure 4.39. 42ft open carriage truck of 1904, drawing 1338.

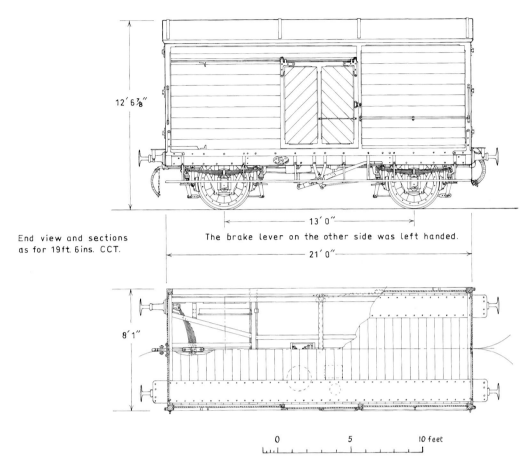

12′ 6⅞″

13′ 0″

21′ 0″

End view and sections as for 19ft. 6ins. CCT.

The brake lever on the other side was left handed.

8′ 1″

0   5   10 feet

Figure 4.40. 21ft covered carriage truck of 1905, drawing 1362.

Plate 4.40. T1 class No 17 with a 21ft covered carriage truck, drawing 1362.   *(J Minnis Collection)*

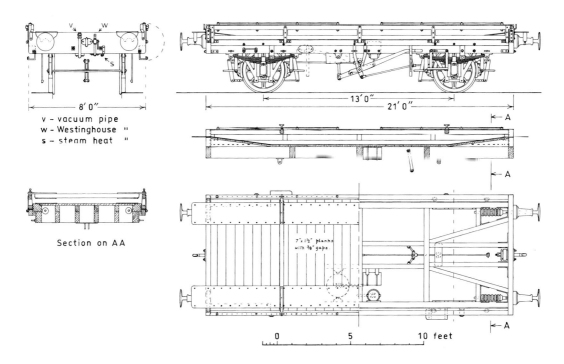

v – vacuum pipe
w – Westinghouse "
s – steam heat "

Section on AA

Figure 4.41. 21ft open carriage truck (low floor) of 1908, drawing 1677.

case these springs provided an added protection. The sides on these had the spaces between the frame members filled in on the inside with oak planks to provide a smooth ramp when side loading. They had stronger springs fitted into wagon-type spring shoes to increase the permitted load from 4 to 6 tons.

The 1901 batch of vehicles was at some time modified to carry 6 tons by having the scroll irons replaced by spring shoes and stronger springs. The date of this is not recorded, but since this alteration is shown on the drawing without any mention of drop ends, it might be inferred that this was prior to 1911.

Prior to 1905, the upright vacuum brake pipes at the ends of carriage trucks had been arranged to pivot sideways to permit loading and unloading. This clearly was a weak point where leakage could occur and in about 1905, in response to Railway Clearing House rules, all these pipes were altered to low level, similar to those that had been introduced on corridor carriages.

A couple of 25ft renewal OCTs were built in 1902, but nothing much is known about them apart from their numbers shown as Appendix item 4.37. They may well have been built using recovered carriage underframes.

In 1904 two more types of OCT were introduced, one 21ft long to drawing 1301, later revised by drawing 1384 (Figure 4.38). The other type was 42ft long to drawing 1338 (Figure 4.39). The 21ft OCT was similar to most others except that the first two built had wagon type springs and 14ft wheelbase while the rest, built in 1905 and 1906,

had scroll irons, 5ft springs and 13ft wheelbase.

The 42ft OCTs, of which only five were built, were again similar to other OCTs apart from the length, which required them to run on bogies. These were structurally very similar to the usual 8ft Fox bogies but with simplified side frames. Because of the length, the drop sides were in two sections; between them at the centre there was a removable steel plate with the pins for retaining the sides when in the upright position. By removing this plate, the complete side between the end posts could be cleared for loading.

Both the 21ft and 42ft types were dual-braked. The Westinghouse brake has been shown in some earlier drawings, and in the 21ft one, using a vertical cylinder with a single piston and a separate reservoir. Another common arrangement was where a horizontal cylinder had two pistons pushing outwards towards the ends of the vehicle. In the case of the 42ft OCT, a horizontal single piston cylinder was used, mounted off-centre, having the reservoir directly attached in place of the second piston. The piston was coupled to the brake cross shaft by a horizontal lever.

As to handbrakes, both types appear to have originally had left and right-handed levers, later altered to both sides right-handed, as mentioned in connection with the 21ft horse boxes.

In authorising renewals in May 1905 the Traffic Committee included ten horse boxes and carriage trucks, all 21ft long with dual brakes. This was interpreted as five of each, the carriage trucks being covered ones to LSWR drawing 1362, as shown in

Figure 4.40. Another five followed in the next year. In most respects they resembled the previous 19ft 6in and 21ft varieties.

More renewals that were approved in July 1907 included three 21ft OCTs with dual brakes. In fact they were built with lowered floors to drawing 1677, signed by S Warner on 23rd December 1907, Figure 4.41. Two more were ordered in the following June, but then the low floor was mentioned in the minutes. The first one, number 40, was lettered for Overton and was reserved to be used between there and Waterloo for carrying a banknote van between Portal's paper mills and the Bank of England. This was a traffic first mentioned in December 1869, when the Traffic Committee had a letter from the Secretary to the Bank of England requesting alterations to the van that conveyed the banknote paper between Messrs Portal's mills and London. It was decided that as the van had been built at the cost of the LSWR precisely as then required by the Bank of England and Messrs Portal, any desired alterations could only be made by those parties, or at their cost. Neither the Bank nor Portal's are able to throw any more light on this slightly intriguing subject. However, there is a relevant entry in the LSWR Road Vehicle Register. Number 163 was a pair horse paper van, assigned to Waterloo and Overton, built about 1866 by Hayes, Stamford for £92 10s, weight 2ton 10cwt 3qtr. It was 11ft 7in long, 5ft 6in wide at the top and 5ft 4in at the bottom, 5ft body height. Front and rear wheels were 3ft and 4ft diameter respectively on a wheelbase of 7ft. It was sold in November 1922.

A design that looks like a CCT, and which was included among them in the Carriage Truck Register as number 57, was a single 46ft 6in Covered Scenery Truck, completed in June 1910, and shown here as Figure 4.42. Some railway companies had several of this type, but the LSWR presumably catered for the needs of travelling theatre companies by using CCTs or other vehicles.

It had the maximum internal width and height, like the CCTs, but without the wheel plates and pin rails, making it more of an ordinary, but long, covered van. The drawings showed normal 16in diameter buffers but the official photograph, which was definitely taken after the vehicle was some years old, shows them cut off at the top to allow a loading board to be laid across between the floor and an end loading dock.

The bogies were ordinary 8ft wheelbase carriage ones with fixed bolsters, the only difference being that the spring trays were partly enclosed at the ends, though the purpose of this is not clear.

This time the Westinghouse brake used a combined cylinder and reservoir. This required the rather odd brake linkage seen in the drawing, converting the single push to an inward pull at each bogie.

After this, no new carriage truck designs were actually built, despite an authorisation in March 1917 for "Twenty CCTs of a new type combining the essentials of the present 24ft special passenger luggage van and the 26ft CCT, such trucks to be fitted with hinged doors at both ends to facilitate the loading of motor cars, etc." This rather curious specification, that appears to merely describe what already existed, was not proceeded with, but was probably overtaken by a requirement in January 1918 to carry out:

"Alterations for the conveyance of aeroplanes: fit end doors to nineteen 6-wheel milk & passenger luggage vans at £63 each, fit end doors to six bogie guard's vans, and remove inside brake, runners for fruit shelves, gas globes, provide either-side hand brake at £75 each. Remove sides and ends from two drop sided 6-wheel wagons at £2 18s 3d each, remove sides and ends from fifty road van trucks at £1 12s 6d each. Remove Westinghouse brake fittings from existing stock and replace on eight 6-wheel milk vans and six bogie guard's vans, at £90 the lot. Costs to be recovered from the Government."

After the First World War, the need for horse boxes and carriage trucks doubtless declined quite rapidly, in any case, no more of either was designed by the LSWR.

Two more photographs that are of interest are Plates 4.43a and 4.43b; both show OCTs that cannot be positively identified. The former was allegedly taken in 1911 showing a wheeled machine gun being loaded over the fixed side rails of a fairly short OCT. This demonstrates the reason for the statement, mentioned earlier, that in 1911 the War Office wrote to the LSWR requesting that OCTs should be provided with "falling down sides". The second photograph not only illustrates troops unloading a limber at the beginning of the First World War from an OCT that looks to be about 19ft long, but also offers a good view of a loading gauge, placed to ensure that any vehicle loaded should not exceed the permitted safe size.

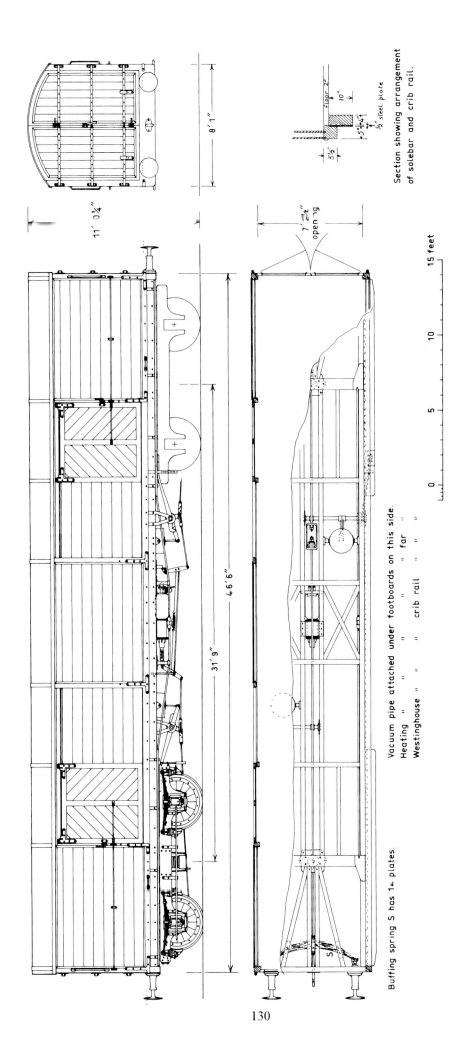

Section showing arrangement
of solebar and crib rail.

8' 1"

11' 0¼"

7' 2½"
open'ng

31' 9"

4' 6' 6"

Vacuum pipe attached under footboards on this side.

Heating   "   "   "   "   far   "   "   "

Westinghouse "   "   "   crib rail "   "   "

Buffing spring S has 1~ plates.

0   5   10   15 feet

Figure 4.42.   46ft 6in covered scenery truck of 1910, drawing 1889.

Plate 4.42. 46ft 6in scenery truck, No 57, drawing 1889.

(National Railway Museum)

Plate 4.43a. Troops loading a machine gun on to a fixed-sided open carriage truck.
("The Wonder Book of Railways", 1911)

Plate 4.43b. Troops unloading a limber from an open carriage truck in 1914. Note the placing of the loading gauge close to the loading dock. *(Underwood & Underwood)*

APPENDICES

Before 1912, each type of non-passenger stock was numbered in its own series from No 1 upwards. In 1912, a new number scheme was drawn up, similar to that for carriages, where each type was put into a distinct section of the number range. In these appendices the column headed "Ren" refers to this scheme, but vehicles were normally only renumbered when they had to go into works for repairs, etc. Thus, many did not get their new number for several years, whilst some were withdrawn without change. The same thing applied when the Southern Railway drew up its own scheme in 1923, with some vehicles retaining LSWR numbers until the late 1920s.

In the remarks the letters mean the following:
B = Broken up   C = Cyphered   W = Withdrawn.

Vehicles were cyphered when they were struck off the Capital Stock register, but were still usable. This was denoted by the prefix 0, for example, No 156 would become No 0156; no further record was made of their final disposal. Normally they could be used until a repair was needed, when they could be sold or broken up without further authorisation.

APPENDIX TO CHAPTER 1 - PASSENGER LUGGAGE VANS

Note: There is no certain record of the existence of any LSWR vehicles in this category before the adoption of automatic vacuum brakes in around 1882. Previously, the traffic appears to have been carried either in goods trains or in Passenger Guard's Vans.

1.1 22ft Luggage Van. LSWR drawing DB97.
Note: The diagram book shows numbers 1 to 5 as being 18ft, but the register has them as 22ft.

Built	No	Ren	
1883	1		C 12/09
"	2		C 12/09
"	3		C 12/09
"	4		C 6/10
"	5		C 12/08
"	6		C 6/10
"	7		C 6/11
"	8		C 6/11
3/83	9	5009	W 10/18 sold Eastleigh
"	10	5010	W 5/18 sold Okehampton
"	11	5011	W 10/18 sold Eastleigh
"	12	5012	W 11/17 sold Basingstoke
"	13	5013	W 7/14 sold Medstead
"	14	5014	W 10/17 sold Milborne Port
"	15	5015	W 7/17 sold Milborne Port
"	16	5016	W 4/17 sold Eastleigh
"	17	5017	W 10/15 sold Winchester
"	18	5018	W 12/17 sold Hayling Island
4/83	19	5019	W 10/14 cabin at Amesbury, underframe to gasholder No 7
"	20	5020	W 12/20 sold Seaton Junction
5/83	21	5021	W 12/17 sold Winchester
"	22	5022	C 7/19 sold 10/19 Winchester
"	23	5023	W 10/16 sold Reading
"	24	5024	W 2/18 sold Whitford (body still used as shed 1984)
"	25	5025	W 12/16 sold Wimborne
"	26	5026	W 6/17 sold Hayling Island
"	27	5027	W 7/17 sold Portsmouth
"	28	5028	W 10/19 sold Battersea
"	29	5029	W 10/19 sold Kingston
"	30	5030	W 1/18 sold Kingston
6/83	31	5031	W 10/17 sold Milborne Port
"	32	5032	W 6/16 sold Basingstoke
"	33	5033	W 11/13
"	34	5034	W 7/17 sold Milborne Port
"	35	5035	W 12/15 to stores van 29s
"	36	5036	W 9/17 sold Milborne Port
7/83	37	5037	W 12/15 cabin at Exeter (was reserved for emigrant train, 1898)
"	38	5038	W 12/17 sold Basingstoke
"	39	5039	W 6/17 sold Exmouth
"	40	5040	W 10/19 sold Eastleigh
"	41	5041	W 7/17 sold Milborne Port
"	42	5042	W 12/19 sold Eastleigh
"	43	5043	W 5/18 sold Okehampton
"	44	5044	W 7/18 sold Hayling Island
"	45	5045	B 7/19
"	46	5046	W 8/18 sold Eastleigh
"	47	5047	to WD Fovant Railway 4/16
"	48	5048	W 12/16 sold Exmouth

22ft Luggage Vans (continued)

Built	No	Ren	
7/83	49	5049	W 5/19 sold Amesbury
"	50	5050	W 12/16 to electrical track stores van 54s

1.2 24ft Luggage Van. LSWR drawing DB97A, SR diagram 926.

Note: Those marked with a * were cyphered, then used between Southampton Docks and Town only.

Built	No	Ren	SR No	
5/87	51	5051	1252	W 9/29
"	52	5052		C 2/20*
	53	5053	1253	W 2/30 to stores van 469s
"	54	5054	1254	to IoW in 4/26, to 2232 in 3/29, W 5/36
"	55	5055	1255	W 3/27 underframe to gasholder 02s in 9/27
"	56	5056	1256	W 5/30
"	57	5057	1257	W 9/28
"	58	5058	1258	W 2/33
"	59	5059	1259	W 9/33
"	60	5060	1260	W 11/27
6/87	61	5061		C 2/20*
"	62	5062	1261	W 9/29
"	63	5063	1262	W 9/25 to stores van 083s
"	64	5064		W 2/23 sold Holsworthy
"	65	5065	1263	W 1/26 (was reserved for emigrant train, 1898)
"	66	5066	1264	W 1/30 underframe to gasholder 01s in 9/31
"	67	5067	1265	W 6/28
"	68	5068	1266	W 1/28
"	69	5069	1267	W 8/30 underframe to gasholder 017s (ex-No 18) in 8/31
"	70	5070		C 2/20*
"	71	5071	1268	W 2/32
"	72	5072	1269	W 2/31
"	73	5073	1270	W 12/30
"	74	5074	1271	W 4/31
"	75	5075		W 12/21 to cabin at Carriage Dept., Barnstaple
7/87	76	5076		C 2/20*
"	77	5077	1272	W 2/33
"	78	5078	1273	W 9/28
"	79	5079	1274	W 10/26 to stores van 64s
"	80	5080	1275	to IoW in 4/26, to 2233 in 2/29, W 5/36
"	81	5081	1276	W 8/33
8/87	82	5082	1277	W 1/27 underframe to gasholder 011s (ex-No 12) in 8/30
"	83	5083	1278	W 4/31
"	84	5084	1279	W 11/28 to stores van 085s
"	85	5085	1280	W 10/32
"	86	5086	1281	W 10/26 underframe to gasholder 013s (ex-No 14) in 2/27
7/87	87	5087		W 5/23 sold Horsebridge
8/87	88	5088	1282	W 11/33
9/87	89	5089		W 7/22 sold Basingstoke
"	90	5090		C 2/20*
8/87	91	5091	1283	to IoW in 4/26, to 2234 in 1/29, 9/33 to Guards van 1016, W 5/37
"	92	5092		W 7/22 to Eng. Dept. 40s
"	93	5093	1284	W 2/33
"	94	5094	1285	W 2/30 to stores van 470s
"	95	5095	1286	W 2/31
"	96	5096	1287	W 5/32
"	97	5097		W 1922 to Carriage Dept. 125s
9/87	98	5098	1288	W 9/29
8/87	99	5099	1289	W 10/33
"	100	5100	1290	W 4/31

1.3 18ft Luggage Van. LSWR drawing DB99.

Built	No	Ren	
1887	205		W 12/09
"	206		W 5/14 sold Bournemouth
"	207		B 6/12
"	208	5191	W 9/1913
"	209		B 12/12
"	210		C 12/09
"	211		W 1/14 sold Gillingham
"	212		C 12/02
"	213		B 6/12
"	214		B 6/12
"	215	5195	W 3/15 sold Sherborne
"	216		B 12/12

18ft Luggage Vans (continued)

Built	No	Ren	
1887	217		C 6/12
"	218		B 12/08
"	219	5197	W c.1913
"	220		B 12/08
"	221	5198	W c.1913
"	222		W 10/15 sold Hayes
"	223		W 12/09
"	224		B 12/08
2/88	103	5103	W c.6/13
"	104	5104	W 11/13 sold Milborne Port
"	105	5105	W c.1913
"	106	5106	W 12/13 sold Medstead
3/88	107	5107	B 6/15
"	108	5108	W c.1913
"	109		B 12/12
"	110	5110	W c.1913
"	111		B 12/08
"	112	5112	W c.1913
"	113		B 12/12
"	114	5114	W 11/16 sold Reading
"	115		C 6/12
"	116		C 6/11
"	117		C 12/09
"	118	5117	W 5/16 sold Bulford
"	119	5118	W 3/15 sold Baynards
"	120		C 12/02
"	121		B 12/12
"	122	5120	W c.1913
"	123		B 12/12
4/88	124	5122	W 3/15 sold Baynards
"	125		B 6/12
"	126	5123	W c.1913
"	127	5124	W c.1913
"	128		B 6/08
"	129		W 12/09 (but 0129 - 18ft fruit van - became SR 2223, W 12/23, cut up 1927)
"	130	5127	W 9/15 sold Brookwood
"	131		B 12/12
5/88	132	5129	W 8/16 sold Dean
"	133	5130	W c.1913
"	134	5131	W 7/16 sold Fort Brockhurst
"	135		W 12/09
"	136		B 1904 (underframe used for new 136/5133 - elliptical roof, to drawing 1318)
"	137		B 6/12
"	138	5134	W 7/16 sold Havant
"	139	5135	W 1/15 sold Kettering
"	140	5136	W c.1913
"	141		W 12/09
"	142	5138	W c.1913
"	143		B 12/08
"	144		C 6/12
6/88	145	5140	W 6/15 to cabin at Eastleigh gas house
"	146		C 6/12
"	147		B 6/08
"	148		C 12/09
"	149		W 3/14 sold Dunsland Cross
"	150		B 6/12
"	151	5144	W c.1913
"	152		W 2/14 sold Bailey Gate
"	153	5146	W 11/15 sold Wimborne
"	154	5147	W 6/16 sold for cabin at Institute Bowling Green
"	155	5148	W c.1913
"	156		C 6/12
"	157		?
"	158		B 6/12
"	159	5149	W 10/15 sold Hayes
"	160	5150	B 5/16
"	161		C 6/10
"	162	5152	W c.1913
"	163		Destroyed in Salisbury smash, 1906
"	164		C 6/11
"	165	5155	W c.1913
8/88	166	5156	W 3/15 sold Baynards
7/88	167	5157	W 10/16 sold Reading

18ft Luggage Vans (continued)

Built	No	Ren	
7/88	168	5158	W c.1913
"	169		B 6/12
5/88	170	5159	W 6/15 to cabin for patrol firemen at Eastleigh Eng. Dept.
8/88	171	5160	W 9/15 sold Brookwood
"	172	5161	W 7/16 sold Wimborne
9/88	173	5162	W 11/15 sold Poole
"	174	5163	W c.1913
8/88	175		W 2/14 sold Bailey Gate
"	176		C 6/11
"	177		?
"	178	5166	W c.1913
"	179		C 6/12
6/88	180		W 4/14 sold Bailey Gate
"	181	5168	W 8/16 to cabin at Swaythling
"	182		B 6/12
"	183		B 6/12
9/88	184		W 2/14 sold Bailey Gate
"	185	5170	W c.1913
"	186		W 1/14 sold Gillingham
"	187	5172	B 6/15
"	188		W 12/14 sold Bailey Gate
"	189		C 6/12
"	190	5174	W c.1913
"	191	5175	W 9/16 sold Wimborne
"	192		C 12/02
"	193	5177	W c.1913
"	194	5178	W c.1913
"	195		C 12/02
10/88	196	5180	W 3/15 sold Baynards
"	197	5181	W 4/16 sold Maiden Newton
"	198		Destroyed in Salisbury smash, 1906
"	199	5183	W 3/15 sold Baynards
"	200	5184	W c.1913
"	201		W 12/14 sold to WD at Addlestone
"	202		W 12/14 sold to WD
"	203		W 2/14 sold Bailey Gate
"	204		B 12/12
1890	226		B 6/12

1.4 22ft 6in Luggage (Milk) Van. LSWR drawing 186, SR diagram 930.

This was the only one built. The drawing is marked "New body for 227 milk van".

Built	No	Ren	SR No	
1893	227	5202	1612	W 6/38

1.5 24ft Luggage Van. LSWR drawing 228 and drawing 874, all SR diagram 927.

Built	No	Ren	Light	SR No	
(a) Drawing 228, fitted with "skew" brake rigging					
7/94	248	5212	O	1301	W 4/34 grounded at Selsey
8/94	249	5213	G	1302	W 12/33 newspaper traffic
"	250	5214	O	1303	W 8/32
"	251	5215	O	1304	W 11/33
"	252	5216	O	1305	W 11/33 altered to gas light 1916, then for newspaper traffic
"	253	5217	O	1306	W 12/26
"	254	5218	O	1307	W 10/36
"	255	5219	O	1308	W 8/34
"	256	5220	O	1309	W 3/35
"	257	5221	O	1310	W 7/36
9/94	258	5222	O	1311	W 2/37
"	259	5223	O	1312	W 6/32
"	260	5224	O	1313	W 8/34
"	261	5225	O	1314	W 8/35
"	262	5226	G	1315	W 8/33 newspaper traffic
"	263	5227	G	1316	W 4/35 newspaper traffic
"	264	5228	G	1317	W 5/33 newspaper traffic
"	265	5229	O	1318	W 4/34
"	266				Destroyed in Salisbury smash, 1906
"	267	5231	G	1319	W 10/36 newspaper traffic
"	268	5232	G	1320	W 7/35 newspaper traffic
"	269	5233	G	1321	W 6/36 newspaper traffic
"	270	5234	G	1322	W 11/33 newspaper traffic
"	271	5235	G	1323	W 2/32 newspaper traffic

24ft Luggage Vans (continued)

Built	No	Ren	Light	SR No		
9/94	272	5236	G	1324	W 1/34	newspaper traffic

(b) Drawing 874, fitted with vertical brake rigging. All oil lit.

Built	No	Ren		SR No		
12/97	101	5101		1291	W 4/36	grounded Winchelsea*
"	228	5203		1293	W 6/38	
"	230	5205		1294	W 12/35	to 998s
"	239	5208		1297	W 9/36	
"	240	5209		1298	W 12/37	
5/98	236	5206		1295	W 12/36	
"	238	5207		1296	W 8/32	
6/98	243	5210		1299	W 12/35	grounded Ashford
"	246	5211		1300	W 2/32	
"	275	5237		1325	W 10/37	
12/99	379	5340		1427	W 2/37	
"	102	5102		1292	W 8/35	grounded Winchelsea

*Note: Despite this register entry, a photograph of the grounded body of SR No 1291 shows it clearly to be of the drawing 636 type.

1.6 24ft Luggage and Fruit Van. LSWR drawing 636, SR diagram 927.

The first 50 (numbers 277 to 326) were shown in the register as marked for fruit traffic. All oil lit.

Built	No	Ren	SR No		
5/96	277	5238	1326	W 3/38	
"	278	5239	1327	W 10/37	
"	279	5240	1328	W 8/32	to stores van 621s (altered to run over Hastings branch 5/28)
6/96	280	5241	1329	W 7/36	
5/96	281	5242	1330	W 9/28	
6/96	282	5243	1331	W 4/34	to mess & tool van 770s
"	283	5244	1332	W 2/37	underframe used for gasholder 07s (ex-No 8)
"	284	5245	1333	W 12/35	
12/96	285	5246	1334	W 12/33	
"	286	5247	1335	W 10/37	
"	287	5248	1336	W 12/33	
"	288	5249	1337	W 1/34	
"	289	5250	1338	W 7/23	damaged beyond repair at Basingstoke 23-5-23
"	290	5251	1339	W 4/32	
"	291	5252	1340	W 10/37	
"	292	5253	1341	W 5/32	underframe to gasholder 04s (ex No 5)
"	293	5254	1342	W 11/38	to mess & tool van 1312s
"	294	5255	1343	W 2/36	grounded Basingstoke
"	295	5256	1344	W 4/38	
"	296	5257	1345	W 6/36	
"	297	5258	1346	W 5/35	
"	298	5259	1347	W 12/36	
"	299	5260	1348	W 9/36	
"	300	5261	1349	W 12/37	
"	301	5262	1350	W 6/38	
"	302	5263	1351	W 12/36	
"	303	5264	1352	W 4/38	
"	304	5265	1353	W 8/32	body put on cosmetic underframe at Haparanda Stn, (St. Germans) 1997
"	305	5266	1354	W 9/36	
"	306	5267	1355	W 9/38	
"	307	5268	1356	W 3/38	grounded Selhurst
"	308	5269	1357	W 6/36	
"	309	5270	1358	W 9/37	
6/97	310	5271	1359	W 5/36	
"	311	5272	1360	W 6/37	
"	312	5273	1361	W 7/37	
"	313	5274	1362	W 11/35	
"	314	5275	1363	W 7/37	
"	315	5276	1364	W 10/34	
"	316	5277	1365	W 8/38	
"	317	5278	1366	W 7/32	
"	318	5279	1367	W 6/36	
"	319	5280	1368	W 6/36	
"	320	5281	1369	W 4/38	
"	321	5282	1370	W 3/38	
"	322	5283	1371	W 9/37	
"	323	5284	1372	W 3/36	
"	324			W 6/07	
"	325	5286	1373	W 9/36	
"	326	5287	1374	W 5/36	
3/98	327	5288	1375	W 2/37	
"	328	5289	1376	W 4/39	grounded Arundel

24ft Luggage and Fruit Vans (continued)

Built	No	Ren	SR No		
3/98	329	5290	1377	W	7/37
"	330	5291	1378	W	9/36
"	331	5292	1379	W	3/38
"	332	5293	1380	W	4/36
"	333	5294	1381	W	2/32
"	334	5295	1382	W	12/37
"	335	5296	1383	W	8/35 to 918s
"	336	5297	1384	W	4/38
"	337	5298	1385	W	2/37
"	338	5299	1386	W	6/38
"	339	5300	1387	W	9/37
"	340	5301	1388	W	7/36 grounded Tulse Hill
"	341	5302	1389	W	12/36
"	342	5303	1390	W	3/35
"	343	5304	1391	W	12/36
"	344	5305	1392	W	7/37
"	345	5306	1393	W	6/38
"	346	5307	1394	W	1/38 grounded Deptford Wharf
"	347	5308	1395	W	2/36 grounded Basingstoke
"	348	5309	1396	W	6/37 grounded Mitcham
"	349	5310	1397	W	2/34
"	350	5311	1398	W	3/38
"	351	5312	1399	W	12/26
"	352	5313	1400	W	1/38 grounded Bromley
"	353	5314	1401	W	6/35
"	354	5315	1402	W	9/36
4/98	355	5316	1403	W	5/36
"	356	5317	1404	W	6/35
"	357	5318	1405	W	8/35
"	358	5319	1406	W	2/37
"	359	5320	1407	W	10/36 grounded Winchelsea
"	360	5321	1408	W	10/35
"	361	5322	1409	W	10/35
"	362	5323	1410	W	11/35
"	363	5324	1411	W	12/32 to stores van 681s
"	364	5325	1412	W	6/37
5/98	365	5326	1413	W	8/38
"	366	5327	1414	W	2/32 underframe to gasholder 08s (ex-No 9) 8/42
6/98	367	5328	1415	W	7/36
"	368	5329	1416	W	6/38 grounded Knights Hill
"	369	5330	1417	W	9/38
"	370	5331	1418	W	9/38
"	371	5332	1419	W	4/36
"	372	5333	1420	W	12/26
"	373	5334	1421	W	4/32 to stores van 623s
"	374	5335	1422	W	8/38
"	375	5336	1423	W	12/35 altered to pass over Hastings branch 2/28
"	376	5337	1424	W	7/35 grounded Hove

1.7 26ft Fruit and Brake Van. LSWR drawing 602.

Built	No	Ren	SR No	
2/95	46	4362	1	to IOW as 1007 in 5/1930, to mess & tools van 1280s in 12/38

1.8 48ft Fruit and Brake Van (and Ambulance conversion). LSWR drawings 791 & 932, SR diagram 868 (Guards Vans), 1190 (Postal Bag Vans), 1145 (Aeroplane Vans).

Built as Fruit Vans to drawing 791, then altered to Brake Vans (drawing 932) in 1901-03. The actual vehicle-to-vehicle renumberings are not recorded. Those shown as broken up (B) in 1903 were actually also altered. The van register shows the first 15 built 1/98 and 2/98, but they were almost certainly 1/99 and 2/99.

Entries in Luggage Van register:

No		No	
		242	W 6/00 converted to ambulance and sold to WD
229	Transferred to Guards Van, 6/02	"	Transferred to Guards Van, 12/01
231	Broken up, 6/03	244	Transferred to Guards Van, 12/01
232	Transferred to Guards Van, 12/01	245	W 6/00 converted to ambulance and sold to WD
233	Transferred to Guards Van, 6/01	"	Transferred to Guards Van, 12/01
234	W 6/00 converted to ambulance and sold to WD	247	W 6/00 converted to ambulance and sold to WD
"	Transferred to Guards Van, 12/01	"	Transferred to Guards Van, 12/01
235	Transferred to Guards Van, 12/01	273	Transferred to Guards Van, 6/02
237	Transferred to Guards Van, 12/01	274	W 6/00 converted to ambulance and sold to WD
241	Broken up, 6/03	"	Transferred to Guards Van, 12/01
		276	Broken up, 6/03

Entries in Brake Van Register. (Note: as mentioned, the 1899 dates are assumed.)

No	Drawings	Built	1912 Ren	
495	791/932	2/99	4690	to aero 2/19, SR 4569, W 1/36 grounded Feltham
496	"	10/00	4691	to aero 5/18, SR 4570, W 1/36 grounded Feltham
497	"	2/99	4692	to aero 10/18, SR 4571, W 6/35
498	"	10/00	4693	SR 313, W 6/36
499	"	10/00	4694	SR 314, W 12/38
500	"	10/00	4695	to aero 10/18, SR 4572, W 2/35
501	"	10/00	4696	to aero 9/18. SR 4573, W 9/35
502	"	1/99	4697	SR 315, W 2/35
503	"	1/99	4698	to stowage 5616 in 1915, SR 4913, new underframe ex-Third 941 in 3/37, grounded Exmouth Jcn 8/40
504	"	1/99	4699	SR 316, W 12/34
505	"	1/99	4700	to aero 10/18, SR 4574, W 4/36
506	"	1/99	4701	SR 317, W 11/35
507	"	1/99	4702	to stowage 5617 in 1915, SR 4914, new underframe ex-Third 952 in 4/38, grounded Exmouth Jcn 8/40
508	"	1/99	4703	to stowage 5618 in 1915, SR 4915, W 2/40
509	"	1/99	4704	SR 318, W 11/35

1.9 24ft Hearse Van. LSWR drawing 884, SR diagram 928.

Built	No	Ren	SR No	
12/99	377	5338	1425	W 5/41 destroyed by enemy action
"	378	5339	1426	W 8/49

1.10 31ft 4in Fruit and Milk Van. LSWR drawings 1115 (body) and 1131 (underframe), SR diagram 931.

Notes: 5119 and 5204 were altered for aeroplane traffic in 10/18.
                  No 120 used the underframe from First No 434, built 1866, broken up 12/02.

Built	No	Ren	SR No	
12/02	120	5119	1633	ren 4575 in 3/28, eitherside brakes 1/32, W 4/40
"	192			W 10/13 to service use as 35s
"	195	5179	1634	W 7/35 to mess & tool van 910s for Engineer's Ironworks, Wimbledon.
"	212			W 10/13 to service use as 36s, SR 29s broken up 6/48
"	229	5204	1635	ren 4576 in 1/26, eitherside brakes 2/32, W 11/39 to Match truck 59SM

1.11 32ft Special Milk Van. LSWR drawing 1598, SR diagram 932 (diagram 1144 as aeroplane van).

Built	No	Ren	Ren date	To Aero van	SR No	
6/07	163	5153	6/13		1641	W 11/41
8/07	198	5182	12/16	8/18	4563	W 10/37
"	266	5230	3/14	10/18	4567	W 3/40
"	324	5285	3/14	8/18	4568	W 9/38
3/08	128	5125	6/14		1638	W 2/41 grounded Petersfield
9/08	111	5111	12/16		1637	W 9/41 to stores van 1642s
"	143	5139	3/14		1640	W 8/41 grounded Richmond
"	147	5141	12/14	10/18	4562	W 12/34
"	224	5201	9/14	10/18	4566	W 8/39
12/08	5	5005	5/16		1636	W 5/39 to stores van 1429s
"	218	5196	12/13	10/18	4565	W 8/41 to stores van 1638s
9/09	129	5126	12/14		1639	W 2/41 destroyed by enemy action.
"	135	5132	10/14	5/19	4560	W 2/41
"	141	5137	11/14	10/18	4561	W 9/41
"	205	5189	8/18		4564	W 8/38
"	223	5200	10/16		1642	W 8/39 to mess & tool van 1414s

1.12 24ft Special Luggage Van. LSWR drawings 1835/6, 2104, 2105, 2571, 2716 & 3072 , SR diagram 929.

Built	No	Ren	SR No	
(a) Drawing 1835/6, all marked for fruit:				
3/09	148	5142	1512	W 7/41 to wireless van 1623s
"	210	5192	1558	W 12/38 to mess & tool van 1362s
12/09	1	5001	1428	W 11/35
"	2	5002	1429	W 6/35 to mess & tool van 655s
"	3	5003	1430	W 11/41 to stores van 1657s
2/10	117	5116	1494	W 8/39
8/10	4	5004	1431	W 5/36 to stores van 994s
"	6	5006	1432	W 4/36 to stores van 993s
"	161	5151	1521	W 4/34 to stores van 782s
6/11	7	5007	1433	W 10/36
"	8	5008	1434	W 11/41 to stores van 1653s

24ft Special Luggage Van (continued)

Built	No	Ren	SR No	
6/11	116	5115	1493	W 2/41
"	164	5154	1523	W 3/41
"	176	5165	1534	W 5/41

(b) Drawing 2104, gas lit, either side brake:

Built	No	Ren	SR No	
10/12	115	5353	1565	W 2/41
"	137	5354	1566	W 6/40
"	144	5355	1567	W 3/37 to mess & tool van 1101s
"	156	5356	1568	W 10/36 to stores van 1071s
"	158	5357	1569	W 3/41
"	169	5358	1570	W 4/34 to stores van 769s
"	207	5359	1571	W 5/41
"	213	5360	1572	W 2/41
"	214	5361	1573	W 4/41 to wireless van 1627s
"	217	5362	1574	W 5/41
5/13		5109	1488	W 8/39 to breakdown van 1444s
"		5110	1489	W 3/39
"		5121	1498	W 10/38 to stores van 1332s
"		5128	1503	W 10/40 to yard wagon 1581s
"		5136	1509	W 7/40 to yard wagon 1566s
"		5138	1510	W 10/40
"		5148	1518	W 2/40
"		5152	1522	W 2/39
"		5166	1535	W 5/40
"		5184	1551	W 1/40 to mess & tool van 1531s
"		5188	1555	W 5/41
"		5363	1575	W 2/41
"		5364	1576	W 5/39
"		5365	1577	W 2/41
6/13		5103	1482	W 6/40
"		5113	1491	W 7/39
"		5120	1497	W 8/33
"		5123	1500	W 2/39
"		5130	1505	W 3/35 to stores van 872s
"		5155	1524	W 9/33 damaged at Victoria
10/13		5033	1459	W 7/40
"		5105	1484	W 12/38
"		5108	1487	W 10/41 to stores van 1683s
"		5112	1490	W 6/42 to wireless van 1737s
"		5124	1501	W 1/41
"		5144	1514	W 3/40 to mess & tool van 1551s
"		5158	1527	W 11/35
"		5163	1532	W 3/40 to mess & tool van 1552s
"		5170	1539	W 8/39
"		5174	1543	W 5/41
"		5177	1546	W 8/39 to breakdown van 1443s
"		5178	1547	W 4/41
"		5191	1557	W 6/41
"		5197	1562	W 10/39 to mess & tool van 1494s
"		5198	1563	W 3/40

(c) Drawings 2104, 2105 & 2571:

Built	No	Ren	SR No	
4/16		5169	1538	W 1/40 to mess & tool van 1533s
5/16		5019	1445	W 4/40
"		5104	1483	W 8/41
"		5106	1485	W 11/41 to stores van 1654s
"		5145	1515	W 11/41 to stores van 1684s
"		5164	1533	W 8/40
"		5171	1540	W 5/39
"		5173	1542	W 12/40
"		5185	1552	W 2/41
"		5187	1554	W 2/41
"		5190	1556	W 8/41
"		5193	1559	W 5/40 to stores van 1559s
6/16		5013	1439	W 1/40
"		5107	1486	W 2/41
"		5118	1496	W 3/39 to mess & tool van 1408s
"		5140	1511	W 11/41 to stores van 1658s
"		5143	1513	W 11/39
"		5167	1536	W 4/41
"		5172	1541	W 5/41
"		5183	1550	W 9/40
"		5195	1561	W 3/41

24ft Special Luggage Van (continued)

Built	No	Ren	SR No	
8/16		5017	1443	W 10/38 to stores van 1333s
"		5135	1508	W 2/41
"		5159	1528	W 3/39
"		5186	1553	W 3/40
9/16		5122	1499	W 12/40 to stores van 1586s
"		5156	1525	W 5/40 to yard wagon 1556s
"		5180	1548	W 6/40

To here were all gas lit, the remainder were oil lit

8/16		5035	1461	W 8/40 to yard wagon 1574s
"		5127	1502	W 8/40 to mess & tool van 1567s
"		5162	1531	W 5/41
9/16		5146	1516	W 5/41
"		5149	1519	W 6/40 to mess & tool van 1557s
"		5160	1529	W 12/40
"		5199	1564	W 3/41
6/17		5117	1495	W 12/40
"		5129	1504	W 1/40 to mess & tool van 1532s
"		5134	1507	W 4/41
"		5147	1517	W 2/41
"		5150	1520	W 9/33 damaged at Victoria
7/17		5047	1473	W 4/41
"		5048	1474	W 2/34
"		5114	1492	W 6/40
"		5168	1537	W 2/41
"		5176	1545	W 4/40
9/17		5016	1442	W 1/41
"		5023	1449	W 1/40 to mess & tool van 1534s
"		5025	1451	W 9/39 to Quainton Road in 1970
"		5032	1458	W 12/30
"		5037	1463	W 12/38 to mess & tool van 1364s
"		5050	1476	W 2/40
"		5131	1506	W 5/41
"		5157	1526	W 8/40
"		5175	1544	W 3/41
"		5194	1560	W 2/41
12/17		5027	1453	W 3/41
"		5039	1465	W 3/40 to mess & tool van 1555s
"		5161	1530	W 8/40
"		5181	1549	W 4/41
"		5366	1578	W 4/41
"		5367	1579	W 1/41
"		5368	1580	W 12/42
"		5369	1581	W 8/41
"		5370	1582	W 11/39
"		5371	1583	W 3/40 to mess & tool van 1554s

(d) Drawings 2105 & 3072. These twenty had 3 mid panels in place of every pair on the other vans; oil lit. All marked for fruit traffic.

6/19		5009	1435	W 11/40
"		5010	1436	W 10/40
"		5011	1437	W 10/47 to mess & tool van 1687s
6/19		5012	1438	W 12/40
"		5014	1440	W 10/40
"		5015	1441	W 3/41
"		5018	1444	W 9/41 to mess & tool van 1685s
"		5021	1447	W 4/41
7/19		5022	1448	W 11/41 to stores van 1655s
"		5024	1450	W 9/39
"		5026	1452	W 12/40 to stores van 1593s
"		5030	1456	W 3/39
"		5031	1457	W 10/40 to open ARP wagon 1745s
"		5034	1460	W 7/41 to wireless van 1622s
9/19		5036	1462	W 12/38 to mess & tool van 1363s
"		5038	1464	W 12/33
"		5041	1467	W 3/41
"		5043	1469	W 1/41
"		5044	1470	W 5/41
"		5046	1472	W 11/41 to stores van 1656s

(e) Drawing 2104 & 2105

10/20		5040	1466	W 3/40 to mess & tool van 1553s
"		5028	1454	W 1/41
"		5045	1471	W 6/39
"		5029	1455	destroyed by enemy action 10/40

24ft Special Luggage Van (continued)

Built	No	Ren	SR No	
10/20		5042	1468	W 5/41
11/20		5049	1475	W 8/39 to breakdown van 1446s
"		5070	1479	W 6/40
"		5061	1478	W 2/40
"		5052	1477	W 8/39 to breakdown van 1442s
"		5090	1481	W 10/40
12/20		5020	1446	W 6/41
"		5076	1480	W 7/40
"		5498	1584	W 9/41 to mess & tool van 1686s, condemned 6/69, to Bluebell Railway
"		5499	1585	W 8/40
"		5500	1586	W 4/41
"		5501	1587	W 5/41 to mess & tool van 1591s
"		5502	1588	W 8/39 to breakdown van 1441s
"		5503	1589	W 1/41 to stores van 104s
"		5504	1590	W 5/40
2/21		5505	1591	W 2/41
"		5506	1592	W 2/41
"		5507	1593	W 6/40
"		5508	1594	W 4/41
"		5509	1595	W 8/34 to stores van 783s
"		5511	1597	W 3/41
"		5510	1596	W 10/39 to service van 1309s
"		5512	1598	W 10/40
"		5513	1599	W 10/40
"		5514	1600	W 7/40
3/21		5515	1601	W 7/41
6/21		5516	1602	W 2/41
"		5517	1603	W 1/36 damaged at Waterloo
"		5518	1604	W 8/39 to breakdown van 1445s
"		5520	1606	W 7/41 to wireless van 1647s
7/21		5519	1605	W 11/40
8/21		5521	1607	W 1/41
"		5522	1608	W 7/41 to wireless van 1648s
"		5523	1609	W 8/40
"		5524	1610	W 8/40
"		5525	1611	W 6/41
12/23			1613	W 10/40
"			1614	W 8/40
"			1615	W 6/40
"			1616	W 6/39
"			1617	W 5/41
"			1618	W 4/41 to wireless van 1628s
"			1619	W 7/39
"			1620	W 12/40
"			1621	W 12/40
"			1622	W 12/40
"			1623	W 4/41 to wireless van 1629s
"			1624	W 4/41
"			1625	W 2/41
"			1626	W 8/40
"			1627	W 2/41
"			1628	W 7/41 to wireless van 1649s
"			1629	W 6/39 to yard wagon 1590s
"			1630	W 8/41 to wireless van 1624s
"			1631	W 11/40
"			1632	W 2/41

1.13 44ft Luggage Van (Mail and Specie). LSWR drawing 2111, SR diagram 940.

Built	No	SR No	
12/12	5341	1680	to DS 3168, 1953
"	5342	1681	to DS 105, 9/49
"	5343	1682	to DS 3007, 1949
1/13	5344	1683	grounded Eastleigh by mid-1945
"	5345	1684	to DS 3059, 1949
"	5346	1685	to DS 3170, 1950
"	5347	1686	cut up at Lancing, 5/47
"	5348	1687	to DS 1778, 1949
"	5349	1688	to DS 3179, 1950
"	5350	1689	to DS 109, 1949
"	5351	1690	to DS 1789, 1949
"	5352	1691	to DS 3203, 1953

1.14 Fruit Van sets - J sets.

(E) indicates elliptical roof. OA and OE show ciphered into a different class.

J1	32ft Brake Third (E) 28, 1310, 4727, SR 112 (W 9/30) and 34ft Third 584, 5492, SR 1672, (W 9/30)
J2	32ft Brake Third (E) 233, 1615, 4728, SR 113 (W 9/30) and ?
J3	32ft 3in Brake Third (E) 695, 1838, Fruit Brake 4729 in 5/22, SR 114 (W 9/30) and ?
J4	31ft 4in Brake Third (E) 1045, Fruit Brake 4730, SR 115 (W 9/28) and ?
J5	34ft Brake Third (E) 1367, Fruit van 4731, SR 116 (W /11/28) and ?
J6	32ft Brake Third (E) 528, 1709, Fruit van 4732 in 5/22, SR 117 (W 9/30) and ?
J7	31ft 4in Brake Third (E) 1325, Fruit Brake 4733 c.1922, SR 118 (W 9/30) and ?
J8	31ft 4in Brake Third (E) 651, Fruit Brake 4734, SR 119 (W 8/30) and ?
J9	32ft Brake Third (E) 457, Fruit Brake 4735, SR 120 (W 9/30) and ?
J10	31ft 4in Brake Third (E) 508, Fruit Brake 4736, SR 121 (W 9/28) and 30ft Third (E) 851, 5421, SR 1659, (W 9/28)
J11	29ft 6in First 0497, 5379, OE8, SR 0112 and 31'4" Third Brake (E) 187, 4737, SR 122 (W 9/30)
J12	29ft 6in First 0516 (or 0506?), 5380, OE9, SR 0114 (W 8/28) and 30ft Third 873, 2 compartment BT 873, 1910 in 7/14, Fruit Brake 4738 in 5/22, SR 123 (W 8/28)
J13	29ft 6in First 0486, 5381, OE10, SR 0118 (W 4/26) and 30ft Third 491, 3 compartment BT, 1700 in 12/15, Fruit Brake 4739 5/22, SR 124 (W 4/26)
J14	29ft 6in First 0527, 5382, OE11, SR 0115 (W 2/29) and 30ft Brake Third 1888, 4740, SR 125 (W 2/29)
J15	32ft Brake Third (E) 283, 1631, 4741, SR 126 (W 9/30)
J16	28ft Saloon 014, Fruit Brake 4706, OV101, SR 011 (W6/29) and 32ft First (lav) 045, Fruit 5378, OE7, SR 0105 (W 6/29)
J17	28ft Brake Compo 0258, 4713, OV108, SR 06 (W8/30) and 32ft Compo 0298, OE40, SR 0102 (W 8/30)
J18	31ft 4in Brake Third (E) 1356, Fruit Brake 4742, SR 127 (W 9/30) and 34ft Third 389, BT 0389, OE41, SR 0127 (W 12/25)
J19	32ft Brake Third (E) 254, 1621, 4743, SR 128 (W 9/30) and 32ft Compo 0324, OE42, SR 0103 (W 9/30)
J20	30ft Third 1354, 3 compartment BT 1354, Fruit Brake 4744, SR 129 (W 1/30) and 34ft Compo 01, OE43, SR 0121 (W 1/30)
J21	32ft Brake Third (E) 236, 1616, 4751, SR 136 (W 9/30) and (but see J31) 32ft 3in Brake Third (E)? 159, 1572, Fruit Brake 4745 in 5/22, SR 130 (W 9/30)
J22	32ft Brake Third (E) 326, 1654, 4746, SR 131 (W 9/30) and 30ft Third 201, Fruit 5451 (1921/2), SR 1664 (W 9/30)
J23	32ft Brake Third (E) 431, 1679, 4747, SR 132 (W 9/30) and ?
J24	30ft Third 285, 3 compartment BT, 1652 in 5/13? Fruit Brake 4748 c1922 SR 133 (W 4/26) and 32ft First 0114, Fruit 5415, OE36, SR 0108 (W 9/30)
J25	32ft Brake Third (E) 384, 1673, 4749, SR 134 (W 12/27) and ?
J26	34ft? OV114, SR 015 (W 2/29) and 29ft 6in First 0503, OE37, SR 0111 (W 2/29)
J27	34ft Brake Third 752, 1867, Fruit Brake 4750 in 5/22, SR 135 (W 2/29) and 29ft 6in First 0508, Fruit 5418, OE38, SR 0116 (W 2/29)
J28	28ft Brake Third 0249, 4712, OV107, SR 03 (W by 5/1922 - see J36) and 32ft First (lav) 0141, Fruit 5414, OE35, SR 0107 (W 9/30)
J29	34ft Saloon 024, 4714, OV109, SR 019 (W9/28) and 32ft First 014, OE44, SR 0109 (W 9/28)
J30	30ft Third 818?, OV115, SR 013 and 29ft 6in First 0515, Fruit 5427, OE45, SR 0117 (W 1/30)
J31	32ft First 0118, 5428, OE46, SR 0110 (W9/30) and 32ft Brake Third 236, 1616, 4751, SR 136 (W 9/30) (but see J21)
J32	30ft Third 1034, 3 compartment BT 1034, 1949 6/16, Fruit Brake 4752 5/22, SR 137 (W 2/29) and 29ft 6in First 0487, Fruit 5430, OE47, SR 0120 (W 2/29)
J33	30ft Third 850, 3 compartment BT, 1901 in 6/16, Fruit Brake 4753 5/22, SR 138 (W 9/28) and ?
J34	30ft Third, 3 compartment BT 783, 1882 in 3/16, Fruit Brake 4726 5/22, SR 111 (W 6/29) and ?
J35	30ft Third 486, Fruit 5373, SR 1644 (W 9/30) and 32ft Brake Third (E) 1357, 4709, SR 102 (W 9/30)
J36	30ft Third 907, 3 compartment BT 907, 1923 9/14, Fruit Brake 4712 5/22, SR 103 (W 9/30) and ?
J37	32ft Brake Third (E) 480, 1698, 4754, SR 139 (W 9/28) and ?
J38	32ft Brake Third (E) 341, 1662, 4755, SR 140 (W 6/29) and 30ft? OE79, SR 0132 (W 6/29).
J39	30ft Third 895, 717, Fruit 5376, OV116, SR 016 (W 9/29) and ?
J40	28ft Saloon 013, GV 4705, OV100, SR 010 (W 9/30) and 29ft 6in First 0518, Fruit 5374, OE3, SR 0113 (W 9/30)
J41	28ft Brake Compo 04, 4725, OV113, SR 09 (W 9/28) and 32ft Third OA62 (ex-Compo), OE77, SR0101 (W 9/28)
J42	30ft Third OA30, OE55, SR 0131 (W 12/28) and 30ft PBV (Caboose) 383, 4589 SR 20 (but see set J47!)
J43	34ft Third 0663, Fruit 5396, OE18, SR 0123 (W 11/26) and 30ft PBV (Caboose) 206, 4476, SR 16 (W 11/26)
J44	30ft PBV (Caboose) 350 or 352, SR 012 and 34ft Third 0662, Fruit 5397, OE19, SR 0124 (W 9/28)
J45	12/08 30ft PBV (Caboose) 368, 4578, SR 18 (W 8/28) and 34ft Third 0567, 5398, OE20, SR 0104 (W 8/28) Set formed 12/08?
J46	5/10 30ft PBV (Caboose) 370, 4580, SR 19 (W 6/29) and 34ft Third OA120 (ex-Compo), OE21, SR 0126 (W 6/27) Set formed 5/10?
J47	9/10 30ft PBV (Caboose) 383, 4589, SR 20 (W 9/28) and 30ft x 7ft 9in PBV 220, 4489, SR 17 (W 10/23)
J48	30ft PBV (Caboose) 402, 4606, SR 21 (W 6/29) and ?
J49	11/08 30ft PBV (Caboose) 409, 4608, SR 22 (W 3/30) and ?
J50	28ft Brake Compo 0252, 4709, OV104, SR 02 (W 9/30) (but see J35 - 4709) and 32ft Third OA124, OE22, SR 0134 (W 9/30)
J51	30ft Third 291, 3 compartment BT 291, 1634 6/15, Fruit Brake 4756 5/22, SR 141 (W 6/29) and ?
J52	30ft Third 892, 3 compartment BT, 1917 in 2/13, Fruit Brake 4757 5/22, SR 142 (W 9/30) and ?
J53	30ft Third 1353, 3 compartment BT 1353, Fruit Brake 4758 in 5/22, SR 143 (W 6/29) and 30ft ex-Second? OE80, SR 0129 (W 12/27)
J54	30ft Third 834, 3 compartment BT 1897 in 6/15, 4759, SR 144 (W 9/30) and ?
J55	34ft Third 763, BT 1874, Fruit Brake 4760, SR 145 (W 7/30) and 34ft Third, OE81, SR 0125 (W 7/30)
J56	30ft Third 196, 2 compartment BT 196, 1604 in 7/14, Fruit Brake 4761 in 5/22, SR 146 and ?
J57	30ft Third 876, 3 compartment BT 1911 in 12/15, Fruit Brake 4762 5/22, SR 147 (W 9/30) and ?
J58	30ft Third 913, 2 compartment BT pre-1904, 1924 7/16, Fruit Brake 4763 5/22, SR 148 (W 4/26) and ?
J59	30ft Third 886, 2 compartment BT, 1913 in 5/14, Fruit Brake 4720 10/20, SR 107 (W 1/30) and ?
J60	28ft Compo 268, Brake Compo 0268, 4724, OV112, SR 08 (W 4/26) and 34ft Third 0107, Fruit 5491, OE74, SR 0122 (W 4/26)
J61	28ft Brake Compo 0253, Fruit Brake 4707, OV102, SR 01 (W 1/28) and ?

Fruit Van sets - J sets (continued)
J62   29ft 6in First 522, Brake Compo 0168, Fruit Brake 4708, OV103, SR 014 (W 9/29) and 30ft Third OA54, OE15, SR 0133 (W 9/28)
J63   32ft Brake Third (E) 38, 1317, 4723, SR 110 (W 6/29) and ?
J64   28ft Compo 270, Brake Compo 0270, 4711, OV106, SR 05 (W9/30) and 29ft 6in First 0488, Fruit 5413, OE34, SR 0119 (W 9/30)
J65   32ft Brake Third (E) 303, 1640, 4721, SR 108 (W 12/27) and ?
J66   28ft Compo 269, Brake Compo 0269, 4718, OV111, SR 07 (W9/28) and ?
J67   34ft BT 709, 1845, Fruit Brake 4719 in 10/20, SR 106 (W 9/30) and ?
J68   30ft Third 904, 2 compartment BT pre 1904, 1920 7/13, Fruit Brake 4722 10/20, SR 109 (W 1/30) and ?
J69   34ft (but rebuilt) Saloon 022, 4715, OV110, SR 018 (W6/29) and ?
J70   30ft Third 274, 2 compartment BT, to body 463, Fruit Brake 4717 10/20, BR 106 and J III Third OA70 (ex Compo), OE60, BR 0128 (W 7/30)
J71   28ft Compo 263, Brake Third 0263, 4710, OV105, SR 04 (W 9/28) and 32ft First 52, OE28, SR 0106 (W 9/28)

The following sets were formed in 1925:
J72   34ft Third 758, Brake Third 2 compartment 1870, SR 020 (W 9/30) and 30ft (ex-Second) Third OA22, SR 0139 (W 9/30)
J73   32ft? 1614, SR 021 (W 9/30) and 30ft Third 413, 413, SR 0140 (W 9/30)
J74   31ft 4in Brake Third 3 compartment (E)? 246, 246, SR 022 (W 9/30) and 30ft Third 190, 190, SR 0141 (W 9/30)

T9 No 337 with 48ft fruit brake van at Petersfield.   *(J Minnis Collection)*

APPENDIX TO CHAPTER 2 - POST OFFICE VANS

All vehicles are 8ft 0¾in wide unless otherwise stated. "$" indicates a "bulge" on one side to accommodate a "newspaper set", the 1912 Register shows the overall width of these as 8ft 6in but the SR diagrams show them as 8ft 6⅞in. All shown at 1923 as gas-lit. IG indicates conversion from plain to incandescent lights. All built at Eastleigh, unless otherwise stated, Wr = built by Wrights. Widths of 7ft 11in are from 1904 Register, diagrams show 8ft 0¾in.

No	Size	Drawing No	Built	Ren	SR No	
1	20ft 4in (?)		Wr 1862	-	-	W late 1899. Noted as on Portsmouth - Southampton service in 1882.
1	48ft	876/880	11/99	5601	4912	IG 11/1910, Chain comm. 11/04, st.ht.8/09, 21T 19C 2Q, £600 central gangways replaced by side ones 7/1913, to Stowage van 1/24, W 8/40, body grounded Exmouth Jcn.
2	20ft 4in x7ft 7½in		Wr 1862	-	-	BU 1900 £487 18 4d
2	44ft (8ft 6in $)	749/755/936	10/00	5602	4906	IG 6/11, Chain comm. 11/03, st.ht.5/09, 21T 9C 0Q. Side gangways both ends, on u/f ex-SECR First 2360 9/36. W 10/43 to 1887s. Restored 3/44, gangways removed some time ?, W 1/55.
3	20ft (or 20ft 4in ?)		Wr 1863			Post Office owned. In 1895 it was Exeter-Barnstaple Bag Tender. Worn out and withdrawn 4/1900, replaced by No 9.
3	44ft (8ft 6in $)	1350/1428-30	11/05	5603	4917	IG 11/11, st.ht.11/09, 21T 6C 0Q. Side gangways. U/f replaced ex-4907 ex-No 4) 11/37. W 12/40, body grounded Redhill. PO owned.
4			?			Converted from a Third in 1866. W 1892 ?
4	44ft (8ft 6in $)	464,618,2250	5/92	5604	4907	IG 11/11, chain comm. 9/02, st.ht. 7/09, 21T 19C 1Q, £586 18 7d. Side gangway fitted after 10/1912 to 1 end only. New u/f ex-SECR Compo 3451, SR 5243 in 1936, W 11/37 u/f to 4917.
5			?			Converted from a Third in 1866. W 1892 ?
5	32ft (8ft 6in $)	DB96,619,2305	12/92	5605	4901	IG 1/08, chain comm. 7/03, st.ht.8/09, 12T 11C 1Q, £465, close-coupled to No 12 in NRM photo in VR period, but to be permanently coupled to No 11 by Minute of 10/1912. Later central gangway sealed. W 11/33 grounded Eastleigh.
6	32ft	DB96	12/81	5606	(4902)	IG 3/09, chain comm. 12/03, st.ht.11/07, £501.4.6d. W 2/28 (Craven)
7	32ft	DB96	12/81	5607	(4903)	IG 3/09, chain comm. 12/03, st.ht.11/07, 14T 1C 1Q, £501.4.6d. W 1/28
8	32ft x 7ft 11in	DB96	5/86	5608	4904	IG 12/11, chain comm. 10/03, st.ht.4/09, 12T 13C 3Q, £432 1 7d, Central gangway and normally coupled to No 12, according to post-1912 Register. Gangway later removed. W 7/31 to M&T 566s.
9	32ft x 7ft 11in	DB96A	6/89	5609	(4905)	IG 5/09, chain comm. 9/05, st.ht.10/07, 12T 12C 3Q, £417.11.7d. Gangway one end only on SR diagram W 2/28.
10	32ft x 7ft 11in	(DB96 ?)	1890	-	-	Chain comm. 1/04, £417.11.7d, Destroyed by fire at Clapham Jcn 30.5.1904. (probably identical to No 9 ?), remains rebuilt to 44ft No 10.
10	44ft (8ft 6in $)	1326/30/33	(10/04)	5610	4908	IG, st.ht.11/09, 21T 13C 3Q, £667 9s 10d. Side gangway both ends. Rebuilt from 32ft No 10. Either side brake 1926. New u/f 4/38 ex- ??, W 8/39
11	44ft (8ft 6in $)	617	10/91	5611	4909	IG 10/11, chain comm. 11/02, st.ht.11/09, 21T 5C 1Q, £629.12.9d, lav. fitted and close-coupled to No 5 after 10/1912, central gangway, (not shown on SR diagram). W 7/33
12	44ft	146	12/92	5612	4910	IG 12/11, chain comm. 12/04, st.ht.6/09, £561.15.11d. NRM photo in VR period shows close-coupled to No 5 with central gangway, then normally coupled to No 8 according to post-1912 Register. Gangways altered from centre to side after 7/1913. To stowage 11/23. New u/f ex-SECR First No 2334 (SR 7292) in 1936. W 11/39
13	44ft (8ft 6in $)	749,755,936	10/98	5613	4911	IG, chain comm. 10/03, fire damaged 1904 but rebuilt. St.ht. (overhead pipes) 3/09, £718.14.6d. Side gangways both ends. Lav added 1937. W 5/39 to 1448s. At Wimbledon in emergency control train.
	56ft x 8ft 6¾in	2191	6/13	5614	4918	IG 6/13 & st.ht. Side gangways both ends. W 10/43 to 1890s, PO owned.
	56ft x 8ft 6¾in	2302/28	3/14	5615	4916	Parcel sorter. IG, st.ht. Side gangways both ends. 26T 2C 2Q, W ?

Ex-Fruit Brake vans, converted to Stowage Vans in 1915 with side gangways at both ends:

No	Size	Drawing No	Built	Ren	SR No	
	48ft x 9ft 1in	2622	1/99	5616	4913	IG. Converted ex-503 , W 8/40, grounded Exmouth Jcn. St.ht. overhead pipes 11/35?. 21T 0C 2Q
	48ft x 9ft 1in	2622	1/99	5617	4914	IG. Converted ex-507, W 8/40, grounded Exmouth Jcn. St.ht. overhead pipes 11/15. 19T 17C 2Q
	48ft x 9ft 1in	2622	1/99	5618	4915	IG. Converted ex-508, W 2/40. St.ht. overhead pipes 11/15. 20T 4C 2Q

Post Office ref. Post 18/21. Roster for October 1903.

BT = Bag Tender, LS = Letter Sorting Van, PS = Parcel Sorting Van,   L&PS = Combined Letter and Parcel Sorting Van.

Service		No	Built	Length (feet)	Use	Gangways	Remarks
Barnstaple - Exeter Bag Tender (daily)							
Barnstaple & Exeter Mail	*The Torrington & Mail*						
Exeter dep 3.10am	Torrington dep 7.40pm	9	1889	32	BT	Rear end	
Barnstaple arr 5.7am	Barnstaple arr 8.14pm						No 9 is fitted with letter sorting boxes.
Torrington arr 6.10am	Barnstaple dep 8.20pm						
	Exeter arr 9.49pm						
Portsmouth Sorting Carriages (daily)							
Portsmouth dep 10.48pm	Southampton dep 1.0am	5	1892	32	LS	Fore end	1 running, 1 spare at Eastleigh
Southampton arr 12.7am	Portsmouth arr 2.13am	8	1886	32	LS	Fore end	
		12	1892	44	PS	Rear end	1 running, 1 spare at Eastleigh
		1	1899	48	PS	Rear end	
Portsmouth - Eastleigh Bag duty (daily)							
Portsmouth dep 12.20am							One end of an ordinary guard's van is used, the other end is used for the Guard and Company's luggage.
Eastleigh arr 1.4am							
South Western TPO Day Mail (except Sundays and Bank Holidays)							
Waterloo dep 5.50am	Dorchester dep 12.32pm						
Dorchester arr 10.7am	Waterloo arr 5.51pm	4	1892	44	L&PS		One running, one spare at Clapham Junction.
		11	1891	44	L&PS		
South Western TPO Night Mail (daily)							
Waterloo dep 9.0pm (Sundays 8.30pm)	Dorchester dep 10.14pm	2	1900	44	L&PS	Both ends	
Dorchester arr 2.33am	Waterloo arr 3.33am	6	1881	32	L&PS	Both ends	
		7	1881	32	L&PS	Both ends	4 running, 1 spare at Clapham Junction.
Waterloo (supplementary) dep 9.58pm		10	1890	32	L&PS	Fore end	
Basingstoke arr 10.42pm		13	1898	44	L&PS	Both ends	
Thence with 9pm TPO to Dorchester							

These carriages on parcel sorting duty only between Southampton and Dorchester.

Bournemouth & Brockenhurst Bag duty (daily) - Conveys Letter Mails							
Bournemouth dep 11.10pm	Brockenhurst dep 1.5am						An ordinary luggage van is used.
Brockenhurst arr 11.43pm	Bournemouth arr 1.39am						

Note: SW TPO Night Mail. The 9.58 departure was the original, running fast to Basingstoke. The 9pm was really the supplementary, stopping at various stations to Basingstoke.

APPENDIX TO CHAPTER 3 - AMBULANCE CARRIAGES

Part 1 – Conversions of Vehicles to Ambulance Trains

3.1 War Office Ambulance Train of 1900.
Five 48ft Fruit Vans, LSWR Nos 234, 242, 245, 247 and 274 were converted into War Office ambulance carriages Nos 1 to 5. Normally kept at Netley Hospital.

3.2 Home Ambulance Train No 10 of 1914.

44ft Passenger Brake Vans Nos 4377, 4547, 4555, 4557, 4646, 4651, 4653.
46ft 6in Brake Third No 1451.
50ft Double Saloon No 4120.

3.3 Home Ambulance Train No 21 of November 1915.

44ft Passenger Brake Vans Nos 4361, 4405, 4442, 4450, 4502, 4518, 4649.
46ft 6in Brake Third No 1450.
46ft 6in Composite No 3095.
48ft Kitchen Brake Van No 4689.

It is not possible to identify which of these PBVs was converted to which purpose.

Part 2 – Carriages Used in CAT No 35 and US Ambulance Train No 62

3.4 Continental Ambulance Train No 35. Formed 10/1917. The formation of vehicles in this train is not recorded.

1912 BTK No	Function	PBV No	SR No	
(a) Built 1906/7 as Brake Thirds to drawing 1487. Rebuilt by LSWR as PBVs, LSWR drawing 3499. SR diagram 869.				
1396	Ward B	4330	319	W 1/45, to 195s
1397	Ward C	4335	320	W 5/41, to Stores van 17s
1398	Ward D	4342	321	W 10/40, to Stores van 1573s
1399	Ward ?	4349	322	W 3/41, destroyed by enemy action
1400	Ward L	4351	323	W 4/46
1401	Ward ?	4354	324	W 12/44, to Stores van 190s
1402	Ward N	4360	325	W 12/44, to Stores van 191s
1403	Ward O	4365	326	W 5/46
(b) Built 1904-1910 as Thirds to drawing 1226 etc				
143	Kitchen A	-	669	W 9/52
144	?	-	670	W 7/50
139	Infectious P ?	-	675	W 9/54
(c) Built 1908 as Brake Thirds to drawing 1569, rebuilt as PBVs by LSWR on return, LSWR drawing 3510. SR diagram 870.				
1465	Infectious P ?	4367	328	W 7/50, to Yard Wagon DS 3177
1466	Ward T	4366	327	W 1/45, to Mess & Tool van 223s, cut up 4/57
1467	Kitchen H	4382	329	W 11/46
(d) Built 1907-1910 as Brake Third to drawing 1568, rebuilt as PBV by LSWR on return, LSWR drawing 3499. SR diagram 871.				
1475	Personnel R	4387	330	W 11/45

3.5 United States Ambulance Train No 62. Formed in 4/1918.

Although listed here in LSWR number order they were marshalled in the train as A10/6201, B/6202, D1/6203, Ward A1/6204, Ward A2/6205, Ward A3/6206, Ward A4/6207, Pharmacy F/6208, Ward A5/6209, A6/6210, Ward A7/6211, Ward A8/6212, Ward A9/6213, Kitchen & Mess D2/6214, Personnel C/6215, Brake & Stores van E/6216.

1912 TK No	Ambulance No	Function	SR PBV No	
(a) Built 1904-1910 as Thirds to drawings 1226 and 1872.			LSWR drawing 3499, SR diagram 869	
107	6210	Ward A6	339	W 8/47
108	6203	Kitchen D1	332	W 10/42 destroyed by enemy action.
123	6214	Kitchen & Mess D2	343	LSWR drawing 3511, SR diagram 871 W 3/46
126	6211	Ward A7	340	W 3/46
142	6202	Staff car B		Probably used briefly for Naval Ambulance Train., then restored to be SR Third 744.
205	6212	Ward A8	341	W 3/52
655	6209	Ward A5	338	W 4/46, to Yard Wagon 170s
668	6213	Ward A9	342	W 3/46
(b) Built 1908 as Brake Third to drawing 1569.			LSWR drawing 3510, SR diagram 870.	
1464	6216	Brake & Stores van	345	W 4/47, to Stores van 447s, cut up 7/61
(c) Built 1907-1910 as Brake Thirds to drawing 1568.			LSWR drawing 3511, SR diagram 871.	
1404	6207	Ward A4	336	W 10/40 destroyed in air raid at Clapham Jcn.
1405	6208	Pharmacy F	337	W 4/46
1474	6206	Ward A3	335	W 5/40 after damage at Clapham Jcn.
1479	6215	Personnel car C	344	W 12/44
1523	6204	Ward A1	333	W 3/46 (seen as Exhibition van in 4/44)
1524	6201	Brake & Infectious car A10	331	W 11/46
1741	6205	Ward A2	334	W 3/46

3.6 This number refers to the drawings and photos of the four variations of vans converted from carriages listed in 3.4 and 3.5 above.

APPENDIX TO CHAPTER 4 - HORSE BOXES AND CARRIAGE TRUCKS

Any LSWR or SR number shown in brackets was allocated but probably not painted on before the next re-numbering or withdrawal.
B = broken up, W = withdrawn, C = cyphered, P = vacuum piped, WP = Westinghouse piped.

4.1 Horse Boxes of Unknown Dimensions.

Built	No	Disposal
?	12	B 1875
?	18	B 1875
?	19	B 1875
1858	62	W pre-4/99 (built at Nine Elms) AVB 1882
1858	64	W pre-6/98 (built at Nine Elms) AVB 1882

4.2 14ft 2in Horse Box of 1861. No numbering known.

4.3 14ft 2in x 7ft 9½in Horse Box. (40 built by Metropolitan and numbered 96 to 135 inclusive.)

Built	No	Disposal (W pre-xxx is stated because a replacement of that number was built at that date.)
1864	99	W pre-12/98, AVB in ?
"	107	W pre-11/95, AVB in 1882
1865	110	W pre-4/96 " "
"	112	W pre-11/99 " "
"	120	W pre-12/92 " "
"	132	W pre-6/97 " "

4.4 19ft 10in Hounds Van. Probably the only one built.

Built	No	Disposal
1865	1	C 12/08 £278 6s 0d.

4.5 15ft 6in x 7ft 10in Horse Box. LSWR drawing 2218.
The entries with a question mark are not shown in LSWR records but have been assumed to be of this type.

Built	No	Disposal
1877	12	B 6/01 £209 6s 6d
"	19	B 6/01 "
"	20	B 6/01 "
"	154	B 6/02
"	155	B 6/01
"	156	B 12/00
1877 ?	157	W pre-4/00
"	158	B 6/02
"	159	B 12/00
1877 ?	160	W pre-6/97
"	161	B 12/01
"	162	B 12/00
"	163	B 12/01
"	164	B 12/00
"	165	B 12/02
"	166	B 6/02
"	167	B 6/01
"	168	B 12/00
" ?	169	W pre-12/96
"	170	B 12/01
"	171	B 12/00
"	172	B 12/00
" ?	173	W pre-5/00
"	174	B 12/01
"	175	B 12/00
"	176	B 12/00
" ?	177	W pre-10/97
" ?	178	W pre-3/00
"	179	B 12/00
"	180	B 12/00
"	181	B 12/01
"	182	B 6/02
"	183	B 12/00
"	184	B ?
"	185	B 12/00
1881	13	B 6/04
"	14	B 12/05

4.6 16ft x 7ft 10in Horse Box. LSWR drawings not known.

Built	No	Disposal
1877	34	B 12/00 £209 6s 6d
"	43	B 12/00
1881	4	B 12/05
"	5	B 6/05
"	9	B 6/04
"	28	B 6/04
"	29	B 6/05
"	30	B 12/03
"	32	B 6/06
"	33	B 12/03
"	199	B 6/03

4.7 16ft x 7ft 10in Horse Box. LSWR drawing 4214.

(It is possible that this drawing equates with DB 86, see next section for DB86A.) These were fitted with vacuum brake through pipes and a single lever handbrake working on one wheel.

Built	No	Disposal
1884	187	B 12/06
"	188	B 6/02
"	189	B 12/06
"	190	B 6/07
"	191	B 6/05
"	192	B 6/06
"	193	B 12/05
"	194	B 12/06
"	195	B 12/05
"	196	B 6/07
"	197	B 12/07
"	198	B 12/02
"	200	B 6/05
"	201	B 6/07
"	202	B 6/07
"	203	B 6/03
"	204	B 12/06
"	205	B 6/06
"	206	B 6/03
1884	207	B 6/05
"	208	B 12/03
"	209	B 6/06
"	210	B 12/05

(total 23, out of 24 ordered 10/83)

The following were probably built to the same design though not recorded as such:

Built	No	Disposal
1885	25	B 12/07
"	26	B 12/07 P 1/92
"	54	B 6/06
"	74	B 6/07
"	93	B 12/06
"	124	B 12/07

Note : All of the following 16ft Horse boxes, although to different drawings and with two distinctly different types of top doors, were similar enough in the essential dimensions to be grouped together by the Southern Railway under diagram 1000. All were built with oil lighting and with a single handbrake lever.

4.8 16ft x 7ft 10in Horse Box. LSWR drawing DB86A.

This is probably a revision of DB86 which might be the same as drawing 4214 above. All vacuum piped and fitted with a single handbrake lever working on one wheel.

Built	No	Ren	SR No	Disposal
x/87	48	048	0201 (2859)	W 7/26
"	49	5699		W 2/18 AVB and WP
"	76	5726	2564	W 6/31 AVB and WP 3/92
"	212	5862		sold 10/21 to Mr Pearce, Camelford WP 1/92
"	213	5863	2677	W 2/31 WP 2/92
"	214	5863		B 1918
"	215	5864		B 2/18
"	217	5866		B 7/17
"	218	5867	2678	W 7/28

16ft x 7ft 10in Horse box (continued)

Built	No	Ren	SR No	Disposal
x/87	219	5868		B 6/15
"	220	5869		sold 10/18 to Mr Sturdy, Wareham WP 1/92
"	221	5870		B 5/16
"	222	5871		B 2/18
"	223	5872		sold 2/19 to Mr Sturdy, Wareham
"	224	5873	2679	W 8/30 WP 1/92
"	225	5874	(2680)	W 8/28
"	226	5875		B 7/19
"	229	5878	(2681)	W 1/23
"	230	5879	(2682)	W 9/28 WP 4/90
"	231	5880	(2683)	W 7/26
"	232			C 6/08
"	233			C 6/08
"	234	5883	(2684)	W 12/28
"	235	5884	2685	W 7/28
"	236	5885		B 5/20
"	237	5886		Sold 5/19 to Mr Sturdy, Wareham
"	238	5887		B 2/18
"	239	5888	2857	?
"	240	5889		B 5/20
x/88	85			C 12/07
2/88	55	5705	2544	W 5/33 WP ?

4.9   16ft x 7ft 10in Horse Box.   LSWR drawing 314.

(All vacuum piped with one side handbrake working on one wheel)

Built	No	Ren	SR No	Disposal
9/92	241	5890		B 7/17
"	242	5891		B 10/21
"	243	5892		Sold 2/19 to Mr Sturdy, Wareham
"	244	5893	2686	W 6/33
"	245	5894		B 7/17
"	246	5895		B 11/21
"	247	5896	(2687)	W 1/28
"	248	5897		Sold 10/17 to Mr Sturdy, Wareham
"	253	5902	2691	W 5/29
"	254	5903	(2692)	W 4/28
10/92	249	5898	(2688)	W 7/28
"	250	5899	2689	W 12/28
"	251	5900	2690	W 8/30
"	252			B 1910
"	255	5904	(2693)	W 3/29
"	256	5905	(2694)	W 1/24
"	257	5906	(2695)	W 9/27
"	258	5907		Sold 5/20 to Mr Worrall, Chichester
"	259	5908	2696	W 8/30
"	260	5909	(2697)	W 4/28
"	261	5910		B 10/17
"	263	5912	2699	W 9/29
"	264	5913	2700	W 1/30
11/92	262	5911	(2698)	W 1/25
"	265	5914	(2701)	W 7/28
2/93	266	5915	(2702)	W 1/28
"	267	5916	2703	W 2/37
"	268	5917	(2704)	W x/23
"	269	5918	(2705)	W 2/28
4/93	272	5921	(2707)	W 5/24
"	273	5922		B 9/16
"	274	5923		B 3/18
"	275	5924	2708	W 2/33
"	276	5925		Sold 10/18 to Mr Sturdy, Wareham
"	277	5926		B 2/18
5/93	270	5919	(2706)	W 9/28
"	271	5920		B 5/17
6/93	278	5927	(2709)	W 8/26
"	279	5928	(2710)	W x/23
"	280	5929		B 12/13
"	281	5930	2711	W 7/32
"	282	5931	2712	W 2/31
"	283	5932	(2713)	W 3/30
"	284	5933	(2714)	W 1/28
"	285	5934	(2715)	W 10/25

16ft x 7ft 10in Horse box (continued)

Built	No	Ren	SR No	Disposal
6/93	286	5935	(2716)	W x/23
"	287	5936	(2717)	W x/23
"	288	5937		B 10/21
"	289	5938	2718	W 11/33
"	290	5939	2719	W 2/33

4.10   16ft x 7ft 10in Horse Box.

Built	No	Ren	SR No	Disposal

(a) LSWR drawings 637 and 730 (AVB with skew brake rigging, single lever handbrake). Those built before 4/96 may have been built to drawing 314, piped only, but later fully AVB fitted, thus becoming equivalent to drawing 637, which was issued about 3/1896.

Built	No	Ren	SR No	Disposal	
7/92	47	5697	(2540)	W 7/28	WP
12/92	120	5770	2605	W 5/32	
6/93	1	5651	2501	W 4/31	WP
"	87	5737	2574	W 2/33	
12/93	82	5732	2570	W 2/33	
"	125	5775	2609	W 3/30	
8/94	68	5718	2557	W ?	
"	84	5734	2572	W 2/33	WP
"	98	5748	2584	W 5/34	
12/94	36	5686	2529	W 3/34	WP
"	59	5709	2548	W 6/32	WP
"	119	5769	(2604)	W 1/25	WP
"	130	5780	2614	W 2/33	WP
"	137	5787	2621	W 7/31	WP
6/95	7	5657	2505	W 9/30	WP
"	21	5671	2518	W ?	
"	52	5702	2542	W 2/33	WP
"	69	5719	2558	W 2/33	
"	128	5778	2612	W 2/33	
11/95	44	5694	2537	W 3/34	
"	97	5747	2583	W 9/33	
"	107	5757	2593	W 8/33	
"	139	5789	2623	W 2/33	WP
4/96	106	5756	2592	W 8/31	
"	110	5760	2596	W 5/33	
"	144	5794	2628	W 2/31	
"	148	5798	2632	W ?	
5/96	83	5733	2571	W 12/28	
12/96	2	5652	2502	W ?	
"	24	5674	2521	W 6/34	WP
"	41	5691	(2534)	W 7/28	
"	77	5727	2565	W 2/33	
"	103	5753	2589	W 8/37	
"	105	5755	2591	W 6/32	WP
"	149	5799	2633	W 9/33	
"	150	5800	2634	W ?	
"	169	5819	2653	W 1/31	
6/97	15	5665	2512	W ?	
"	40	5690	2533	W 2/33	
"	57	5707	2546	W ?	
"	61	5711	2550	W ?	
"	63	5713	2552	W ?	
"	67	5717	2556	W 2/32	
"	91	5741	2578	W 6/32	
"	116	5766	2602	W 6/32	
"	126	5776	2610	W ?	
"	127	5777	2611	W 2/37	
"	129	5779	2613	W 6/32	WP
"	132	5782	2616	W ?	
6/97	135	5785	2619	W ?	
"	160	5810	2644	W ?	WP
10/97	70	5720	2559	W 2/32	
"	71	5721	2560	W 2/33	
"	72	5722	2561	W 2/33	
"	94	5744	2580	W 2/33	
"	114	5764	2600	W 8/31	
10/97	131	5781	2615	W 2/33	
"	140	5790	2624	W 2/33	
"	146	5796	2630	W 4/32	
"	147	5797	2631	W ?	
"	177	5827	2661	W ?	WP
2/98	17	5667	2514	W 7/32	

16ft x 7ft 10in Horse box (continued)

Built	No	Ren	SR No	Disposal
2/98	60	5710	2549	W ?
"	145	5795	2629	W 4/34
4/98	75	5725	2563	W 2/33 WP
"	100	5750	2586	W 2/33
"	108	5758	2594	W 7/33 WP
"	136	5786	2620	W 3/32
5/98	95	5745	2581	W ? WP
6/98	8	5658	2506	W 2/33
"	31	5681	2525	W ?
"	53	5703	2543	W 10/31
"	81	5731	2569	W 2/33
"	101	5751	2587	W 2/34
"	115	5765	2601	W 5/31
"	134	5784	2618	W 2/33
"	121	5771	(2606)	W 7/28
"	122	5772	2607	W ?
"	123	5773	2608	W 5/34
"	142	5792	2626	W 6/32
"	152	5802	2636	W 6/32
"	153	5803	(2637)	W 10/25 WP
"	186	5836	2670	W 7/32
8/98	64	5714	2553	W 2/33
12/98	78	5728	2566	W ? WP
"	86	5736	2573	W ?
"	99	5749	2585	W 6/32
"	102	5752	2588	W 8/31
"	104	5754	2590	W 6/52
"	151	5801	2635	W ? WP
4/99	18	5668	2515	W 2/33 WP
"	23	5673	2520	W 7/34
"	27	5677	2522	W 2/33
"	62	5712	2551	W 5/31
5/99	66	5716	2555	W 2/33
"	79	5729	(2567)	W 7/28
"	90	5740	(2577)	W 7/28
6/99	109	5759	2595	W 9/30
"	143	5793	2627	W ?
9/99	3	5653	2503	W 2/33
"	35	5685	2528	W ?
"	42	5692	2535	W 4/39
"	46	5696	2539	W 10/31
"	58	5708	2547	W ?
12/99	133	5783	2617	W ?

(b) LSWR drawings 637 and 780 (AVB with straight brake rigging, single lever handbrake.)

Built	No	Ren	SR No	Disposal
12/98	291	5940	2720	W ?
"	292	5941	2721	W ?
"	293	5942	2722	W 9/37
"	294	5943	2723	W 6/52
"	295	5944	2724	W 9/37
1/99	296	5945	2725	W ?
"	297	5946	2726	W 6/52
"	298	5947	2727	W ?
"	299	5948	2728	W ?
"	300	5949	2729	W ?
"	304	5953	2733	W 11/29
"	305	5954	2734	W ?
"	306	5955	2735	W 6/32
"	307	5956	2736	W 8/31
"	308	5957	2737	W 7/32
"	309	5958	2738	W ?
"	310	5959	2739	W ?
"	311	5960	2740	W ?
"	312	5961	2741	W 6/52
"	313	5962	2742	W ?
"	314	5963	2743	W ?
"	315	5964	2744	W ?
"	321	5970	2750	W 6/52
"	322	5971	2751	W ?
"	323	5972	2752	W ?
"	324	5973	2753	W 4/32
"	325	5974	2754	W 8/38
2/99	301	5950	2730	W 4/32

16ft x 7ft 10in Horse box (continued)

Built	No	Ren	SR No	Disposal
2/99	302	5951	2731	W ?
"	303	5952	2732	W ?
"	316	5965	2745	W ?
"	317	5966	2746	W 2/31
"	318	5967	2747	W ?
"	319	5968	2748	W ?
"	320	5969	2749	W 8/31
"	326	5975	2755	W ?
"	327	5976	2756	W 6/32
"	328	5977	2757	W 2/30
"	329	5978	2758	W ?
"	330	5979		B 9/21
"	337	5986	2765	W 6/32
"	338	5987	2766	W ?
"	339	5988	2767	W ?
"	340	5989	(2768)	W 7/28
3/99	331	5980	2759	W 6/52
"	332	5981	2760	W 5/30
"	333	5982	2761	W 1/34
"	334	5983	2762	W ?
"	335	5984	2763	W 6/25
"	336	5985	2764	W ?

(c) LSWR drawings 892 and 780 (AVB with straight brake rigging, single lever handbrake.)

Built	No	Ren	SR No	Disposal
11/91	141	5791	2625	W 8/31 WP (The build date must be a clerical error or it is a rebuilt vehicle)
11/99	11	5661	2509	W 2/33
"	50	5700	2541	W ?
"	92	5742	2579	W ? WP
"	111	5761	2597	W ?
"	112	5762	2598	W ?
"	113	5763	2599	W ? WP
"	118	5768	2603	W 2/33
"	138	5788	2622	W 6/32
"	184	5834	2668	W 11/31 WP
3/00	22	5672	2519	W ?
"	65	5715	2554	W ?
"	89	5739	2576	W 7/32
"	96	5746	2582	W ?
"	178	5828	2662	W 7/31
4/00	6	5656	(2504)	W 2/26
"	16	5666	2513	W ?
"	88	5738	2575	W ?
"	157	5807	2641	W 6/52
5/00	10	5660	2508	W ?
"	45	5695	2538	W ?
"	56	5706	2545	W ?
"	80	5730	2568	W ?
"	173	5823	2657	W ?
6/00	183	5833	2667	W 6/32
10/00	43	5693	2536	W ?
12/00	34	5684	2527	W 6/32
"	156	5806	2640	W 5/32
"	159	5809	2643	W after 1946
"	162	5812	2646	W 3/32 WP
"	164	5814	2648	W ?
"	168	5818	2652	W ? WP
"	171	5821	2655	W ?
"	172	5822	2656	W 11/31
12/00	175	5825	2659	W 6/32 WP
"	176	5826	2660	W ? WP
"	179	5829	2663	W 4/31 WP
"	180	5830	2664	W 11/30 WP
"	185	5835	2669	W ?
6/01	12	5662	2510	W 7/32
"	19	5669	2516	W ?
"	20	5670	2517	W 3/34
"	155	5805	2639	W ?
"	167	5817	2651	W 4/36
10/01	161	5811	2645	W 6/31 WP
"	163	5813	2647	W ?
"	170	5820	2654	W ?
"	174	5824	2658	W ? WP
"	181	5831	2665	W ?

16ft x 7ft 10in Horse box (continued)

Built	No	Ren	SR No	Disposal
All vehicles of 1902 are recorded as fitted with Bartrum's patent tethering apparatus				
1/02	341	5990	2769	W ? WP
"	342	5991	2770	W ? WP
"	343	5992	2771	W ? WP
"	344	5993	2772	W ? WP
"	345	5994	2773	W ? WP
2/02	346	5995	2774	W ? WP
"	347	5996	2775	W ? WP
"	348	5997	2776	W ? WP
"	349	5998	2777	W ? WP
"	350	5999	2778	W after 1947 P, dual brakes 8/06

(d) LSWR drawings 1085/780 (AVB with straight brake rigging, Westinghouse piped, single lever handbrake)

Built	No	Ren	SR No	Disposal
3/02	351	6000	2779	W ?
"	352	6001	2780	W ? dual brakes 8/06
"	353	6002	2781	W 6/32 dual brakes 8/06
"	354	6003	2782	W 7/31 dual brakes ?
"	355	6004	2783	W ?
4/02	356	6005	2784	W ?
"	357	6006	2785	W ?
"	358	6007	2786	W ? dual brakes 8/06
"	359	6008	2787	W ?
"	360	6009	2788	W 2/32
5/02	361	6010	2789	W ?
"	362	6011	2790	W ?
"	363	6012	2791	W ?
"	364	6013	2792	W ? dual brakes 9/06
"	365	6014	2793	W after 1947
6/02	54	5804	2638	W ?
"	158	5808	2642	W 6/32
"	166	5816	2650	W after 1947
6/02	182	5832	2666	W 2/32
10/02	165	5815	2649	W ?
"	188	5838	2671	W ?
"	198	5848	2672	W ?
"	366	6015	2794	W ?
"	367	6016	2795	W ?
11/02	368	6017	2796	W after 1945
"	369	6018	2797	W after 1945
"	370	6019	2798	W ?
"	371	6020	2799	W ? P, dual brakes ?
"	372	6021	2800	W ?
"	373	6022	2801	W ? P, dual brakes 12/06
"	374	6023	2802	W ?
"	375	6024	2803	W ?
12/02	376	6025	2804	W ? P, dual brakes 9/06
"	377	6026	2805	W ?
"	378	6027	2806	W 5/37
"	379	6028	2807	W ?
"	380	6029	2808	W ?
"	381	6030	2809	W ? P, dual brakes ?
"	382	6031	2810	W 7/31
"	383	6032	2811	W 2/32
"	384	6033	2812	W ?
"	385	6034	2813	W ?
"	386	6035	2814	W ? P, dual brakes ?
"	387	6036	2815	W ?
"	388	6037	2816	W ?
"	389	6038	2817	W ? P, dual brakes ?
"	390	6039	2818	W ? P, dual brakes ?
5/03	199	5849	2673	W ?
"	203	5853	2674	W ?
"	206	5856	2675	W ?
12/03	30	5680	2524	W ?
"	33	5683	2526	W ?
"	208	5858	2676	W ?
6/04	9	5659	2507	W ? dual brakes
"	13	5663	(2511)	W 10/24 dual brakes
"	28	5678	2523	W ? dual brakes
"	73	5723	2562	W ? dual brakes

4.11   21ft Horse Box. LSWR drawings 1364 (and 1371 for u/f), 1401, 1953/4. SR diagram 1001.

All dual braked and oil lit. Approximate withdrawal dates derived by Glen Woods from Carriage Working Notices.

Built	No	Ren	SR No	Disposal
(a) Drawings 1364 & 1371				
6/05	191	5841	2836	late 1954
"	200	5850	2843	mid 1950
"	207	5857	2848	mid 1954
12/05	4	5654	2820	mid 1954 altered to Hearse van 6/16
	5	5655	2821	W 1/51 Gas lit 11/17
"	14	5664	2822	mid 1950
"	29	5679	2825	W 2/50 Gas lit 11/12
"	193	5843	2838	late 1948
"	195	5845	2840	mid 1949
"	210	5860	2850	mid 1954
5/06	32	5682	2826	W 10/53
"	54	5704	2828	W 10/56
"	192	5842	2837	W 12/55 or 12/56, records differ.
"	205	5855	2847	mid 1950
"	209	5859	2849	W 5/57
12/06	93	5743	2831	W 6/57
"	187	5837	2833	late 1954
"	189	5839	2834	late 1950
"	194	5844	2839	mid 1952
"	204	5854	2846	W 9/52
6/07	74	5724	2829	W 11/54
"	190	5840	2835	late 1951
"	196	5846	2841	late 1954
"	201	5851	2844	W 7/59
"	202	5852	2845	W 5/53
12/07	25	5675	2823	late 1956
"	26	5676	2824	W 5/56
"	85	5735	2830	W 6/57
"	124	5774	2832	late 1948
"	197	5849	2842	late 1951
6/08	48	5698	2827	W 10/52
"	211	5861	2851	late 1950 Gas lit 7/14
"	227	5876	2853	mid 1955
"	232	5881	2855	Westinghouse brake removed 12/15 for Army Ambulance, refitted 7/16. W ?
"	233	5882	2856	W 2/50
2/10	252	5901	2858	late 1951

(b) Drawing 1953 (the differences from the above were internal, including steam heating)

Built	Ren	SR No	Disposal
11/13	5865	2852	late 1950
"	5877	2854	W 1/56
"	5888	2857	W 9/52

4.12   This item number refers to the 14ft Open Carriage Truck of c.1840. No details are known.

4.13   26ft Open Carriage Truck. (No drawings known.)

Built	No	Disposal
1860	69	B 12/00

4.14   14ft 6in Open Carriage Truck. (No drawings known.)

Built	No	Ren	Disposal
1861	76		W c.1901
1861	78		W 12/02
1868	47		W 6/03
1870	31		W 6/01
x/93	45	6313	W 9/19 (sides not hinged)

4.15   22ft Open Carriage Truck. (No drawings known.)

Built	No	Disposal
1864	91	W 12/00

4.16   14ft 6in Covered Carriage Truck. (Incomplete drawing in Metropolitan collection.)

Two built but no details available, although one was probably No 101.

4.17 16ft Covered Carriage Truck. (Incomplete drawing in Metropolitan collection.)

Two built but no details available.

4.18 19ft Open Carriage Truck. (No drawings known.)

Built	No	Disposal
1870	33	W 12/00

4.19 19ft 6in Open Carriage Truck. (No drawings known)

Built	No	Disposal
1870	11	W 6/03
" ?	18	?
"	61	C pre-1908

4.20 17ft x 7ft 6in Covered Carriage Truck. LSWR drawing 1894.

At least four were built but only two numbers are known.

Built	No	Disposal
1874	28	W 6/02
"	39	W 12/02

4.21 16ft Covered Carriage Truck. (No drawings known.)

Ten ordered from Birmingham RC&W Co, Smethwick. (Two to cost £131 5s each and 8 to cost £123 5s each, see the next entry for 19ft 6in CCTs. The Register shows all ten valued at £167 18s 6d.)

Built	No	Disposal
1883	97	C c.1904/5 to vacuum cleaner truck 23s SR V4, W 12/37
"	98	C c.1904/5 to vacuum cleaner truck 24s SR V3, W 5/38
"	99	C c.1904/5 to vacuum cleaner truck 25s
"	100	C c.1904/5 to vacuum cleaner truck 26s
"	101	C c.1904/5 to vacuum cleaner truck 27s SR V9, W 4/34
"	102	B 12/05
"	103	B 12/05
"	104	B 6/06

4.22 19ft 6in Covered Carriage Truck. (No drawings known.)

Built by Birmingham RC&W Co (see note for 16ft CCT).

Built	No	Disposal
1883	105	B 6/06
"	106	B 6/06

4.23 15ft 4in Open Carriage Truck. LSWR drawing DB88A (9ft wheelbase).

Built	No	Ren	Disposal
1889	27	6297	W 3/18
" ?	30		C ?
" ?	50		C ?

4.24 15ft Open Carriage Truck. (No drawings known, 9ft wheelbase.)

Built	No	Ren	Disposal
1890	55	6323	W 7/19
"	82	6348	W 9/17

4.25 22ft Open Carriage Truck. SR diagram 1084 (hinged sides).

Built	No	Ren	SR No	Disposal
With 12ft 6in wheelbase				
1891	54	6322		W 12/13
1900	91			C ?, to SR 0402 then 4023, W 5/36
4/02	59	6326	3958	W 8/28 P
12/03	19	6290	3957	W 3/36 P
With 12ft 3in wheelbase (or were these 20ft long?)				
?	69			W pre 1912
1/93	6	6280		W 3/18

4.26 16ft Open Carriage Truck.   LSWR drawings 317 & 790, SR diagram 1080.

Drawings 317 and 790 apply to vehicles as shown, but the other vehicles listed were probably virtually identical, certainly both the LSWR and the SR included them on the same diagrams.
P = Westinghouse piped when built, unless a date is given.

Built	No	Ren	SR No	Disposal
Drawing unknown				
12/89	63	6329		W 8/17 P 3/92
8/90	49	6317		W 12/13 P
1/91	1	6276		W 1/15 Westinghouse fitted 1/1914
"	21	6292		W 2/18
"	25	6295		W 2/18
Drawing 317				
11/92	29	6298		W 5/17 P
"	46	6314	3905	W 4/25 P
5/93	107	6363		W 2/18 P
"	108	6364		W 2/18 P
"	109	6365		W 12/13 P
"	110	6366		W 4/16 P
"	111	6367		W 3/21 P
"	112	6368		W 7/19 P
"	113	6369		W 2/18 P
"	115	6371		W 2/21 P
"	117	6373		W 10/17 P
"	118	6374		W 2/18 P
"	119	6375		W 9/16 P
"	120	6376		W 10/17 P
"	121	6377		W 10/17 P
6/93	93	6359		W 4/16 P
7/93	7	6281		W 3/18
"	85	6351		W 7/17 P
12/93	44	6312		W 2/18 P
x/93	34	6303		W 7/19 P
"	42	6310	3904	W 6/31
10/95	70	6336	(3911)	W 1/23
12/95	10	6284	3901	W 3/32
"	24	6294	3902	W 9/29
12/95	51	6319	3907	W 9/31
"	74	6340	3912	W 9/31
2/96	32	6301	3903	W 7/24
"	38	6307		W 4/16
"	52	6320	(3908)	W 12/23
6/96	14	6287		W 12/22
"	53	6321	(3909)	W 2/25
11/96	84	6350	3914	W 12/24
Drawing 790				
5/99	137	6378		W 12/21
"	138	6379	3916	W 3/27
"	139	6380		W 12/22
"	140	6381	3917	W 2/25
"	141	6382	3918	W 6/31
"	142	6383	3919	W 5/31
"	143	6384		W 4/16
"	144	6385	3920	W 4/25
"	146	6386	3921	W 1/28
"	147	6387	3922	W 7/31
6/99	148	6388	3923	W 5/25
"	149	6389	4017	W 7/31
"	150	6390		W 12/22
"	151	6391	3924	W 11/29
"	152	6392	3925	W 4/28
"	153	6393	3926	W 2/25
"	154	6394	3927	W 7/31
"	155	6395	3928	W 7/24
"	156	6396	3929	W 8/28
Drawing unknown				
6/02	65	6331	3910	W 1/32 P
"	94	6360	3915	W 3/24 P
12/02	78	6344	3913	W 11/34 P
6/03	47	6315	3906	W 1/28 P

4.27 14ft 6in Open Carriage Truck. (No drawings known, 9ft wheelbase.)

Built	No	Ren	Disposal
1893	45	6313	W 9/19

4.28   19ft 6in Covered Carriage Truck.   LSWR drawings 611, 786, etc, SR diagram 1140.

Built	No	Ren	SR No	Disposal
1892	57	C 6/10	0401 (4609)	W 2/26 to 0749s
Possibly to drawing 578:				
1893	4			C 12/06
"	22			C 12/02, converted to vacuum cleaner truck 26s, SR V8
Drawing 611				
9/93	122	6619	4508	W 9/33 P
"	125	6622		B 6/18 P
"	126	6623		B 5/16 P
"	127	6624	4511	W 9/29 P
"	128	6625	4512	W 6/31 P, sold
"	129	6626		B ? P
"	130	6627	4513	W 5/30 P, either side handbrake
"	131	6628	4514	W 9/28 P
"	132	6629		B 5/16
"	133	6630	4515	W 9/29 P
"	134	6631	4516	W 9/29 P
"	135	6632	4517	W 6/31 P
"	136	6633	4518	W 9/33 P
10/93	123	6620	4509	W 7/31 P, sold
"	124	6621	4510	W 6/31 P, sold
Drawing unknown				
6/97	12	6602	4501	W 5/32
"	60	6608	4505	W 10/37
12/97	16	6603	4502	W 7/28
Drawing 786				
3/99	157	6634	4519	W 3/33
"	158	6635	4520	W 2/29
"	159	6636	4521	W 11/29
"	160	6637	4522	W 12/32
"	161	6638	4523	W 4/32
6/02	28	6605	4503	W 8/35
12/02	39	6606	4504	W 3/30
6/04	97	6609	4506	W 12/36 Dual braked
"	98	6610	4507	W 2/32 Dual braked, to vacuum cleaner van V8 (replacement)

4.29 19ft Open Carriage Truck. SR diagram 1081 (10ft 6in wheelbase).

Built	No	Ren	SR No	Disposal
x/95	3	6278		W 3/18
5/96	23	6293	3933	W 7/24
"	37	6306	3934	W 9/33
6/97	2	6277		W 6/15
11/97	64	6330	3935	W 6/24
12/97	86	6352		W 3/18
x/99	13	6286	3932	W 8/31
"	88	6354		W 5/17
5/99	80	6346	3937	W 11/28
6/00	72	6338	3936	W 8/27
9/00	33	6302		W 12/22
6/01	31	6300		W 3/18
"	76	6342		W 6/18
"	89	6355		W 6/15 P

4.30 18ft 9in Open Carriage Truck. SR diagram 1081 (10ft 6in wheelbase).

Built	No	Ren	SR No	Disposal
x/96	26	6296	3931	W 8/28
6/97	67	6333		W 6/15
6/98	75	6341		W 7/19
12/98	17	6289	3930	W 9/25

4.31 19ft 6in Open Carriage Truck. SR diagram 1081.

Built	No	Ren	SR No	Disposal
1/96	43	6311		W 12/22
5/99	41	6309		W 2/21
12/99	62	6328	3939	W 9/31 (might have been 19ft 4in long.)

4.32 19ft 4in Open Carriage Truck. SR diagram 1081.

Built	No	Rcn	SR No	Disposal
6/99	58	6325	3938	W 8/28
1901	77	6311		W 444

4.33 25ft 11in Fish Truck. LSWR drawing 921.

These were 5 Ton Fish Trucks constructed on the underframes of old carriages.

Built	No	Underframe built	Broken up
1900	162	1866	12/12
"	163	1873	6/12
"	164	1873	12/12
"	165	1877	12/12

4.34 24ft Fish Truck. LSWR drawing 931, 2087.

These were built as Fish Trucks but converted to OCTs to drawing 2087 in 1912. They were then to have drop ends and sides so as to make them convenient for War Department use.

Built	No	Ren	SR No	Disposal
11/00	166	6401	3960	W ?
"	167	6402	3961	W 4/25
"	168	6403	3962	W 4/25
5/00	169	6404	3963	W ?
7/00	170	6405	3964	W ?
"	171	6406	3965	W 11/27
9/00	172	6407	3966	W 10/27
"	173	6408	3967	W 4/25

4.35 26ft Open Carriage Truck. LSWR drawings 1034 & 2066, SR diagram 1086.

All provided with drop ends and sides so as to be convenient for War Department use. All those below are shown in the Register as Westinghouse piped. Load 6 Tons.

Built	No	Ren	SR No	Disposal
Drawing 1034				
8/01	174	6409	3990	W 9/31
"	175	6410	3991	W 5/32
"	176	6411	3992	W 8/34
"	177	6412	(3993)	W 8/30
"	178	6413	3994	W 11/30
"	179	6414	3995	W 8/30
"	180	6415	3996	W 8/33
"	181	6416	3997	W 11/30
"	182	6417	3998	W 8/30
"	183	6418	3999	W 1/37
"	184	6419	4000	W 3/32
"	185	6420	4001	W 9/31
"	186	6421	4002	W 9/31
"	187	6422	4003	W 11/32
"	188	6423	4004	W 6/33
"	189	6424	4005	W 8/31
"	190	6425	4006	W 4/38
"	191	6426	4007	W 8/31
"	192	6427	4008	W 10/31
"	193	6428	4009	W 8/31
"	194	6429	4010	W 9/28
"	195	6430	4011	W 11/32
"	196	6431	4012	W 10/31
"	197	6432	4013	W 12/31
"	198	6433	4014	W 4/31

Drawing 2066 (all with either side handbrakes)				
8/12		6335	3976	W 3/38
"		6279	3971	W 8/31

Built	No	Ren	SR No	Disposal
26ft Open Carriage Truck, drawing 2066 (continued)				
8/12		6397	3986	W 4/36
"		6398	3987	W 10/31
"		6399	3988	W 2/35
"		6400	3989	W 3/36
9/13		6370	3982	W 5/38
"		6372	3983	W 3/36
6/14		6317	3973	W 3/36
"		6322	3974	W 4/38
"		6365	3980	W 7/37
"		6434	4015	W 1/38
"		6435	4016	W 5/38
5/19		6276	3969	W 4/34
"		6277	3970	W 6/36 to 1281s
"		6307	3972	W 4/36
"		6333	3975	W 4/36
"		6355	3977	W 3/38
7/20		6358	3978	W 5/38
"		6359	3979	W 2/38
"		6366	3981	W 4/38
"		6375	3984	W 3/38
"		6384	3985	W 4/38

4.36 26ft Covered Carriage Truck. LSWR drawing 1035, SR diagram 1142.

All Westinghouse piped, one side lever handbrake. Load 4 Tons.

Built	No	Ren	SR No	Disposal
9/01	199	6639	4534	W 12/36
"	204	6644	4539	W 10/35 sold
"	205	6645	4540	W 6/35 sold
"	206	6646	4541	W 9/38
"	207	6647	4542	W 9/38
"	208	6648	4543	W 1/37
"	209	6649	4544	W 9/41 to 1640s
"	210	6650	4545	W 9/36
"	211	6651	4546	W 12/36
"	212	6652	4547	W 1/40
10/01	200	6640	4535	W 12/36
"	201	6641	4536	W 12/36
"	202	6642	4537	W 12/38
"	203	6643	4538	W 2/37
"	213	6653	4548	W 9/38
10/01	214	6654	4549	W 9/38
"	215	6655	4550	W 10/35 sold
"	216	6656	4551	W 10/37
"	217	6657	4552	W 10/33 sold
"	218	6658	4553	W 12/26
"	219	6659	4554	W 1/38
"	220	6660	4555	W 9/37
"	221	6661	4556	W 9/38
"	222	6662	4557	W 1/37
"	223	6663	4558	W 8/37 sold

4.37 25ft Open Carriage Truck. SR diagram 1084 (16ft wheelbase - or 15ft?). (Load 4 Tons.)

Built	No	Ren	SR No	Disposal
4/02	92	6358		B 5/16 P
12/02	15	6288	3968	W 4/32

4.38 21ft Open Carriage Truck. LSWR drawings 1301 and 1384 , SR diagram 1082.

(Drawing 1301 had 14ft wheelbase, 1384 had 13ft.)

Built	No	Ren	SR No	Disposal
(a) Drawing 1301				
6/04	77	6343	3947	W 2/36
"	95	6361	3950	W 5/31
(b) Drawing 1384				
6/05	8	6282	3940	W 11/30
"	71	6337	3946	W 9/30
8/05	50	6318	3944	W 12/34
"	56	6324	3945	W 1/35

161

Built	No	Ren	SR No	Disposal
21ft **Open Carriage Truck** , drawing 1384 (continued)				
8/05	87	6353	3949	W 4/32
3/06	36	6305	3943	W 5/38
"	96	6362	3951	W 8/30
10/06	30	6299	3941	W 1/34
"	35	6304	3942	W 9/31
"	79	6345	3948	W 3/29

4.39   42ft Open Carriage Truck. LSWR drawing 1338, SR diagram 1087.

Built	No	Ren	SR No	Disposal
12/04	20	6291	4018	W 6/32
"	66	6332	4019	W 9/31
"	68	6334	4020	W 2/32
"	81	6347	4021	W 7/31
"	83	6349	4022	W 1/33

4.40   21ft Covered Carriage Truck. LSWR drawing 1362, SR diagram 1141.

All dual braked with either side hand brakes. Load 4 Tons.

Built	No	Ren	SR No	Disposal
3/05	99	6611	4526	W 8/33
"	100	6612	4527	W 4/32
"	101	6613	4528	W 3/33
12/05	102	6614	4529	W 3/33
"	103	6615	4530	W 10/33 sold
6/06	104	6616	4531	W 3/33
"	105	6617	4532	W 11/33 sold
"	106	6618	4533	W 5/34 sold
10/06	4	6601	4524	W 3/35 to 862s
"	22	6604	4525	W 5/31

4.41 21ft Open Carriage Truck (low floor). LSWR drawing 1677, SR diagram 1083.

All dual braked, either side handbrakes. Load 6 Tons. Tare 7T 8C 3Q.

Built	No	Ren	SR No	Disposal	Note of 1908 usage
3/08	40	6308	3952	W 5/34	Marked for use between Overton & Waterloo for Banknote paper van.
"	61	6327	3954	W 2/35	
"	90	6356	3955	W 7/32	
12/08	48	6316	3953	W 8/35	
"	91	6357	3956	W 3/36	

4.42 46ft 6in Scenery Truck.   LSWR drawing 1889, SR diagram 1143.

To carry 6 Tons. Dual braked.

Built	No	Ren	SR No	Disposal
7/10	57	6607	4559	W 6/35

ADDENDA TO PREVIOUS VOLUMES

Those readers who have read either of the previous volumes might be interested in some items that have come to notice since they were published.

First of all some corrections to *LSWR Carriages in the 20th Century*:

Pages 202-205. 56ft brake thirds listed in Appendices 6.17 and 6.19. The SR renumberings of all of these two types should read 30xx and **not** 15xx as shown.

Page 180, Figure 10.6. The two embossed windows on the kitchen side are each too wide. They are drawn as 2ft 6in and 1ft 7½in wide, but in fact, these were the dimensions over the window openings. Hence, the panel lines embracing these windows should have been 2ft 10½in (11.5mm) and 2ft 0in (8mm) apart. For model makers, the glass, frames and the smaller ventilator should be adjusted to suit.

Some caption errors were introduced at too late a stage to be corrected:
- Page 18. The title should be 51ft.
- Page 47. The title should be 56ft.
- Page 139. The LSWR drawing number should be 1736.
- Page 160. The date should be 1918.

Next, in *LSWR Carriages, Volume 1*, there was a description starting on page 73 of a 25ft Family Carriage of 1876 (shown in figure 3.22). Since that was written, the surviving body has changed hands and the latest owner has done further research and restoration work on it. Some of his findings have been most interesting.

When painted with the colour described in the book, the owner says that it appeared rather pink and fleshy, but that the colour changed substantially when varnished. It became richer and warmer, almost terracotta. It will be recalled that many photos of LSWR trains show distinct variations in carriage colours. This probably reflects, apart from weathering and dirt, the fact that carriages would often receive additional coats of varnish rather than be stripped back and repainted.

More careful stripping of the paintwork revealed hitherto unknown details of the lining. Round the droplights, door louvres and top panels, the red lining was not in contact with the dark brown, but separated from it by about 1/8 inch of salmon. Thus, at a droplight, the sequence was: varnished droplight frame, salmon moulding (not really a bolection), brown line, salmon line, red line, then the main salmon of the door frame. At the louvres, the sequence was the same except that it started with the salmon louvre instead of the varnished frame. In the top panels it was: salmon panel, brown edge of fascia, salmon line, red line then the main salmon of the fascia.

Another interesting find was made by a fellow member of the South Western Circle, Mr A Westlake, who came across an illustration and article in *The Engineer* for 15th February 1878 describing the Royal Saloon Carriage which was illustrated in *LSWR Carriages, Volume 1* on page 81 (Figure 3.28). When I prepared my drawing from measurements of the body, I was only able to base the Cleminson underframe on those of some other companies. The drawing in *The Engineer* (reproduced on the next page) shows some differences in the underframe, which is drawn in considerable detail. There were also a continuous lower footboard, four short waist level handrails, and commode handles by the doors. I feel that the roof shape as drawn does not fully conform with what I saw on the surviving body, and that there are some slight dimensional discrepancies. The roof lamp tops shown are of a different pattern from the usual ones. The royal crest, garter and crown without supporters, is shown in the door lower panel. As the drawing is side elevation only with a plan of the Cleminson trucks, it does not show the unusual feature of the inward curvature of the sides at each end. The only photograph of this carriage that has come to light is the very distant view at Plate 8.7.1 during its use as an Engineer's Inspection vehicle.

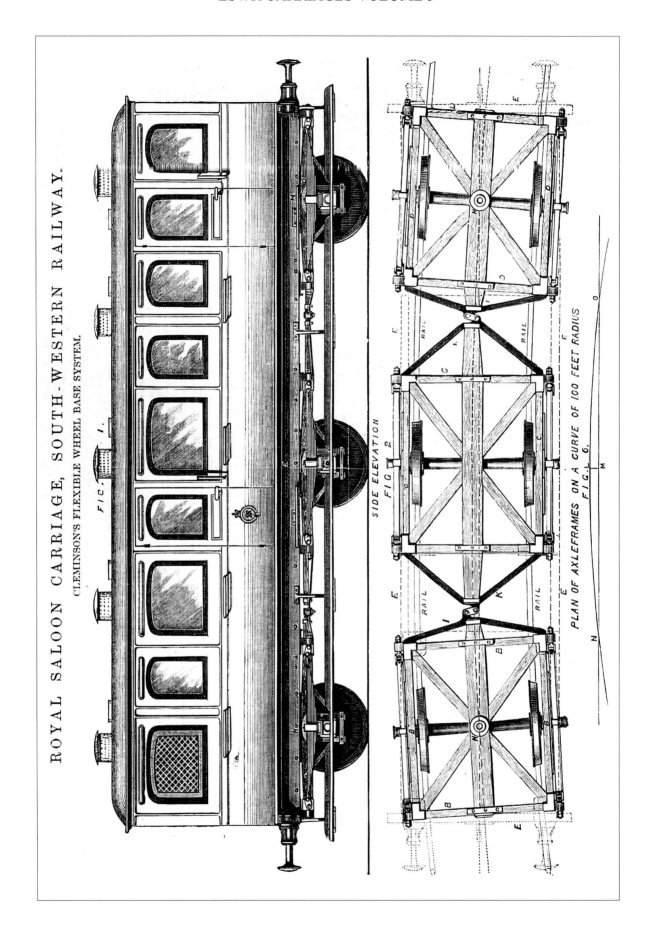

ROYAL SALOON CARRIAGE, SOUTH-WESTERN RAILWAY.

CLEMINSON'S FLEXIBLE WHEEL BASE SYSTEM.

FIG. 1.

SIDE ELEVATION
FIG. 2

PLAN OF AXLEFRAMES ON A CURVE OF 100 FEET RADIUS
FIG. 6.